RESTORING PRIDE

Used by permission of Rowman & Littlefield Publishing Group.
All rights reserved

RESTORING PRIDE

THE LOST VIRTUE OF OUR AGE

RICHARD TAYLOR

 Prometheus Books

59 John Glenn Drive
Amherst, New York 14228-2119

Published 1996 by Prometheus Books

Restoring Pride: The Lost Virtue of Our Age. Copyright © 1996 by Richard Taylor. All rights reserved. No part of this publication may be reproduced, stored in a retrieval system, or transmitted in any form or by any means, electronic, mechanical, photocopying, recording, or otherwise, without prior written permission of the publisher, except in the case of brief quotations embodied in critical articles and reviews.

Inquiries should be addressed to
Prometheus Books
59 John Glenn Drive
Amherst, New York 14228–2119
VOICE: 716–691–0133, ext. 210
FAX: 716–691–0137
WWW.PROMETHEUSBOOKS.COM

22 21 20 19 18   10 9 8 7 6

Part Three of this volume is in part adapted from Richard Taylor, *Virtue Ethics* (Interlaken, N.Y.: Linden Book Co., 1991), and is used with permission of the publisher.

Library of Congress Cataloging-in-Publication Data

Richard Taylor, 1919–
    Restoring pride : the lost virtue of our age / Richard Taylor.
        p.   cm.
    ISBN 978–1–57392–024–7 (alk. paper)
    1. Pride and vanity. I. Title.
BJ1535.P9T39   1995
179'.9—dc20   95–35985
                                                                    CIP

Printed in the United States of America on acid-free paper

He who lets the world, or his own portion of it, choose his plan of life for him, has no need of any other faculty than the ape-like one of imitation. He who chooses his plan for himself employs all his faculties.

—John Stuart Mill

CONTENTS

7

Part Two: Pride and the Rule of Manners

Part Three: Happiness

PREFACE

The themes of this book result from years of observing people and my effort to understand why their lives take the directions they do. Some of these people have been men and women of great creative achievement while most, of course, have not.

What is it, then, that sets the former apart? The answer is, in short, that they invent their own lives, while the others fall into the lockstep of custom, thereby letting society more or less choose their lives for them. This latter approach to life I call "willing slavery."

The philosophers of classical antiquity were profoundly aware that there are two kinds of truth; namely, facts of nature, which are simply given, and facts of custom, which are human creations. Thus it is a fact of nature that a given person is male and not female, but a fact of custom that he is married. Both are indeed facts, or truths, but they are of different kinds. Similarly, it is a fact of nature that the earth's surface is mostly water, that the sun rises (or appears to rise) in the east, and that we are all mortal. However, it is but a fact of custom that all persons are equal, that all are endowed with certain human rights, that criminals ought to be punished for their deeds, and so on.

Facts of custom are important. Indeed, some of them are basic to civilized life. But the mischief begins when these are treated as fixed truths. Thus the sometimes violent conflict over abortion results from treating the rule of the sanctity of human life and the rule of a woman's right to her own body as though these were natural truths, when both are the creations of custom. Conflicts, sometimes bloody ones, similarly arise between nations when purely customary notions concerning equality, human rights, and justice are treated as fixed truths.

Creative people do not fall into this kind of trap. They treat custom for what it is worth, but supplement it with principles of their own making, thereby enabling their gifts to flourish. The result is, notwithstanding the rule of custom to the contrary, people are not equal. Some are better as human beings than others. It is time we recognized this, and stopped thinking that there is some kind of nobility in grinding everyone down to the same level. Perhaps then we can see more clearly what makes some people genuinely superior to the rest, and perhaps more people, who would otherwise be destined to willing slavery, will then emulate them.

PART ONE

WHAT IS PRIDE?

INTRODUCTION

The ideas that will unfold in these pages will be greeted by many with shock, as being "elitist." So let it be made clear at the outset that these ideas *are* elitist. There is no attempt here to be politically correct, or to defend any popular ideology.

We should face the fact that some people are better as *human beings* than others. Everyone knows that this is true, and while it may be good social policy to pretend otherwise, much is also lost. That is, some people are in fact wiser, more creative, more resourceful, and, in general, more competent in some or many of the ways that count in the world. The corollary of this is that some people are foolish, uncreative, unresourceful, and incompetent in some or even all of the ways that count in the world.

The good—that is, those who stand out as resourceful and creative human beings—are entitled to take pride in themselves, for pride is the justified love of oneself. All people, including simpletons, love themselves, but only in the case of the proud is such love justified. What justifies it is personal excellence, that is, actual achievement of the kind that sets such people apart from others. Examples of the proud include Ludwig van Beethoven, Socrates,

Abraham Lincoln, Malcolm X, Willa Cather, Nelson Mandela, Pablo Picasso, and Amelia Earhart. These people are very different from each other, but what they have in common is this: each, in his or her own way, has excelled, and that excellence is based on some gift or strength which its possessor used to achieve something of lasting significance—musical genius in Beethoven's case, intelligence and the power to galvanize followers to the pursuit of an ideal in the case of Malcolm X, courage in the case of Amelia Earhart, and so on. Thus the proud rise above ordinary people, and are quite literally superior to them; but their superiority rests not on class, power, or wealth, but on being gifted in some way and then applying those gifts to personal achievement.

The fact that pride is here illustrated with the names of the famous does not mean that it is a virtue reserved for the famous. Greatness is not always recognized, and sometimes foolish people gain fame through their sheer folly, as in the case of some witless daredevil who makes his name known far and wide by going over a great waterfall in a barrel. Fame he has, but greatness he has not, and should he survive such a pointless stunt his sense of pride would be misplaced, for it would rest upon no personal achievement at all. Sometimes, again, fame is the reward of a mere accident of birth, as in the case of some athlete of minimum skill whose prowess results from little more than his sheer bulk.

Persons quite unknown, on the other hand, often possess greatness that matches that of the most deserving heroes. Their names are sometimes little known simply because the world does not know what they have done. One thinks, for example, of a truly great teacher, who inspires and enriches the lives of generations of students. Her abilities may be as rare and precious as those of a Beethoven, notwithstanding that her name will remain forever relatively unknown.

The reward of personal excellence is not fame, but pride. You are proud, not because of the applause of others, or even the applause of the whole world, but because of what you genuinely *are*—provided, of course, that you are gifted in some significant way and that you do something with that gift.

Some people, no doubt, are born, and destined, to be common, to live out their lives to no significant purpose, but that is relatively rare. What is more to be lamented is that so few people do anything with the strengths that nature has given them. As the ancient Stoics expressed it, most of us have mingled in our being the powers of the gods and the mindless impulses of the beasts, and we tend to rest effortlessly on our dead kinship with the latter instead of nourishing and perfecting the divine element in us. Most people have the power to be creative, and some have it in a god-like degree. That is what the pagan philosophers of antiquity were referring to when they wrote of human goodness and happiness. But many people—perhaps even most—are content with the passing pleasures and satisfactions of the animal side of our nature. Indeed, many people will account their lives to be successful if they get through them with only minimal pain, with pleasant diversions from moment to moment and day to day, and the general approval of those around them. And this, notwithstanding that they often have within them the ability to do something which perhaps no human being has ever done. Merely to do what others have done is often safe, and comfortable; but to do something truly original, and do it well, whether it is appreciated by others or not—that is what being human is really all about, and it is what alone justifies the self-love that is pride.

While the gifts and powers that can enable certain persons to make something truly worthwhile of their lives are extremely various, and unevenly distributed, the *manners* possessed by proud people are all the same. Therefore, there is much to be said about these, and what is said will apply to all. We cannot, of course, offer an extensive guide to manners, covering just about every situation that is likely to arise in one's life. Such a guide would be tedious and pointless. What we can do, however, is to formulate the single *rule* of manners, which is beautiful in its simplicity but often not easy to live by, and we can then illustrate it with situations that are fairly typical.

Finally, we shall tackle the question that has always been at the very heart of all moral philosophy and is, indeed, the most important question that anyone can ever ask: What is human happiness? People take for granted that they know the answer to this, though in fact very few do. The reason there is so much confusion and error here is that people tend to embrace, without much thought, superficial conceptions of happiness and then, imagining that they know the answer, they cease looking for it. Thus, many people identify ultimate happiness simply with the possession of wealth. Probably no idea has ever been more totally discredited, and yet it persists and is even widely taken for granted. The disastrous result is that many people—most, probably—having all their lives pursued some specious notion of happiness, go to their graves never having tasted genuine happiness or fulfillment.

All three of these ideals—personal excellence, manners, and happiness—are intertwined. None of them, especially the first and third, can be entirely understood apart from the others. Happiness without personal excellence is quite impossible, for genuine happiness is a kind of fulfillment. But it is not enough simply to understand these two ideas. We are social beings. We have to live together in order to have any kind of civilized life at all. So the manner in which a proud and happy person does this is important, and it is easy to fail here. Thus manners, and the simple rule of manners, are critical to a whole life that is at once a life of pride and fulfillment.

PRIDE AND THE DOCTRINE OF EQUALITY

The claim, implicit in all egalitarian philosophy and in popular religion, that fools are just as good as their opposites flies in the face of empirical fact and, indeed, no one really believes it anyway. We have been *taught*, for political and social reasons—some of them perhaps good reasons—to talk that way, to declare that no one is really any better as a human being than anyone else; that we are really equals, notwithstanding appearances. But everyone knows that this is not true. It is simply another comfortable falsehood—comfortable, that is, to those among us who are fools, or who are singularly lacking in the gifts of intelligence, creativity, and resourcefulness that are the marks of great persons.

This is not to say, of course, that such distinctions of better and worse can be made along the lines of race or class, for they cannot. The marks of personal excellence are numerous. Some are possessed by some persons and others by others, with the result that those who rise to any kind of greatness are often very different. Still, they all stand out as superior human beings.

It must also be stressed that egalitarianism is no doubt essential to public policy. No social and political arrangement can work well unless people, notwithstanding their differences, are all treated the same. No one gets more than one vote; no one, by virtue of special wisdom or other gifts, can receive favorable treatment under the law. In the eyes of the law we are all the same. The mischief begins only when this basic foundation of public policy is treated as a kind of natural truth, for it is, in fact, not a truth but a falsehood.

This elitist way of viewing people, and life, is not new. It was considered obvious in classical Athenian culture, to which most of what is precious in our own culture can be traced. Indeed, the writings of the moralists of that day—Plato, Aristotle, the Stoics, and others—cannot even be understood apart from these presuppositions. The primary problem of all ethics was, to the thinkers of that period, that of describing the nature of human excellence, of what it is that lifts some persons above the rest and, through the discovery of this, to set forth the conditions of human happiness. Clearly, these are ideas very much worthy of our thought.

So what we are going to do in this book, first of all, is to defend and illustrate this ancient way of looking at people and at life and, more to the point, to explore the ways in which you can raise yourself up to a level of goodness that will entitle you to genuine pride. You can do little about those gifts that nature has bestowed upon you, or withheld. You can never become great in the art of music, literature, politics, or whatever if you lack the gifts for success in those realms. But, unless you were born a fool, there are gifts that you do have, many or few, and your task, then, is to nourish and perfect those gifts. Your reward will be some measure of achievement and greatness—not, perhaps, in such things as wealth and position, but in something far more precious; namely, greatness as a human being.

You are given yourself, and you can either do something with it, or you can choose not to. You can spend your life in ignorance and folly if you wish. Many—indeed most—do. And you can, following that path, console yourself with comforting platitudes to the effect that, notwithstanding your folly and ignorance, you are really just as good as anyone else. In other words, you can lie to yourself, and even, with the help of the dedicated egalitarians among us, convince yourself of that falsehood. But, alternatively, you can set for yourself an ideal of personal excellence, and achieve it. Form in your mind a clear idea of what it means to be a genuinely superior human being—superior, that is, *as a person*, and not merely as an adherent to this or that religion, ideology, or group—and then make of yourself that human being. Then, and only then, can you be proud. Your reward may not be honor, riches, or glory—things that are bestowed by others, or more often withheld—but a kind of inner glory and richness. You will see yourself not merely for what you may appear to be to others, but for what you in fact *are*, for what you have made yourself become, and the result, if what you then are is something truly worthy and wonderful, will be pride—that is, the justified love of yourself.

Directions cannot be given for achieving personal excellence, because we are all different. The gifts and potentialities of one person are not those of another. Indeed, each person is unique. His or her gifts and abilities are probably not exactly matched by anyone else on earth. And from this it follows that one person's excellence is his or hers alone. No one can tell you how to achieve yours. Your task is simply to find the one or few things that you can excel in, and then make it your primary business in life to excel in those ways. To do otherwise, to disregard the treasures with which you are at least potentially gifted, is simply to waste your life—a path to nothingness that is, alas, only too common. People often, and perhaps usually, do not nourish what they have, but instead fall back on what is common, pleasant, easy, or, worst of all, expected. They simply fall into step with what others are doing, absorb their values from others instead of creating their own, pattern their lives after the common mold—and then hear with comfort the egalitarian teaching that no one is any better than anyone else anyway. Their own lack of achievement, they conclude, is no fault. The common herd of human beings sets the standards and the rules, glorifies them as the very teachings of some god, and those who might, through hard work and the cultivation of their special gifts, try to rise above this herd, to become literally better than these, they dismiss as having failed in advance. If no one is, or can be, any better as a person than anyone else, then there is no point in trying, is there?

COUNTERFEIT PRIDE

The word "pride" has come to be used so loosely that it has virtually lost the overwhelmingly important meaning it once had. It has degenerated to little more than an exhortation. We are told to *be proud*, of this, that, or the other—indeed, of everything. The downtrodden are urged to be proud, likewise the forsaken, the ignorant, the weak, as if these conditions might themselves be sources of pride. But when everyone is expected to be proud of everything, then there really is nothing left to be proud of, nor can a truly proud person be distinguished from anyone else.

To see how meaningless the word has become, consider the following descriptions:

1. These people are poor, illiterate, hopelessly ignorant, and guided by superstition. About all they have is their pride.

2. It's impossible to make any kind of conversation when George is there, because he just takes over. All he hears is his own voice, and if you offer an idea of your own he only hears as much of it as he needs to prompt a fresh stream of talk about himself. He's terribly proud of his abilities, more apparent to him than to

others, and of his wit and talent for scintillating talk, even though he really has neither.

3. When Susan learned that her husband had had an affair she refused to have anything to do with him forever after. Any communication had to go through her lawyer, and when friends tried to raise the possibility of reconciliation she just told them to stay out of it. This was too bad, because it actually had been a pretty good marriage and he had made clear that he would like to get back together and try to make it work. Susan, though, chose battle, instructing her lawyer to inflict every damage he could. "After all," she said, "I have my pride."

4. Ben likes to be in charge. He's never happier than when he's at work, because there are seven people under him. He is constantly inventing things for them to do, often useless things, just so he can be giving orders He has always said that he wished he could have been a police chief. In a restaurant he usually takes forever to order, making the waiter stand by, no matter how busy he is, and then he is likely to have it returned to the kitchen for being not properly prepared. It's just his pride. It is impossible to imagine him being modest or humble or taking anyone's advice on anything.

5. Kay is very proud of her achievements, and never misses an opportunity to call attention to them. Her paintings have received decent recognition and even been sold for fairly good prices, and you cannot be in her company long without these things coming out, usually without much subtlety. I think she seeks out well-known artists, not to learn from them, but just so she can drop their names. In a social gathering the name dropping becomes almost rapid fire. She is a talented painter and justifiably proud, but she would probably become much better if she concentrated more on her work and less on how she appears to everyone else.

6. Carl is too proud to admit that he can be mistaken. If you try to correct him he just doesn't hear you. He constantly screws up grammar but there would be no point in anyone trying to correct it. He would resent it. If he says something that is clearly mistaken, or even absurd, then he either defends it or pretends to have said, or meant, something else.

In these six descriptions the word "proud" is applied in various ways, and many people would find nothing terribly incongruous in any of them. The word has become hardly more than a vague expression of praise and, as such, has almost lost the very precious meaning it once had.

At this point, obviously, we need a definition of pride. It is *the justifiable love of yourself.*

It would be idle and off the track to quibble here, for what we are concerned with is not a mere word and its meaning, but rather, a very important idea, which this definition captures. To be proud, in terms of this ancient and precious concept, is not merely to love yourself in some perhaps childish, arrogant, or conceited way, but to have the kind of love that is justified by the kind of person you are. And it is a difficult thing to do, because to become that kind of person is difficult and rare.

Consider our first brief description, of the downtrodden ones. If there is really any pride in them, then there is no hint of what it could be based on. Ignorance and illiteracy are hardly virtues. Pride, in this description, is nothing but a buzz word, signifying nothing, a way of trying to find worth where there apparently is none. The underlying explanation for this fairly common type of description is the need people have to find something positive to say about everyone, even when nothing positive is apparent. The same thing is at work in common euphemisms, as when retarded children are described as "special children," the poor as being somehow the "salt of the earth," and so on. Perhaps this way of trying to view things positively and covering over what we wish were not there serves some useful function in enabling people to get along, but when the concept of *pride* is enlisted to this end then the price paid is dear. We totally lose sight of what pride is.

Or consider George the garrulous of our second description. He is described as proud of his abilities. But is he? Quite the contrary, he is constantly seeking the authentication of those abilities from others, precisely because he doesn't entirely believe in them himself. Someone possessed of genuine abilities need not be constantly trying to draw attention to them, especially when such an effort takes the form of self-directed talk. Someone who is genuinely proud of an achievement can take inward satisfaction in it, can reflect, in silence, that what he or she has done is very good, and, for whatever it is worth, be pretty sure that it will not go unnoticed by others. But George, by continuously drawing attention to himself, is in effect soliciting praise which he would not need if he were himself confident of his worth. He is saying: That is pretty good—*don't you think?* The expressions of appreciation, probably rendered out of mere politeness, are nothing but fuel which, in the absence of anything better, serves to carry along his weak sense of self-worth.

Susan, the injured wife, has similarly substituted something for pride which in fact gets in the way of it. What is called pride here is hardly more than a shield to protect a damaged self-image. Pride and magnanimity are indeed difficult in the face of rejection, but it is seriously wrong to look at some perhaps understandable substitute for pride and call it by that name. The need to nourish a shattered ego is no sign of a justified love for oneself, but the very opposite. It arises from a serious self-doubt. And the impulse to vengeance should never be labeled as pride, for a justified self-love cannot possibly express itself in hatred for others. The two cancel each other.

Then what about our fourth example, Ben? No, there is no trace of pride in him, either. He imagines that love for oneself is to be measured by his contempt and disdain for others, and he is so carried away by this that he is not even entirely aware of the extent of that abuse. He knows that the waiter is standing by, at his behest, but has not noticed how harried he is, because it doesn't matter to him. He wants someone to be bound by his will and whim, and that he easily achieves here—the waiter has no choice. That those he supervises must bow and scrape is to him evidence of his superiority, so he need not ask himself whether this superiority is genuine. The appearance is good enough, and in case he should learn of some merit in one of these that is lacking in himself—a superior education, for example—then this will seem to him to prove that he is still the better person, notwithstanding. Indeed, it is his delight to find that one of those under him has a Ph.D.

What Ben does, in short, is try to measure his worth not in comparison to the worth of others, but by an accidental relationship to them. What matters to him is, as in the case of George, not his own worth, upon which a genuine self-approbation could be based, but the mere appearance of it, an appearance that rests on nothing more than his having a role that permits him to tell others what to do. He loves a kind of reflection of himself, not so much a reflection of how he looks to others, much less to himself, but of how he looks in his relationship to others. The mirror of this reflection is that pattern of relationships, nothing more. Yet it is absurd to suppose that there can be any but the flimsiest connection between the roles in which people are cast—police officer, supervisor, whatever—and their own worth as persons. No one would covet the role of police officer but for this confusion. A policeman can, indeed, under certain fairly common circumstances, make *anybody* stop and, at least briefly, do as told, but so what?

And what about our artist? Someone with artistic genius does, indeed, have a genuine and justified basis for self-love. To be able to do something well is an indisputable source of personal pride, the more so, perhaps, if the ability is rare and its fruits precious.

But Kay, in our fifth example, does not really have this or, to whatever extent she does, does not rest her love upon it. The judgment and approval of other people who matter is by no means an insignificant measure of worth. It would be without significance only if it came from persons who do not matter, that is, from vulgarians who know nothing about what they are appraising. But Kay is not content with competent praise. Indeed she seeks to impress others, not just by what she does, but by her mere acquaintanceship with those who do it *better*. And this betokens not a love for herself as an artist, but the lack of it. She has to make do with whatever reflection of worth she can derive from those accidental associations.

Nor does Carl, in our last description, come even close to embodying any genuine pride. He doesn't even know himself. He is so bent upon concealing his ignorance from others that he conceals it from himself. Others see through him almost at once, while he never does. They see him as someone who clumsily tries to cover over his mistakes, even his smallest intellectual errors, while he does not acknowledge even to himself that any mistake is made. He does not hear a correction if it is offered or, if he does, pretends that it is misplaced. The next day he will mangle the mispronounced word again or make the same error of fact. Nothing has penetrated his closed mind, not even an inward glance at himself.

What Carl does is try, ineptly, to impress *others*. What matters to him is not his own self-approbation, which is essential to genuine pride, but the approval of everyone else. His love for himself, such as it is, is thus entirely borrowed: If *they* think he is good—that is, in this case (and absurdly), not fallible—then that will be good enough for him. His love is not for himself, but simply for how he appears, and it does not matter to him that the appearance is faked. So far is this from being proud, in any significant sense that concerns us here, that it tends almost to the opposite. A fool who feigns wisdom is a fool twice over.

These descriptions thus illustrate some of the counterfeits of pride. Someone who is genuinely proud resembles none of these people. A proud man has no need to dominate, welcomes corrections, cares little about the approval of others, is soft-spoken and does not call attention to himself.

It is important, then, that we now look closely at this idea, to see just what genuine pride *is*. This concept was so important in the social life and thought of the ancient Greeks, the true fathers of our secular and scientific culture, that they thought of it as underlying all the other virtues. The corruption began when the religious culture born in the Middle East began to overwhelm the heritage of the Greeks. Indeed, pride came to be, in teachings of Christians, the first of the seven deadly sins, and to this day people are not sure whether it is a sin or a virtue. Proud people are both lauded and scorned, as the meaning of the term shifts back and forth, and the original meaning, basic to everything that follows in these pages, becomes quite lost to view.

THE MEANING OF PRIDE

Everyone extols pride as a virtue, yet hardly anyone has the least idea what it is. We speak, with approval, of taking pride in one's work, or family, even of pride in one's country or race—things over which one has little choice. Why should one be proud of being, say, Hispanic, when this is but a biological fact of origin? Worse yet, people are sometimes praised for their professed pride in something that is in the clearest sense undesirable. Fat people, for example, are sometimes exhorted to exult in their very obesity.

Genuine pride is a lost virtue. I say *lost*, because it was clearly understood by our cultural ancestors, the pagan Greeks of antiquity. Aristotle described the proud person as having a "great soul," and indeed we derive our very word "magnanimous" from that idea. No thinker of classical antiquity doubted the value of pride, nor were they in the least confused about what it is. Pride was for them the appreciation of one's own special worth and superiority over others. To be proud is to believe that you are in the clearest and truest sense *better* than ordinary people, and to be *correct* in so believing. Pride, in short, was for Aristotle and every other moralist of his culture the justified love of oneself. And the operative word here is *justified*.

Judeo-Christian culture, on the other hand, which eventually met, clashed with, and overwhelmed Greek culture, regarded pride as a sin, an arrogant attempt to be god-like. Pride was for Christians the very first of the seven deadly sins. In place of the pursuit of self-love and the ideal of rising above the meek and relatively worthless horde, Christians elevated the meek and lowly, declaring these to be the very salt of the earth! There has probably never been in history so complete and lasting a transformation of values, or indeed, a reversal of them; for we have here not simply a change or evolution of some ideal, but the utter destruction of it and replacement by its opposite!

The result is that today pride is first extolled as a virtue, in deference to our Greek origins, but then, in deference to our religious inheritance, condemned as a sin; finally, as if to combine these opposites, it is spoken of as if it were something to be nourished in everyone, with no regard whatever to merit.

The Athenians thought of themselves as obviously better than others, for whom they invented the word "barbarians," and educated Athenians never doubted their superiority to those who were ignorant, weak, and incompetent. What, indeed, would be the point of becoming educated, of improving one's mind or soul by literature, rhetoric, and, eventually, science, except to make oneself better?—a question which, indeed, still needs asking.

Christians, on the other hand, declared each and every human being, even the despised, to be a creature of God, to be in some sense God's very *image*, from which it of course follows that no one can be any better a person than any other. Utter equality is implicit in this religious tradition and it is an equality that is ensured not by the possession of reason, or the power of thought, or aesthetic awareness, or any other uniquely human capacity, but by the mere fact of being born! And today, indeed, it is extended, by those who take this teaching literally and seriously, even to those merely conceived and not yet born, for the minute and unformed fetus is declared to have the same worth as the noblest person ever to walk on earth.

So now we are in the extraordinary, even bizarre, position of combining two totally different and even incompatible ideals and praising both as if they were one. And few people have noticed the incongruity, even the impossibility, of this. Thus a stupid or an ignorant person, or someone completely lacking in taste and refinement, can declare himself proud, and no eyebrows will be raised. On the contrary, such a declaration, even from so absurd a source, meets with nods of approval. For someone of common tastes, values, and worth to say, "At least I have my pride," is as outrageous as a grossly obese and intemperate person declaring, "At least I have my health," or someone whose entire life is marked by silliness and manifestly stupid choices declaring, "At least I have my wisdom." We see at once the contradiction in these latter declarations, and anyone, in those circumstances, who uttered one of them would be thought pathetic. Why, then, do we fail to see the contradiction in the first? Genuine pride is not merely a *feeling* that you have about yourself. It is a *belief* that some, but not all, persons have about themselves which is *true*, the belief, namely, that they are possessed of some virtue or excellence that is not common to many

The nature of genuine pride is thus clear. It is the love of oneself that rests upon some strength or excellence—some *virtue*, in the ancient sense of that term—which is not common to all, something that enables its possessor to stand out among the multitude. A fine athlete can take pride in his or her prowess, for the virtue is perfectly manifest, but someone who merely aspires to such excellence cannot, for such a person has not yet achieved the excellence which is its foundation. A woman of buoyant health and beauty can take pride in this, but it is a perversion of the idea to exhort the plain or homely to do so. Someone who is plain, disposed to illness, and of fragile strength should surely avoid self-effacement, should no doubt accept such limitations in a stoic spirit; but such a one should certainly not be urged to be proud on the very basis of such limitations. They are, in the very strictest sense, *faults*, or shortcomings, and nothing is achieved by pretending otherwise. A man who, by his energy, resourcefulness, intelligence, and command of his field creates a great industry justifiably loves himself for what he *is*. He is not reduced to nourishing some inner sense of pride in himself as if he were possessed of greatness when there is in fact no visible sign of it, for his achievement lies before him. Another man who aspires to greatness of this kind but repeatedly fails, and fails precisely because he lacks the wit and resourcefulness to carry it off, can console himself and blame circumstances, but he cannot be proud, at least not in that area, however much he may wish to be. Other examples come readily to mind—the first woman to become a fighter pilot, the baseball player whose achievements are proclaimed in the Baseball Hall of Fame, the writer or composer or painter whose creations become lasting cultural treasures: people such as these are and should be proud. But people who fall short of these and all other ideals of personal excellence and virtuosity have no business being proud, and whatever may be the ethical and religious teachings to the contrary, pride should not be urged upon them.

Some might want to insist, of course, that there is in each and every single human being *something* to be proud of. But this is no generalization drawn from experience. On the contrary, experience refutes it. Most people are, in the most ordinary sense, very limited. They pass their time, day after day, in idle, passive pursuits, just looking at things—at games, television, whatever. Or they fill the hours talking, mostly about nothing of significance—of comings and goings, of who is doing what, of the weather, of things forgotten almost as soon as they are mentioned. They have no aspirations for themselves beyond getting through another day doing more or less what they did yesterday. They walk across the stage of life, leaving everything about as it was when they entered, achieving nothing, aspiring to nothing, having never a profound or even original thought, doing what those around them are doing, getting through life with as little discomfort as possible, and finally leaving behind not so much as a durable memory of themselves. It is, indeed, almost as if they had never been. This is what is common, usual, typical, indeed normal. Relatively few rise much above such plodding existence. They have self-love, to be sure, but in spite of the almost universal conviction that all these masses of people ought, and even deserve, to be proud, they cannot be. The conditions for genuine pride simply do not exist here. For pride is the *justified* love of yourself, and the only thing that can justify such love is your own personal excellence, your own achievements, your own special worth, something which is not the common lot of all.

This does not, of course, mean that true pride requires the recognition of greatness. Strength and virtue are generally honored, but not always, and sometimes your unique worth can be hidden from everyone but yourself. Honor is often posthumous, and probably much more often it never comes at all even though deserved. Heroes die unsung, and so do great artists. Not every profound thought finds expression, and persons of genius are sometimes struck down before a single fruit of their great souls finds expression. None of this detracts from the virtues of their possessors, however. Worth can only be measured by what one *is*, not merely by what one is seen by others to be. Had Plato's *Republic* perished in the rubble of his culture the loss to the civilizations that followed would have been immense, but such an accident would have detracted not at all from Plato's intrinsic greatness or worth. What is important is that here was a man who could create such a work, and whose pride was therefore not misguided. The greatness of such an achievement is inherent to it, as is the virtue of its author. Similarly, had Martin Luther King been murdered on his way to the march on Washington where he delivered, without notes or text, the speech that has come to be known as "I have a dream," then this would have been a gap in our history and would have diminished his fame, but it would not have diminished his greatness in the slightest. For the point remains that here was a man capable of such a feat, of creating something profoundly moving and beautiful, which no one else on earth could have done. Others could have inspired the civil rights movement, and of course many others did participate in those momentous events, but only he could create the speech that has reverberated in our minds ever since. His stature would have been no less had no one ever heard it. In the same way, Mozart's genius was not lessened by his early death, nor Beethoven's by his deafness, and the virtues of Helen Keller shine through the handicaps which, in lesser persons, would have been overwhelming.

It is thus not at all trite to say that goodness is its own reward, provided goodness is taken in the sense outlined here. Usually it is not. Goodness is usually thought of as goodness to others, that is, altruism—a shift of meaning that again reflects our religious heritage. To say that goodness in this sense, or unselfishly doing good for others, is its own reward is trite indeed, and quite simply false. It is a way people have of exhorting you to be unselfish or self-sacrificing without expecting anything in return—a manner of behaving that is useful indeed to everyone else but hardly useful to you except, perhaps, in terms of the nods of approval from those you so selflessly serve. To talk like this is much like telling a slave that he already has his reward in his very toil.

The reward of personal excellence is your knowledge that you possess it. That reward is, in other words, pride. If others heap honors on you for your achievements this is, of course, not unpleasant, but a proud person does not need this. Such a person knows his or her worth, without needing others to proclaim it. If you do a great deed—for example, save the life, health, or fortune of some deserving person through your own strength and wit— then the deed is done, and you know it, without needing praise. You already have your reward. And the beauty of your deed is not that someone was rescued from disaster, no matter how overwhelmingly important that may be to others. Its beauty lies in the strength and wit that you displayed, and that is *your* blessing.

Nor do great deeds need to be directed to the benefit of others, though this is how they are usually thought of. When we think of great deeds we are apt to think of the leader who saves his nation from disaster, the selfless risk of life to rescue a stranger, lifelong dedication to relieving the downtrodden, and so on. But the beauty of a deed is not in its fruits but in the character it displays and this requires no participation of others. A poem of unique worth requires no audience to be what it is, nor does the poet require applause in order to rejoice in the creation of it. Thus did Emily Dickinson write essentially for herself, and her genius was displayed in these poems themselves, not in the presentation of them, for she kept them mostly to herself. Even if they had never been seen by another's eyes they would nevertheless have remained what they were, as would their creator. Similarly, the philosopher who thinks profoundly and truly is no less a philosopher for keeping his thoughts to himself. His contribution to culture is less for that, and so is his fame, but not his profundity and acumen. Van Gogh, whose paintings are sold at auctions for millions today, sold only one during his lifetime, for forty-five dollars. His aspiration was to paint, not to sell paintings. Genius is sometimes content with itself, and this is not hard to understand when you realize that things of great worth should be brought about for what they are and not for some additional ornamentation that they do not need. Glenn Gould's chief aim in life was to render Bach's music with perfection, and he so despised an audience that he finally refused to go before one, in spite of the clamoring of those who knew what he, virtually alone, could do.

The blessings of the proud are thus precious indeed, but they are inner blessings. For it must be remembered that pride is the justified love of oneself, and all that justifies such love is excellence or virtuosity that is genuine, whether recognized by anyone else or not. To be loved by others is doubtless a reason to rejoice, but it is not by itself a reason to be proud. That will depend on *why* you are loved by others, and when you know that, then you will know whether or not to deem yourself a proud person. You can find the answer to that only in yourself. Others can bestow honors, but they cannot bestow excellence or pride. That must be your work, and yours alone, provided you have what it takes to do it.

Thus far the meaning of pride has been illustrated mostly in terms of great and sometimes dramatic achievements—the creation of great works and the doing of earth-shaking deeds. But this is not essential to the idea. You take pride in yourself for what you are, and what you are is, indeed, proved by what you are capable of doing; but what you do with uncommon skill may be something the great worth of which might be known to few besides yourself. The fruits of the kind of character in which one justifiably takes pride need no recognition by others. However sweet may be others' acclaim, the justification of your love of yourself requires no authentication by them. What is required is only that such self-love be justified, that is, that you be correct in your assessment of your worth, and this might sometimes be true even in the face of your being repudiated by all. The approbation of others does, to be sure, enhance your confidence in your own self-approbation, but that is not what it rests on. If you know that you are very good at something, perhaps uniquely so, then you still know it even when the rest of the world does not. And it is this knowledge, and this alone, upon which pride rests.

Personal excellence, therefore, requires no recognition, no authentication by others. More than this, it need not even be recognizable; that is, a person's worth often rests upon some strength or ability which the world might not recognize as of much value even when clearly displayed. Genius, even great genius, can be in small things, in things that most persons might regard as even insignificant. What is required for personal excellence is that its possessor be able to do something with extraordinary skill. It need not be some great or dramatic thing.

For example, there are people who have an uncanny ability for parenting. They are not merely parents, for there is no creativity or merit in that; anyone can beget children. They are *good* parents, in ways that are not easily described and cannot be reduced to formulae. Such people, by a kind of natural talent, consistently make the right choices with respect to raising their children. They do things right where others, with every good intention, consistently blunder. Such an ability, precious both in itself and in its fruits, is nowhere regarded as a mark of genius, even though it is far from common. It is, nevertheless, a source of pride in its possessors, and quite properly so. They know that they are very good at something that many attempt and relatively few really succeed at. They have, therefore, a *justified* or well-founded love for themselves, and it is no less justified for being virtually unrecognized and even unrecognizable by others. People are often admired for their parenting skills, but they are never thought to be heroic for that. Such pride, accordingly, comes from within, not from the plaudits of others.

The same is true of numberless other skills, things quite commonly done but rarely done well. One thinks of the expert at gardening, the person with the "green thumb," an expression that is meant precisely to convey that the talent thus displayed is inherent and not something merely learned from others through imitation. Or consider such examples as the chess expert, or a fine pianist, whose endless practice simply hones a natural ability rather than bestowing it, or someone gifted at acting, or dancing, or one possessed of great wit who sees through the ordinary to the subtle. Others hear the same words and sounds and see the same sights, but this person effortlessly sees beyond these to what others do not see, to shades of meaning, hidden absurdities, and all the nuances, the perception of which distinguish someone of great wit from virtually everyone else. Those who are blessed with such gifts almost never receive great honors for them, and they even, sometimes, do not even receive significant notice, yet they are precious things and very proper sources of pride. The very word *gifts* implies much about them; namely, that they are precious, and that they are not the result of the kind of effort and practice that anyone with the requisite energy and determination might have. Gifts of this kind are neither earned, deserved, nor labored for, nor is there any giver of them. They are simply abilities that in whatever way set one apart from and above the ordinary run of humankind. Such things as clumsiness, dullness, and stupidity are never described as gifts. They are quite literally faults or defects, qualities which, to the extent that they set their possessors apart from others, also set them beneath them.

GOODNESS

Think of two people, very different from each other, whom we'll simply call Ms. A and Ms. B.

Ms. A's life is governed by benevolence. She is by nature sympathetic and sensitive to suffering of whatever kind, whether in people, even total strangers, or in animals, and much of her time and energy are spent trying to lessen it. Although not wealthy, she gives all she can to charitable organizations, sends money abroad where famine has spread, gives to animal shelters, helps the homeless and the sick. Her hand goes, as if by impulse, to her checkbook at every report of need. She is a person of limited personal achievement. One can point to nothing of much worth that she has wrought. She lives a simple, unimaginative, pedestrian life, going day in and day out to the boring job she has held for thirty years, doing each day more or less what she was doing the day and, indeed, the year before. What matters to her is not herself and her fortunes, but others. She is, in the fullest sense, devoted to others, even to the world, wherever anything that she can do will amount to help. She is a warm-hearted, compassionate, loving human being, the epitome of what one would call a *good* person.

Ms. B, on the other hand, is concerned primarily with herself. She is not indifferent to suffering and need, and contributes, when asked, to organizations that exist to alleviate these, but this is not at all the direction of her life. She is a writer, highly successful in terms of the quality of her work. Her days are spent writing, all other concerns, even concerns for family and day-to-day responsibilities, being secondary to this. Her books, novels, and poems have earned her a glowing reputation in the literary public and in the circles of academe, and some of the best reviewers and scholars have hailed her as among the century's few writers of lasting worth. She is gifted, brilliant, creative, and driven; she is, in short, a *good*, outstanding specimen of humanity.

Now note that these two people are utterly different in their values and the directions of their lives, one of them living primarily for others, the other primarily for herself and her creations. And yet, each, precisely because of these totally different attributes, is correctly described by the same adjective, *good*. No one could dispute that the first is, indeed, a good woman—the epitome of human goodness. But no one could dispute, either, that the second is a good woman—among the very best, an ornament to her nation and culture. But it is a totally different sense of goodness.

Now nothing in the pages that follow will be understood unless these two totally different kinds of human goodness are kept apart. The first is simply *benevolence*. The second is *personal excellence*. One can easily have one, and fall far short with respect to the other. A Picasso can be quite lacking in the goodness of Mother Teresa, and conversely, Mother Teresa can be quite lacking in the kind of goodness or human worth so dramatically displayed in a creative genius like Picasso. Both are paradigms of what is good, but in two totally different senses of goodness.

The pagan philosophers of antiquity, some of whose reflections are everlasting treasures—Socrates, Plato, Aristotle, and those who followed in their steps—*always* had personal excellence in mind when they thought of human goodness. Thus, when Aristotle spoke of a *good man*, he was not, even remotely, thinking of a man who is benevolent. He was thinking of someone more like Alexander the Great, someone who is capable of achieving great things. When Plato spoke of a good ruler, he meant, to be sure, one who is just—but justice was for Plato a kind of personal excellence, a condition of its possessor. It was not defined in terms of how such a person treated others. And when Socrates spoke of a good man he, too, had personal excellence in mind, and nothing else. Personal goodness was for Socrates the possession of a certain kind of mind, namely, one characterized by wisdom, and had little to do with the quality of the heart, that is, benevolence.

This notion of human goodness was virtually lost with the advent and spread of Christianity, a religion unknown to the classical moralists just mentioned. For the teaching of Christianity was totally different, indeed even antithetical to this concept. Human goodness came to be defined in terms of how one treats *others*, not in terms of what one does with *oneself*. The antithesis is perfectly illustrated by the Sermon on the Mount, in which personal worth and excellence are *dismissed* in favor of their opposites. It is the meek, the poor, the downtrodden who are declared good—indeed, the very best, the "salt of the earth." Such utterances would have been incomprehensible to the Greeks; indeed, they would have been flat contradictions. By good, as applied to persons, the Greeks meant, quite simply, the *superior*—superior not in social status but in terms of personal achievement, intelligence, and creative power. The good, the Greeks thought, were those who make the great difference between being civilized and being barbarians or, indeed, between being fully human and being akin to animals.

Today we think of human goodness in the sense fostered by religion. Most people are unable to disentangle themselves from this notion, with the result that the insights of the ancient pagan philosophers are not only unappreciated, they are totally misunderstood. We find Aristotle alluding to a good man, for example, and then describing such a man's contempt for slaves and other inferior people, and it seems to make no sense. It in fact makes sense to anyone capable of going back to the original, Greek sense of human goodness. Modern readers of Aristotle might, having finally understood what Aristotle was saying, want to disagree with it, but they would at least understand what was being said if they could for a moment rid themselves of the meaning of human goodness first fostered by religion.

Although we, of this Christianized culture, think of human goodness almost entirely as benevolence, the original meaning of the term has not vanished entirely Thus, when the Marine Corps advertises that it is looking for "a few good men" it is not meant that the Corps is seeking recruits from the tender-hearted. The Marines are looking for some superior men—superior in strength and courage. When a police officer is killed in the line of duty and the mayor extols him as having been "a fine man," he is not primarily praising his benevolence. He is saying that the officer was an outstanding specimen of manhood. And when the editor of a great newspaper slaps one of his reporters on the back and exults, "you're a good man, Ed," the reporter is not being praised for having a warm heart, but for doing something extraordinarily well, better than could be expected from most others.

It would be idle and off the track to argue over which is the true meaning of human goodness. *Both* are correct. The very same word *good* is used to express two totally different ideas, and it is used correctly in either case. Some persons, contemplating human nature generally, will admire the warm-hearted or compassionate, while others will have a preference for persons of significant achievement, but this is not a difference of opinion between them. It is simply a difference in what they value most.

Nor do we mean, by calling attention to this distinction, to raise the question of which is *better*, benevolence or personal excellence. That is obviously something on which intelligent people can disagree, without either of them being mistaken.

We are here calling attention to this distinction of meanings, this profound ambiguity, only in order to avoid confusion, a natural, almost inevitable confusion which, unless understood, would lead any reader to miss entirely the point of all that follows.

In these pages, human goodness will mean personal excellence, as it did to the Greeks. Aristotle declared that a proud or magnanimous man must, first of all, be *good*—for otherwise, of course, he would have nothing in himself to be proud *of*. And what he meant was that such a man must be superior to others in some worthwhile way. And this is what all the Greeks meant by being possessed of virtue—a word that will rarely be used in the discussion to follow, simply because its corruption by religion has been even more thoroughgoing than the corruption of the idea of human goodness.

GOODNESS AND
HUMAN SUPERIORITY

The fact that the term *good* can be applied to a person in two totally different senses—the Greek sense of personal excellence, on the one hand, and the Christian sense of benevolence, on the other—gives rise to another point that is in serious danger of being misinterpreted. This can be clarified as follows.

In describing someone as *good* we shall, in these pages, usually mean that there is something about this person, other than the benevolent treatment of others, that is outstandingly good; that is, we will be using the word in the Greek sense of personal excellence. Thus, saying that someone "is a good woman" will not mean that she is sweet and kind. Any simpleton can be sweet and kind. It will mean that she has some strength, virtue, or excellence that sets her apart—for example, that she has extraordinary judgment in some area or other, or that she is highly creative, or that she is a fine painter or musician or composer or author—something of this sort.

The immediate implication of this is that some people are better than, or superior to, others, and this is a way of speaking that is in some circles highly unpopular. It is dismissed as "elitist" or "undemocratic." And that is where the misinterpretation comes in.

45

Consider first, that some people are, in plain fact, better than others. This means nothing more than that, with respect to certain strengths or valuable abilities, some people excel while others do not. To deny this would be simply silly. Not everyone has excellent judgment, though some do. Not everyone is gifted with a high degree of intelligence, though some are. Or, with respect to any pursuit or ability that is universally honored—such as the power to create things of great worth, to create lasting art, literature, music, and so on—some people have such an ability to a very high degree, while others do not. Those who possess such creative power to a high degree are relatively few, while those who do not are overwhelmingly numerous—this being, again, a matter of fact. The only way such an observation could be attacked as dubious would be by misinterpreting it, or reading into it some claim that it does not contain.

Beethoven, for example, was uniquely gifted with respect to his creative power in music. Anyone appreciative of that power and its fruits is inclined to regard its possessor as almost godlike, so extraordinary were his achievements. Had Beethoven lacked that gift, then his works—his sonatas, symphonies, and so on—would never have existed, nor would anything quite like them ever have come into being. They were all due to him. So it can be truly said that, with respect to this art and this creative power, Beethoven was superior, vastly superior, to virtually the entire rest of humankind. And, since those creations of his are, by universal consent of persons capable of appreciating them, things of great and lasting worth, then their creator, the man who brought them into being, is someone of great and lasting worth, a person who is in the fullest sense a better man than the overwhelming majority of those who walk on earth. This does not, of course, mean that he was a good man in the sense of being sweet and compassionate, for he was not known for those qualities, but that he was possessed, to a high and almost unique degree, of a singular personal excellence.

Now, one is likely to ask, isn't *everyone*? That is, is there not something that virtually *everyone* does well? And if so, does not this alleged superiority of a Beethoven evaporate after all?

One sees in this sort of remark a strained effort to preserve an egalitarian point of view at whatever cost. It would not have the least plausibility to anyone not thus motivated. In the first place, it probably is not even true that everyone does something especially well. Many perfectly normal and ordinary people seem to have no special abilities at all. They are born, live out their perfectly ordinary lives, and die, having had virtually no effect on the world beyond those who happened to know them. There is, of course, nothing wrong with this, but it is not compatible with the claim that everyone does something or other exceptionally well, and that, therefore, no one can be superior to anyone else with respect to any abilities or special gifts.

But—and this is the more important point—even if we were to grant this claim, it would not follow that no one is really superior to anyone else. That is, even if we were to suppose that everyone, or nearly everyone, does something especially well, or that we are all of us gifted with respect to something or other, that would hardly make us all equals. The Beethovens, Picassos, Shakespeares, and Aristotles would still stand out as superior beings, as better specimens of humanity than virtually all the rest. And in general, with respect to any group of people, there will still be some few who are better than the rest; not merely better with respect to this or that, but better human beings, superior to the others.

The reason for this is that some abilities or capacities are worth more than others. Some are, indeed, immeasurable treasures to their possessors, while others are of trivial significance. It is this fact that enables us, with universal consensus, to single out certain individuals as persons of greatness.

This can perhaps best be seen through an illustration.

Thus there exists somewhere a man who is the slingshot champion of the world. He was briefly brought to public attention on television years ago and then immediately all but forgotten.

He has loved slingshots since he was a kid, and all his life has entertained himself with them. He always has one with him and, at any opportunity, continues to hone his skill. He can hit virtually anything within range with one try. He can toss a can into the air and hit it with his slingshot before it falls to the ground. He can shoot from a variety of positions, or with either hand, between his legs or even from behind his back, with deadly accuracy.

Now this man is, to be sure, superior to everyone else in the world with respect to this ability. Does this mean that someone of universally recognized greatness, such as Beethoven, is no better than this man? Does it all just come down to saying that Beethoven is the better composer, while the slingshot champion is the better with slingshots—and that, beyond this, neither is better than the other?

Hardly, for while skill with a slingshot, even great and unique skill, is to some extent entertaining to its possessor and perhaps a marvel to onlookers, it hardly compares in its worth to the creative power of Beethoven. This is simply obvious. A Beethoven is a credit not only to his culture but to the whole of humankind, and no one would withhold the description of him as a great man. His greatness as a person rests upon his possession of virtues or creative powers that are inherently great and good.

No one, on the other hand, would want to describe the slingshot champion as a great man, just because of his skill with a slingshot; for while this skill may be great, impressive, and unique, it is one of little inherent value. Its possessor is no ornament to his culture or to humankind. He is but a person who has honed a relatively insignificant, albeit entertaining, skill to perfection.

Some persons will, of course, at this point say, "Yes, but who's to be the judge of which abilities are precious and which are not?" But to make that kind of remark, and expect to be taken seriously, would simply mark one as invincibly vulgar, even beyond hope. No person of even elementary intelligence would suggest that the gifts of a Beethoven amount to no more than those of a slingshot expert, except, perhaps, to prolong an argument. The suggestion is merely silly.

This brings us, finally, to the possibility of truly dangerous misinterpretation. For someone, led to this point, is sure to say that this philosophy is elitist, and is thus incompatible with the most basic of democratic values. Taken seriously, it would therefore threaten the most basic of human values and even the faith in democratic society. All people are equal, no one can in the final analysis be a better human being than the rest, no persons or groups of persons have any natural superiority over others—all these are just ways of saying the same thing, and are affirmations of the values upon which rest the most precious of democratic ideals, such as the basic human rights of everyone, and so on. If some persons were, by their very natures, superior to others, if some were considered better as human beings, then the supposition of basic human rights shared by all would be destroyed. Carried to its logical conclusion this elitist philosophy would justify the division of society into the deserving few and the relatively worthless masses, the latter to be ruled and exploited for the benefit of those who have been somehow deemed worthy. The belief in the natural superiority of any group or class, and the consequent natural inferiority of all the rest, cannot be made compatible with democratic society or even with the most basic principles of public policy and ethics upon which contemporary progressive societies rest. It is more akin to the ugly expressions of despotism and fascism against which people have struggled throughout human history This conception of human nature thus has no place in the thinking of enlightened people.

What has happened here is that the equality of rights has been totally confused with the equality of human beings, when in truth they are utterly different.

In the first place, it is a simple *fact* that people do not all possess the same abilities, and that the vast array of talents and capacities that people do possess are, by almost universal consent, of unequal worth. Some are honored for what they can do, and are long remembered for what they have done, while most, quite properly and correctly, are not. This is but an observation of fact. And this is no less true in a democratic society than in others; indeed, the bestowal of honor and tribute, *where it is deserved,* is far more likely to occur within a democratic society than any other. Fascists do not regularly honor the good. They honor fascists and thugs. The suggestion, therefore, that any recognition of the natural superiority of some is incompatible with democratic ideals is simply false. To a large extent a background of democratic principles is essential to this philosophy, however derisively it may be dismissed as "elitist."

And in the second place, the affirmation of the equality of human rights does not at all rest upon any assumption of the equality of worth in human beings. The Beethovens, Picassos, and Aristotles among us have but one vote each, must obey the same laws as everyone else, and can claim no special treatment in any court of law. This is exactly as it should be, for human history has shown that such policy works. To confer rights on some and withhold them from others opens the door to endless abuses and misery. So, whether human beings are in fact all of equal worth or not makes no difference with respect to human rights. All people must, under law and public policy, be treated as equals—which is to say, treated as if they were all of equal worth, whether in fact they are or not. The justification of this is pragmatic, and it is overwhelming.

So the lesson is, for the proud: Uphold at whatever cost the equality of rights for all persons, resisting any effort anywhere to compromise it. And then, having made sure of that, do what you can to nourish those capacities in you which mark you as good, that is, better as a specimen of humanity. There can be no other genuine basis for pride. Pride is pride in *yourself,* that is, in what you are, and you are without any basis for it if all you are is common. Just as an idiot cannot take pride in his idiocy, nor a vulgarian in his lack of taste and refinement, no one can take pride in the mere fact of his humanity. Being human is something that the best share with the worst.

PERSONAL SUPERIORITY

The quest for personal excellence seems to run directly counter to certain social values that have been ingrained in us from childhood. Excellence is something that admits of degrees, and the fact that personal excellence must be sought and cultivated implies that one might fail to achieve it and, indeed, that one might fail even to seek it. The fact that this kind of excellence being alluded to here is *personal* suggests, quite correctly, that some people might be better *as persons* than others. This is not only antithetical to the egalitarianism that is thought to be essential to democratic values, but also to an ancient cultural tradition according to which all persons are inherently equal. This has been expressed in a religious context in the claim that all are equal in God's view or, similarly, that all persons, regardless of any circumstances of their births or their lives or what may happen to them, reflect an image of God and are, indeed, created by God in that image. This view of human nature finds its most eloquent expression in the Sermon on the Mount, in which the very least among us—the meek, the poor, and what the world might regard as those of little worth—are declared to be not merely equal to the best, but actually *better* than they. They are, in this brief discourse which is generally thought to be the foundation of Christian social ethics, declared to be *better* than all the rest, to be blessed beyond measure, the salt of the earth and its rightful inheritors.

So deeply ingrained are these egalitarian values that they are, by most people, simply taken for granted. You are not allowed ever to consider yourself better as a person than anyone else. You may be more learned, more beautiful, wiser, stronger, more courageous, and so on through every imaginable virtue, but no matter what these may be, or how justified your claim to embody them, none of them can make you one whit better as a person than the poorest, most foolish, ignorant, and intemperate wastrel. That person will always be your equal, no matter what, and you must not allow yourself to think otherwise.

Such, at any rate, is how we have all been taught to think. The presupposition of absolute equality runs through all our speech and thought, and anyone who raises a doubt about it is viewed with a suspicion of basic evil and bad motive. People who have made themselves wise, learned, creative, resourceful, and strong are admired for possessing these virtues, but they must never speak as though such qualities bestowed any value upon themselves as persons.

There is obviously a great deal of hypocrisy here. It has to be granted that a presupposition of equality must, as a practical matter, govern all social and political policy and the application of law. No one can be deemed to be entitled to more votes for the possession of superior wisdom, even though it is obvious that some people do cast their votes more wisely than others. One cannot claim exemption from taxes merely on the basis of virtues, no matter how impressive these may be. Nor can anyone claim exemption from the application of criminal statutes.

But the principle of human equality embodied in such policies as these rest entirely on practical considerations of overwhelming importance, not on any fact. To treat people differently, solely on account of their different degrees of goodness, would give rise to numberless questions and problems impossible to resolve and, worse yet, would open the gates to all kinds of abuse and exploitation. *Who's to say?* This is the first question that arises, and the question itself throws into doubt any proposed social or political policy that would rest upon distinctions of personal worth.

A presupposition of human equality is thus absolutely essential to a well-ordered and stable social and political life. The mischief begins, however, when such a claim, whose value is purely pragmatic, is taken to express some natural truth. For it is plainly not a truth. Since some people achieve personal excellence through the cultivation of their creative powers—that is, through wisdom, strength, resourcefulness, and imagination—while others do not, it does follow that some persons are better than others. They are not better merely in the sense of being more skilled at this or that activity, or merely by being richer, or from any other accidental consideration. They are superior as persons. They have a degree of personal worth that is lacking in others.

That is the fact, and it is up to a proud person, that is, anyone who is genuinely better than others, to find some way of acknowledging this *without* implying that he or she rejects egalitarianism as a practical principle of social, political, and legal policy. The claim of superiority suggests insufferable arrogance. Thus even if you are clearly entitled to make such a claim you should under no circumstances do so, except to yourself. The egalitarian ideology is so firmly entrenched, and so tenaciously held, that people generally will not permit it to be questioned. And if you question its truth *in your own favor*; that is, if you suggest that other people may be inferior to you as persons, then you will risk being reviled as an elitist or even a fascist, no matter how vehemently you may proclaim the egalitarian principle as essential to social and political life.

But there can be nothing wrong with your aspiring to be a better person than you are, which is to say, one who exercises his capacities for a creative life, and there can thus be nothing wrong with your aspiring to be a better person than those who simply allow their capacities for a creative life to stagnate and die. You have in you something that can be regarded as being, if not divine, at least something uniquely human and good. It resides in the power of your mind to think and act creatively. It is this that makes you a person in the first place. You are not a person just by virtue of having two arms and two legs and an upright stature, or whatever else distinguishes you biologically from other creatures. There is no uniquely human worth in these. Your worth as a person lies within you and, unless you treasure it and cultivate it, it dies, and, with it, whatever worth you ever had. Your primary business in life should be to not let this happen. Whatever may be the solicitations of the world—the temptations of wealth or power or status or recognition or whatever—you will, if you have any sense of personal worth, scorn these in favor of the only thing that this sense of worth can rest upon. You should not, indeed, really cannot, love *yourself* for your wealth or status or power, however much these may impress others. But you can love yourself for what you are, provided what you are is worth loving. If it is, your self-love will be justified, and you will be proud.

So, if you see a man, frightfully obese, stuffing his mouth with every kind of injudicious food and rendering his condition even worse, you need not say: I am superior to that man. But you can certainly say, if it is true: I am not, like him, a glutton.

And if you see women sitting around a table, playing some mindless card game, giggling and chattering about nothing of significance, killing half a day in essentially pointless activity, you need not say: I am better than these. But you certainly can say, in case it is true: I am not, like them, silly and unthinking.

And if you see a pompous man, puffing himself up, talking much and hearing nothing, calling attention to his power and position, insensitive to those around him, then you need not say to anyone: I am a better person than he. But you can say, in case it is true: I am not, like him, a pompous bore.

Conversely, if you see someone doing something very well, displaying creative gifts that have been cultivated to a high degree of excellence—a musician, for example, or a writer, or the pursuer of things more plebeian such as horticulture or skilled parenting, or whatever may rest upon creative powers that have not been allowed to atrophy—then admit, with some sense of shame, that you are not as worthy as a person as she. And do something about it. That ought, by nature, to be your primary business in life.

LIVING FOR YOURSELF

If a man is described as someone who just "lives for himself" it has a decidedly negative connotation, primarily that of selfishness in its worst sense. You think of someone disregardful of others in his drive to fulfill his own wants, and of these wants themselves as being less than noble. You imagine him, perhaps, as ambitious for personal status and gain, and willing to achieve these at the expense of other people.

There is, however, another sense of living for oneself that is quite the opposite of this.

To begin to see this other meaning, think, for example, of a mother who is described as living for her children. Here the image is one of unselfish devotion. This mother wants what is best for her children, and unhesitatingly forfeits some of her own fulfillments in favor of theirs. She rejoices in their achievements and, to the extent that they grow up to be fine, honorable, and creative men and women, she is herself fulfilled.

If, on the other hand, this mother spent her energy trying to satisfy the least worthy of her children's needs, then she would not, except in a debased sense, be thought of as someone who lived for her children, or even really cared much for them. Thus, if she imposed little discipline on them, yielded to their cravings for junk foods and toys, and had no concern for nourishing worthy inclinations and capacities, she would not be a mother who lived for her children. She would instead resemble a slave to them.

Similarly, if a man is described as living for his wife, for example, the image is again one of unselfish devotion. He sees in her what is noble and good, and his life is centered around these. Again one could give a different and debased meaning to the expression, by thinking of a man who simply lavished upon his wife the satisfactions of her most childish and foolish desires and whims, but that is not the meaning that first springs to mind.

Let us, then, think of living for yourself in this nobler way, which is really what the expression should mean, if you think about it. If you *really* live for yourself, then you will certainly *not* fit the image of being disregardful of others in a headlong drive to satisfy your ambition for wealth, power, and status. Indeed, that is the description of someone who does *not* live for himself, but lives for those things—wealth, power, and status. To live for yourself is to devote your strength, energy, and thought to what is *good* in yourself, and to make it better. It is a quest for personal excellence and nobility. That is something you are capable of attaining; so if you are really concerned with yourself and, literally, with your own good or well-being, then that is what you will try to achieve, putting everything else aside in order to do it. And this means, of course, putting aside any fondness you might have for such things as wealth and status, in favor of what really matters to you, namely, yourself. No one was ever made better as a person by the acquisition of money, or a more powerful position. On the contrary, these are strong forces for the corruption of whatever is good in you. Therefore, if you really, in the strictest sense, "just live for yourself," then you will scorn specious externals such as these, no matter how they might glitter and tempt you. There is something that glows with more beauty than these, and that is your own nobility as a person.

And just what is that? Of what does this nobility consist? Well, consider that which is best in you, that which sets you apart, not only from all the other creatures on the earth, but from the mass of humankind who are foolish, shallow, absorbed in petty things, and who live just for themselves in the debased sense. What you find, by this simple guide, is that you have the capacity to think, rationally and perhaps profoundly; you have a love for what is true, even though it may be a trivial truth, or an unwelcome one; and you have the power to create something— something which, but for you, would never exist anyplace on the face of the earth. These are the kinds of things that set you apart as good—not necessarily good in the sense of being benevolent, but good in the sense of being an outstanding specimen of the human race. You do not *have* to be ordinary. You do not *have* to be another nothing, or someone who counts for so little because you make no difference anywhere. What your thought, reason, and creative power achieve may or may not dazzle the world. The chances are overwhelming that it will not. But that is of little importance. What is important is that you, as a person, will have done something worthwhile that perhaps no one else could do. You will have left the mark of your nobility and goodness on something, and even if it turns out that only you ever see or appreciate that mark, you still will have succeeded in everything that counts. You will indeed have lived for your *self*, and justified your love for yourself. And you can be proud.

CREATING YOUR OWN LIFE

Human creative effort is exercised in many directions— poetry, music, graphic art, innovative businesses; the list is very long. Sometimes it attracts little attention, because the result does not immediately affect many lives, as in the case of many gifted teachers, parents, and so on; but creativity of this kind need be no less fulfilling. Sometimes, indeed, people find deep fulfillment in the humblest of projects, which still require their unique creative gifts even though they are of little interest to most people. These are the putterers and inventors of all kinds. Their goal is not primarily to draw applause or to enrich themselves, but just to show *themselves* that there is something quite original that they can do, and which few, if any, others can do. They do not merely laboriously assemble something, but carry out some imaginative dream. Having done it, they can note, with deep satisfaction, what they have wrought, with the realization that, but for them, it would never have been done. Such, for example, is the horticulturist who creates a new plant variety, the naturalist whose industry and vision bring about a wildlife sanctuary, and so on. These people, sometimes hardly known, nevertheless fulfill what is uniquely human in us all and thereby give their lives the only true meaning they can have. To do otherwise, to just passively receive pleasant sensations, to eat and drink and reproduce, to merely get through life with the minimum of pain and boredom, is to be no better than a dumb animal.

Quite apart from any inventory of creative goals, there is one creative pursuit that is open to anyone possessed of imagination, intelligence, courage, and a correct conception of what life is all about. That pursuit is the creation of a life—one's *own* life. You have within you the power to do something that few others, and possibly no one else, can do. It may be something that, perhaps unpredictably, will leave a mark on the world and make your name known for generations, or more likely, it will turn out to be something that is more or less unnoticed by the rest of the world. That does not matter. It will be noticed by *you*, and you are the only person on earth who needs to be impressed. For remember, you are your own judge, and a severe one. What the rest of the world thinks of you is of little importance. It has its own concerns and values. But what you think of yourself is of overwhelming importance, for you, too, have your own concerns and values. You need only make sure that what concerns you tests and fulfills your own, perhaps unique, creative power, and that your values lie in this direction. You do not have to take your values from others. You do not need to merely absorb what the world offers like a sponge, or imitate others like an ape; however pleasant may be their applause (if it is ever given), the only person whose applause you will really ever need is your own. It is your life, and you are the final judge of it. If you make of your own life a work of art, and it becomes beautiful in your eyes, bearing in mind that your standards are high and severe, then what do you care if the world is blind to the worth of what you have created? You will have satisfied the judge who counts, for that is no one but you.

All this sounds straightforward, perhaps even easy, but do not be fooled. This is the way of the proud, and it is uncommon and difficult. It requires you to cast aside something you have been taught to do almost from the moment you first drew breath. It requires you to disregard, as truly worthless, what others may think of you, and to set your own standard. You have a life to live; that is easy enough. But to create your own life is hard indeed, even though it may be a life of utter simplicity

Most people can never, even for a moment, disentangle themselves from the restraints imposed by those around them, nor can they disregard their approval. From the moment they began to understand their parents' smiles and frowns they have needed the moment-to-moment approval of everyone, even strangers. This is what they are deeply conscious of whenever they are with others, and their lives revolve around ways to get it. They wish to look good—to whom? To everyone, and this often means to everyone *but* themselves. Uppermost in their minds, whether conscious or not, are the questions: How do I look to them? What sort of an impression am I making? How do I stand in relation to all these people? These concerns govern their behavior. This is why they try to appear witty, or profound, or talented—whatever. They want those around them to think of them in these ways.

Thus, when people, even those unknown to each other, are thrown together in some sort of social situation, where conversation is called for, each vies with the others to be heard, to be clever, to elicit approval. They all instantly begin to silently compare themselves with the rest, with respect to their station in life, their worldly achievements, their wealth or power or position, and each tries by every means to appear good in these ways—to appear, indeed, somewhat better than is justified. A man of wealth and power misses no opportunity to drop hints of this; a woman of artistic achievement hopes that conversation will take a direction enabling her to call attention to this; someone accustomed to moving in the circles of the famous and near-famous misses no opportunity to allude to them, to "name drop," as it is called. The intention is not to call attention to these famous persons, but rather, to oneself as someone who moves in those circles. And why? Because this, it is hoped, will impress others, gain their approval and perhaps even envy.

But you need no special settings or situations to discern this overwhelming need of the multitude to impress others. These people measure their entire worth by what others think of them. In other words, instead of creating their own lives, they let the world create their lives for them. Instead of responding to what they themselves might want, if they but allow themselves to be what they are, they respond to what everyone else wants of them. If wealth is applauded, they seek wealth or, at least, the appearance of it. If status is applauded, they seek this. If piety is upheld, then they feign piety. How they choose, how they vote, what they do with their time, what they do on Sunday, how they dress, how they speak, indeed, how they think and feel—all these are in effect decided by those around them, that is, by everyone *else*, rather than by the only persons entitled to decide them, that is, themselves.

You see this in the simplest, day-to-day things. People often furnish and decorate their dwellings not merely for their comfort and pleasure, but for what others will think. If their furnishings inspire admiration and envy in others then they are well pleased with them. People sometimes pay extra for houses on streets that are associated with status. They want an address that will be noticed, and reflect well on them. They dress much the way others dress, and would feel mortified appearing in a garment that is worn or currently unfashionable, however satisfactory such a garment would otherwise be.

All this is so obvious and even banal that it would be hardly worth noting, except to call attention to one thing. These are not the proud. They would of course deny this, with vehemence, for few people would deny themselves the virtue of pride, but in fact they are not proud in any true sense of the word. They take their values from others, and their love for themselves rests overwhelmingly on what others think of them rather than on what they think of themselves. Looking good in their own eyes simply reduces to looking good in the eyes of everyone else. If they have the applause of the world, then they feel justified in applauding themselves. But they have thereby subordinated the judge who really counts.

If you can at some point look clearly at your own life, and if you can in truth declare to yourself that this life, that is, the way you have lived and the things you have achieved, are your own creation, then you can love yourself justifiably. You can be proud. But if to any extent the way you live your life is a response to how others would have you live it, it really is not your life at all, and there is nothing in it to form a basis of pride. Indeed, to the extent that your actions and pursuits are your responses to the will and the approval of other people, you are the very opposite of a proud person, for you are the slave of others. A willing slave, to be sure—but a slave, still.

LIFE AS ART

We are much absorbed in things around us. Our energy and creative thought are directed to externals. We want to make something new, erect great edifices, create new businesses or revamp old ones, invent machines, design electronic wonders that disclose things hitherto undreamt of. But we should remind ourselves that the materials for creating something truly worthwhile, and more precious than anything the world holds, lie very close at hand. They lie in ourselves.

Thus instead of supposing that a work of art must be something that all can behold—a poem, a painting, a book, a great building—consider making of your own life a work of art. You have yourself to begin with, and a time of uncertain duration to work on it. You do not have to be what you are, and even though you may be quite content with who and what you are, it will not be hard for you to think of something much greater that you might become. It need not be something spectacular or even something that will attract any notice from others. What it will be is a kind of excellence that you project for yourself, and then attain—something you can then take a look at, with honest self-appraisal, and be proud of.

The alternative is not very inviting. That is to live out your life, willy nilly, doing nothing with yourself except going from one day to the next, absorbed in externals, and then, in that inevitable evening of your life, looking back and seeing nothing in yourself, having done nothing with yourself to be proud of. But of course, just as people do not like to dwell upon their own death, neither do they like to look back on their own lives. They would rather dwell on the things around them, things they have affected, things they have wrought, and find their pride in these—in their children, their business, the scenes of their endeavors, everything but themselves.

Of course, as we have noted, the clearest way to prove your own personal excellence is by what you do, by your visible achievements. But the point to be made is that these should be the signs and symbols of what you are, and it is what you are that counts, not just the things you do.

You can, in other words, up to a point, *invent* or *create* your own life. You perhaps cannot be just anything you might aspire to be; you can find out, if you do not already know, by trying. But there is some personal excellence that can be yours. Perhaps you can be a great writer, a composer, a profound thinker, perhaps you can design a new enterprise in which your genius is displayed. Or perhaps it will be something far less dramatic, something that will be little appreciated except by you—yet it is you, as the judge of yourself, who counts. Perhaps your fulfillment will be as a great teacher, though one who, because of the blindness of most people, is not recognized. Perhaps you will learn things of great interest and significance to you, about which the rest of the world cares little or nothing. But the point is this: There is something, whether it is of the least significance to others or not, that you can become; something that, once achieved, you will find deeply and lastingly satisfying. You can then approach the evening of your life knowing, whether anyone else knows it or not, that you did it, and you can be proud. You will then measure your life not by years, but by what is in it, by what you yourself put in it, and then you will more than be at peace with yourself. You will be proud.

Another aspect of such a program of self-creation is that you can, at any point, start over. You need not invent your life once and for all; you can reinvent it as you go along. Just as you need not take your ideals from those around you—from your family, your group, your religion or whatever—so do you also not need to be stuck with whatever point you have gotten to. We are not omniscient. We go off in wrong directions, what we think we wanted turns out to be empty when achieved. And then it is time to start again. Have you failed as a writer? You need not be stuck with that role. Did you become a physician because everyone else praised that goal, and you just took their word for it? You need not be stuck with that, either. It is never too late for a new start, building on what you have but finding or, better, creating something new to become. Has your marriage failed? Then face the fact, and start over. Are you lonely and abandoned? You need not accept it. But through all these possible changes in the circumstances of your life—what are referred to as the externals—bear in mind that your primary interest must be in yourself, and what you are going to do with *that*. Look at yourself—not just at your place in the world, or at what to date you have done, but at who and what you *are* as a person. Are you pleased with what you see? Are you proud? If so, then you are blessed indeed. If not, then do something about it. Do not be tempted to take pride in putting up with what you are, and imagining that mere endurance is a virtue worthy of anyone's aspiration.

THE REINVENTION OF LIFE

Creative effort does not always produce the kind of result hoped for. Painters constantly modify what they are creating and sometimes cast it aside to begin all over. Composers and writers do the same.

It is the same with one's life. Rather few of us have the creative power or desire to express ourselves in such familiar areas as painting, music, and literature, but each of us has a life to live and the option of making of it a work of art. Most people just live out their lives more or less along the lines that are given to them by others. They lack the courage to strike out on their own, to find within themselves and within their imaginations and innermost aspirations an original ideal of what they should make of themselves. But if you can shake yourself loose from the dead weight of the conventions that have been imposed on you, if you have the heart for risk and are willing, in this sense, to risk your life to achieve something that is truly your own, then you have at hand all you need for a creative life, a life that will be the fulfillment of yourself rather than of what everyone else expects of you. Or you can, if you lack the courage to be different, recline on the soft and comfortable bed of inherited custom and convention, go into an undisturbed sleep there, and let what is unique and precious in you simply die. That is the easy road, not usually chosen but simply accepted as given. The reward of it is that you will disturb no one, elicit criticism from no one, be deemed safe and blameless by all, and will even receive the praise of everyone, for you will have left unchallenged the rules, customs, and values that *they* have given you. And you will, of course, have become a slave without knowing it. The idea of a proud slave is of course a contradiction, but so is the idea of a proud person beholden to convention. You may take deep satisfaction in leading a life based more or less on the values others have given you, for we are social beings, and we like to fit in, accommodate ourselves to the rest, and bask in their approval. You can indeed do that, as most do, and be deeply self-satisfied; but you cannot be proud. You can tell yourself, a thousand times over, that you are proud, and you can be utterly convinced of it, even glorying in your sense of pride. But your pride will be illusory, for your love of yourself will not be justified by what *you* have done. It will be derived only from the delicious approval of others.

The world is sometimes shaken and the course of history altered by one proud person giving his or her own life a new and hitherto untested direction, but that is not what is fundamentally important. What is important is that this life itself—in the biographical rather than the biological sense—is redeemed by its possessor. That person decides to be a slave no more, to do his or her own bidding rather than the bidding of everyone else, to find the true self and become it.

Malcolm X, after years of being nothing but a thief, his vast talents lying untested, remade himself while in prison and, upon emerging, became one of the most dynamic leaders of this century. He had a vision of what he could be and, against overwhelming pressures and obstacles, made it real. His life became his own work of art, so that eventually, looking out a window at Harvard University, where he was about to speak, he saw the roofs of Roxbury, scene of his criminal past, and had driven home to him what he had, by himself, done with himself.

The story repeats itself throughout history. Gautama Buddha left the comfort of princely luxury to become a mendicant and, through his own contemplation and thought, find the meaning and purpose of his own life and, thereby, an appropriate goal for humankind. He totally transformed himself not by heeding some plan handed to him by a rich religious tradition, but by discovering his own true ideal. And having made of his life this work of art, he transformed the lives of millions, with insight so profound and liberating that we draw inspiration from it still.

Epictetus was a Roman slave who discovered that he had it within himself to rise, as a person, above the emperors of the world, not in worldly glory but in a personal excellence so vivid that, in time, even the emperor Marcus Aurelius was converted to his Stoic philosophy. What Epictetus discovered, following the inspiration of Socrates, was that he was himself his most precious possession, far more important than all the goods of the world, and that it was therefore his mission to perfect himself. You do not let your most precious possession simply rot, through corruption or neglect. You tend and perfect it, and conform it to the ideal standard that your mind and reason disclose.

Other examples come easily to mind. Gandhi's life, for example, presents the same pattern. He was a lawyer who could have rested content with the relative security that his education made possible, but he had a different vision of himself and followed it, eventually challenging the British Empire and winning, simply on the strength of what he was and what his millions of followers saw in him.

St. Augustine led a dissolute and intemperate life of pleasure and would certainly have gone to his grave a wasted talent, having done nothing except live life out; but he had a vision, radically changed the direction of his life in the light of that vision, and became a towering father of the church. He thought that his vision, and the words he imagined he heard, were vouchsafed by God.

This is, of course, dubious, to say the least. The important point is that, from whatever incentive, St. Augustine was able to reinvent his life in a most dramatic way. His theology, for better or worse, still drives the thinking of the church, as it will for centuries to come.

Of course history and contemporary life, too, provide numerous familiar examples of people who, by remaking themselves, alter the world forever. Abraham Lincoln educated himself and, through the combination of his wisdom, strength, sensitivity, and a pride that was graciously blended with humility, became an inspiration to the world. Martin Luther King, Jr.'s, brief career is similar. He could have rested on the comfort and security of his education and an established position in the church, but instead chose nonviolent resistance and jail in the pursuit of an ideal.

Examples such as these are misleading, however, if they suggest that personal fame, resulting from an impact on the world, are what count. What matters is not the effect upon the world of what you do with your life. What counts is simply what you do with your life. Do you merely live it, or do you create of it something different and precious? Can you, looking at your life, feel only the pride of a simpleton, or is it the pride that is justified by what you have actually done? Do not think just of what you have done with the things around you, nor even of what you have done for the betterment of the world, but of what you have done *with yourself*. For personal pride is nothing but the justified love *of yourself*. The pride you take in other things—in your possessions, power, wealth, children, and family—is something else.

There are countless relatively unknown people who have, sometimes late in life, gained this kind of vision of personal excellence, and then had the strength and courage to embrace it. A retired man begins piano lessons and, late in life, with no expectation or interest in becoming a virtuoso, nevertheless makes of himself a significant pianist. Another, successful and comfortable in business, abandons it to become a rabbi. A grandmother, having fulfilled her family role and seen her children into adulthood and independence, joins the Peace Corps. Former president Jimmy Carter, leaving behind positions of vast power, became a poet whose published works, though doubtless not great, are nevertheless of significant literary worth. There are men who, finding themselves alone in their sixties, have remarried and started new families. A man leaves a position of great prestige in the corporate world and devotes much of what remains of his life to something he has loved since childhood, namely, blue birds, creating ever expanding nesting trails and carrying the love for them to classrooms and other audiences. He thus leaves his imprint on the world of ornithology, but what is more important, he creates his own ideal life and lives it as he wants to.

It might seem that people of modest personal achievement have little in common with the great historical examples I have given, but in fact, they have everything in common that counts. What all these people do, whether they are remembered for it or not, is to reinvent their own lives. Not content with what they are, they become something else, and what is significant is that the ideal they carve out is uniquely their own. Creativity is what is excellent in the human species, and possessed by no other creature. It needs no justification to anyone except its possessor.

You do not need to be what you are. Even if you are accepted and perhaps admired or even envied by all, you do not need to be what you are, and you should not let the comfort of widespread approval reduce you to comfort with yourself. Are you doing today exactly what you have done for years? If so, then you are stagnating, and it means little that you may be doing very well whatever it is you have been doing for years. Your days are just going by, each like the others, none of them adding anything to you except the accumulation of the days themselves. The easy thing is to be content with that, and to fill what might otherwise be dull or boring days with distractions or pleasures; but that does nothing for you, except get along a bit further in life without the burden of boredom. Is there not something, perhaps something that the world attaches little importance to, that you have always wanted to be? Then try it.

Has your marriage become loveless, a routine going through familiar motions? Then leave it and start another. Courage is a virtue, but endurance is not, and mere duration of a marriage, perhaps over decades, is no proper source of pride, contrary to what virtually everyone imagines. The only proper basis for pride is yourself, and whether pride can rest upon this or not depends entirely on what you do with yourself. Enduring what you would not originally have chosen, simply because it is widely thought to be admirable, is not doing something with yourself, but the very opposite.

Has your work lost its meaning, so that it simply repeats itself day after day? Perhaps it is a role that is considered enviable and pays a lot of money. Perhaps you are a physician of standing, or an attorney—whatever. The work can still have become meaningless so far as your capacity for personal creativity is concerned. Consider that you are not compelled to stick with it. Did you always really want to be a poet? Or to farm? Or to become expert in something you perhaps know little about—natural history perhaps, or philosophy, or whatever? Take seriously the question: Can I do it? Do not let the values of others determine your answer. Do not worry that you might cease to be noticed, or even that you might appear a fool in everyone's eyes but your own. The only judge whose opinion matters to you is you, but make sure that this judge is a demanding one. This judge, if a wise and proud one, does not care whether you are rich or poor, whether you are admired or ridiculed. This judge is concerned only with what you are *as a person*; with what you are capable of becoming *as a person*; and with whether, through your own creative power, you in fact become that person. If you can, and if the ideal that guides you is truly your own, and not something handed down to you by tradition or church or family or whatever, then your reward will be fulfillment and pride, no matter what you may be lacking in the esteem of others, about which you should care nothing.

WHAT IS GREATNESS?

The great men and women of history are judged by their impact—battles and wars won, books that altered the course of things, inventions, and so on. But personal greatness is something quite different from this and often forgotten, or indeed never known to any except its possessor. And it is within the reach of nearly everyone—everyone, that is, who is capable of creating a personal ideal and then achieving it.

Abraham Lincoln, for example, is remembered first of all for his leadership in a great and terrible war and for his emancipation of slaves. But another person could have done those things. So think, instead, of the man who composed the address at Gettysburg—a speech of about two minutes in length. No one else in the history of the world could have created that brief and trenchant speech, one that will inspire everyone who encounters it for as long as the English language endures. And this was achieved by a man who had barely a year of formal schooling. He alone created in himself a man of greatness: he formed an ideal of what a person should be, then slowly and laboriously molded himself to that ideal. Lincoln created in himself a work of art. He became the man who composed the Gettysburg Address; had he not written it that speech would never have existed at all. But bear in mind, too, that had it never been heard—had its author been assassinated en route to the battlefield, for instance, and the speech then lost forever—it would still have been exactly what it is and would have expressed, albeit for no one ever to see, the personal greatness of its author.

So greatness, as thus understood, is within the reach of anyone having the will, determination, and imagination to achieve it. It need not be measured by the acclaim of others. Lincoln's greatness as a person would not have been lessened had his famous address, once composed, never been heard or seen by anyone, or even if he had never gained the fame associated with the presidency. Fame is but the public recognition of greatness. Personal greatness is something within a person, and it may be—in fact, it often is—quite unknown to all but its possessor. What matters is what you are, that is, what through your own creative effort you become. That vast numbers of others should see this is of secondary importance. Someone of total obscurity can embody it. Personal greatness is thus its own reward, and does not depend on recognition by others. Applause and recognition may be pleasant, but the reality that draws it—and which may fail to draw it—is the genuine treasure.

This hardly means that any fool can declare himself a person of greatness. Sometimes the multitude applauds things of specious worth, and it is of the nature of the fool to do so consistently. There is, of course, no way of proving, other than by the judgment of the wise over time, what is and what is not of great worth. It is something that all of us must decide for ourselves, and we can, of course, be wrong. But someone who is genuinely wise and imaginative is far more likely than the fool—indeed, almost sure—to be right about what is of great worth; indeed, only the fool would say that there is really no way of distinguishing the wise from the foolish.

Lincoln composed a two-minute address of wondrous beauty and perfection. This was an expression of his greatness, the sign of it; it was not the foundation of it, for that lay within him. You have it within you to do something similar; not to compose a speech of great historical significance, perhaps, but you can create something that is new and precious, something that will serve as a sign, to you if to no one else, of a kind of greatness that lies within you. But to do that, you must first have the will and the determination to do it, and the imagination to discover what it will be, and the wisdom to know that it is of great worth. Do not wait for others to tell you that, and above all, do not turn to others to find it for you, for then it would no longer be yours.

ANONYMOUS GREATNESS

While it is hard to separate the ideas of personal greatness and fame, we have tried to emphasize that the two are not only not the same, they are often not even connected. Greatness must not be measured solely by its impact or the recognition it brings its possessor, for these are but the occasional effects of greatness. Since personal greatness is a quality of its possessor, it can exist and never be recognized by others at all except, perhaps, by a very few.

Here are a few illustrations of this. Each is true, and each illustrates a kind of strength that is uncommon but which, because of circumstances, brought little or no fame to its possessor.

The first example is that of a mother whose son was, at a very early age, diagnosed as autistic and hopelessly retarded. The prognosis of experts was that he would never achieve anything of significance and would be unlikely to be able to remain long in a regular school at any age. They strongly recommended that the boy be institutionalized, thereby sparing his mother and other family members the discouragement that would certainly accompany any attempt to salvage him. His mother, extraordinarily gifted at parenting, dismissed all this and devoted her enormous abilities and energy to nurturing her son and helping him find in himself some strength or ability that might save him. And she succeeded. The boy grew up to graduate from a demanding preparatory school as its valedictorian, and then to gain admission, with scholarships, to several outstanding universities.

The second example is of a man convicted of a sexual offense who spent seven years in prison before winning parole. While imprisoned he perfected his skills and knowledge of the uses of computers, as well as his writing skills, and cast about as well for other areas into which to direct his intelligence and interests. When finally paroled he found himself unemployable in all the areas where his talents lay, simply because of his criminal record, so he prepared himself for an entirely new livelihood, in which he was totally inexperienced; namely, that of long-distance truck driving, from which he was not hopelessly barred by his record. He now gains a decent living from this and, in spite of the obstacles, he has created a normal and fulfilling life, with home, wife, and children.

The third example is of two United States Congressmen, relatively unknown except to their constituents until scandal brought them to public attention at about the same time. One was discovered to have, as his paid assistant, a woman whose role was simply to be his mistress, and the other was disclosed in the media as a homosexual. The first of these appeared before television cameras tearful and contrite, virtually begging the forgiveness of his wife and all those who had believed in him. The second proclaimed his homosexuality without shame or apology, and led the Fourth of July parade in his home district, ignoring the jeers of some of those along the parade route.

The fourth example is, again, that of a man convicted of a felony and sent to prison, this time for mismanagement of corporate funds. While in prison he used every available minute to improve himself, through rigorous exercise, study, and planning, all with a determination to make a fulfilling life for himself from the day of his release. He never regained the status he had once had in the world of business, but he was not defeated, either. He freely conceded what had happened, did not pretend to any innocence of the offense for which he has been convicted, believed in himself and his still great abilities, asked others to do the same, and built a decent and acceptable life for himself.

These are not accounts of greatness in the extraordinary sense, nor do their subjects deserve any special place in history. Each of them, however, illustrates the worth of personal excellence and the beauty of personal pride. In each of these examples, with the glaring exception of the congressman who had hired his mistress at public expense, one can see a kind of strength and resourcefulness that is not the common possession of everyone. Few mothers could, through the gift of outstanding parenting skill, bring a child to the level of achievement that this one did. Few people treat prison life as affording an opportunity to hone one's strengths and skills. And the gay congressman illustrates the true and often misunderstood nature of pride, for he totally dismissed, as not suited to himself, the rules of custom and religion that the world tries to force upon us all. His defiance of these came at a time when homosexuality was still deemed deeply shameful and most persons of such orientation felt obliged to conceal it. But this congressman, exhibiting pride in himself for what he was—a highly intelligent and resourceful representative of his constituents—gained their acceptance and was never afterward defeated at the polls. His fellow congressman, who had chosen the path of penitence and remorse, thereby destroyed utterly his political career.

However much we may praise confession, contrition, and self-abasement, what the world really holds in esteem is pride. But to be genuinely proud you must first find something in yourself to be proud of. No one honors those who do not honor themselves, nor do we honor those whose feigned pride rests upon no genuine personal strength. No matter what we may have been taught by custom to say of the equality of the foolish and the wise, of the weak and the strong, no one really believes it.

SUPERIORITY AND DISPLAY

Everyone enjoys the sense of superiority, whether in the small things, such as skill at a game, or in the larger gifts and talents that set one apart. To be highly skilled at some relatively insignificant activity, such as checkers and bowling, is pleasant and gives zest to what might otherwise be a dull existence, but things like this add little or nothing to one's excellence as a person. To be highly intelligent, creative, and resourceful in any of those areas around which life itself turns, on the other hand, is not merely pleasant. Such abilities are profoundly gratifying as marks of a genuinely superior human being. You can love checkers, but you can hardly take deep pride in yourself as a person for being good at the game. But if you are good at music, for example, or at science, and, devoting yourself utterly to the pursuit of something like this, you finally excel as a composer, for example, or a researcher, then you are right in taking pride in what you are. You are, to the degree that you succeed in something like this, a person who counts, who is important, and genuine pride rests upon the realization of this.

Superiority is one thing, however, and the display of it something quite different. Indeed, if you are a truly proud person you have no interest whatever in exhibiting your worth to those who stand to you as lesser people.

Suppose, for example, that you have, through imagination and resourcefulness, created a thriving business of some sort, with many employees who must, in some sense or other, look up to you. They are aware of what you have done, and what it took to do it, and they are at least dimly aware that they probably could not have done anything comparable. Now your temptation will be to act arrogant in their presence, to let it be constantly obvious who is in charge and to whom all these people are beholden. But if you are proud, you must not do this. Pride and arrogance not only do not go together, they are antithetical. No truly proud person can be arrogant. Arrogance is the mark of insecurity, of someone whose self-esteem is to some extent lacking and who must, therefore, reinforce it by display.

Women of humble origin who marry wealthy and powerful men are sometimes arrogant, trying thus to compensate for the lack of esteem which they have always felt. Men of modest intellectual achievement who find themselves in positions of authority as, for example, university deans or lower court judges, sometimes display the same fault. Examples can be found all over. But if you want to see a truly proud person, then find someone who, through his or her own vast resourcefulness, has created something of impressive worth, or has won a position of great authority and power, but who acts with modesty and constant consideration toward everyone else, especially those in a lesser position. This person's goodness and superiority are perfectly evident to all, including their possessor, who feels not the slightest need to remind others of them.

It is not hard to illustrate these points from life. If you observe people in their various roles, some important and some not, you will find examples everywhere. On the one hand there will be those whose self-love must be constantly reinforced by the deference of others, people who cast themselves in the role of having position and power in order to obtain this deference, thereby easing their own insecurity. On the other hand, you will find persons of great power and authority who appear bent on minimizing the appearance of this, though these are less common. These are the truly proud, whose love for themselves is justified by what they know themselves to be, and who have no need whatever to have others prove anything to them.

A striking example of this contrast is provided by the airline industry. This is a intensely competitive area, and nearly every airline constantly struggles just to keep going. Failures and bankruptcies are common. Among the airlines, one that totally collapsed was run by an executive notorious for his arrogance. He was universally disliked, most especially by his employees. He was a man who had struggled and fought his way to the top from his beginnings as a street kid, where he had learned that he had to fight for anything he was going to get. He sought self-worth first through dramatic achievement, and second, through the display of it, reducing others in order to elevate himself. The airline failed. Of course there are many factors responsible for this, but the low esteem in which he was held by those vast numbers on whom he depended was a large one. Treating his employees more or less as his adversaries, he made himself one in their eyes.

In contrast, another airline has succeeded spectacularly. When every other major carrier was losing money, this one alone was profiting and expanding. The chief executive of this airline, whom everyone has rightly credited with its success, is a man both proud and self-effacing. He is perfectly aware of his great abilities, and takes no credit for his stunning success. Instead, he credits his employees, declaring that these fine and dedicated people are the airline's real heroes, the ones who deserve all the credit, and the ones the company must try to please. And he acts on that policy. The result, of course, is that he is looked up to and admired by everyone, because his strengths and virtues are so perfectly obvious. He has no need to call attention to them. When he speaks, it is with total confidence and authority, and yet totally devoid of the kind of display that one finds in those who, wielding great power, think that the demeanor called for is arrogance.

The point being made here applies not only in the larger spheres of life but everywhere. The proud never swagger, and never invite attention to themselves or their achievements. They have no need to. They wish primarily to look good in their own eyes, and have little need for the admiration of others.

Thus, when you enter a restaurant, for instance, you are instantly placed in the special position of customer, while another person automatically becomes someone to wait on you and try to please you. You become, in short, someone who is, to that very limited extent, the superior. And many people, thus placed, almost automatically assume a role of mild arrogance. The words "please" and "if I may" disappear from their speech, and they say simply "I'll *have* (this or that)" or, which is vastly worse, "gimme . . . (whatever)." Even in the least imposing circumstances, for example, in a fast-food restaurant, where one is dealing with people working for a minimum wage, a proud person does not say "gimme the ham on rye," or anything comparable. Such a person says "I would like," or, "may I have . . . please." Courtesy is *never* misdirected, even to total strangers, even to persons to whom one has every right, by both nature and custom, to feel superior. To slip into even the smallest appearance of arrogance, or to take advantage of what is, by custom, a position of superiority, as when dealing with subordinates, waiters, clerks, and so on, betrays a lack of civility to which only someone insecure in his or her own strengths is tempted. And this, in spite of the fact that civility and unwavering courtesy and considerateness are not really expected in most such situations.

Another type of situation in which a reminder of these principles is needed is one involving frustration. It is, for example, sometimes deeply frustrating to make airline reservations, purchase the tickets, and so on, because of the complex and arcane rules governing these things, and on top of this, airline travel sometimes involves delays, misdirected luggage, and so on. A typical response of a traveler is to berate whatever clerk he happens to be dealing with, especially when dealing by telephone. A proud person does not do this, primarily because it is stupid and pointless. The clerk is not the author of those many rules that must be enforced. And the executives who are responsible are well shielded from your anger. The woman at the other end of the telephone line, whom you berate for the problems being thrust upon you, may very well be a single mother, struggling with an inadequate salary to keep her children fed and clothed and to pay the rent and so on. Nothing but the utmost courtesy is appropriate, whatever the level of your anger and frustration. And, on the other side of the situation, when the service you receive is excel-' lent, and your needs are well met, then the expression of appreciation is in order, even though what you are getting is nothing more than the service you reasonably expect. Courtesy and civility, let it be said once again, are never misdirected. Arrogance always is. It is the refuge of the weak and the incompetent.

One last illustration of all this may be useful.

When the news was released that the president of an outstanding university was being considered to replace the president of an even greater university, she was asked by the press for her reaction to this quite stunning development. Responding, she said almost nothing about herself or the qualifications that put her in this enviable position. Instead she spoke of the gratitude and honor she felt, gave no hint whatsoever of what significant things she might be able to do in such a role, but instead spoke of the institution she was already serving; of its excellent faculty, students, and administrators; and how reluctant she would be to leave all this. She spoke, in short, as of woman of deep and justified pride, whose strengths are sufficiently obvious so that she had no need to invite attention to them. It was a perfect performance, entirely worthy of the literally outstanding person that she is.

You do see this sort of thing sometimes, and whenever you do you recognize that you are seeing a proud person, whose pride and superiority are beautifully evident through the modesty that brings them to focus.

GENUINENESS AS A MODEL

Most people are in fact two people. There is, on the one hand, the person you actually are. On top of this is likely to be the person you wish to appear to be to others. A *genuine* person is one in whom these two are really one and the same. What this genuine person is is exactly what he or she appears to be. And the point of making this distinction is that, while not all genuine persons are proud—for there are, after all, genuine fools—the proud are always genuine. You will, if you are proud, never try to appear to others as something the least different from what you in fact are.

The reason for this is evident to anyone who reflects on it. You of course love yourself—every proud person does. But you are proud only if that love for yourself is justified by what you are. This is simply the definition of a proud person. A fool can love himself, but no fool can be proud, for the love is not justified. Fools have nothing to be proud of. Only the good, that is, the best, have this.

Thus, if you are proud, loving yourself for what you are, then at the very least you have nothing to hide. You have no need to appear to be anything but what you are. Someone of significance or perhaps even great achievement, while having no temptation to display this, certainly has no inclination to conceal it.

If, on the other hand, you are a fool, in whatever degree—and most people are, at least to some degree—then you try to appear as someone different, more or less, from what you actually are. Thus, you pretend to know more than you actually do, concealing ignorance even in matters about which you could not be expected to be knowledgeable. Or you pretend to some position or status that exceeds what you actually are. Thus someone quite ignorant of music comments on a performance in a manner calculated to convey the impression of sophisticated judgment, or someone ignorant of art bandies about the names of artists, from the same motive.

Dissimulation always fails. One who pretends is very soon seen to be someone who pretends. Even children see through it. And when a fool thus tries to conceal his foolishness, he loses twice over; for first of all, he is seen to be phony, and second, he is seen to be a fool.

For instance, someone quite ignorant of music comments, upon overhearing a bit of a recording by another pianist, that this performer plays as well as Rubenstein—a remark quite meaningless as it stands and made only to impress. Or someone who has worked in some governmental capacity—perhaps on a board of inquiry or the like—alludes casually to his golf games with the governor, a person he has in fact never seen. Or someone who was sent by his company to participate in a symposium sponsored by a prestigious university alludes to his days there, as if to imply that he is an alumnus.

The proud never do this. They have no need to fabricate virtues, for those they possess are real, whether apparent or not. Proud people wax knowledgeable with respect to those things about which they *are* knowledgeable, and readily admit ignorance about anything else. Pretending to be what you are not, even in the smallest and seemingly insignificant way, is a mark of insecurity, of a sense of shortcoming. If you are ignorant of something, as everyone is, your job is not to try to conceal it but to correct it.

The sad thing about not being genuine is that, in trying to conceal what you really are from everyone else, you are likely to conceal yourself from yourself. Self-knowledge becomes thereby virtually impossible. Being primarily concerned with how you appear to others, you become absorbed in these appearances yourself and rarely get a glimpse of the person behind them.

This is why it is impossible to form any true friendship with persons who are not genuine. You never get to know that person, who in fact never gets to know himself. Whatever this person says is said mostly for effect, and you therefore do not know whether to take it at face value. Genuine people, on the other hand—that is, those who appear, for better or worse, to be exactly what they are—can form actual friendships, for each knows the other for who that other is. What is said between them need not be met with skepticism, for no effort is ever made simply to "look good." A proud person, who is also genuine, is good, and has no need at all to try embellishing this. Such goodness is not, of course, perfection, for no human being is without fault, in the literal sense of that term; that is, no one is without defect. The fact that no one is omniscient ensures this. But the proud know that they are strong, that is, that they are intelligent, skilled, and creative in ways unique to themselves, and so have no need to mask over any existing shortcomings. A superb athlete need not also be a superb musician, and vice versa; someone who knows much need not know everything; and even the wise are entitled to occasional folly. A true friend sees all these things, the good and the bad, for exactly what they are. The important thing is that true worth, and not just the appearance of worth, is there.

WEALTH AND DISPLAY

The possession of riches is, we have noted, no proper basis of pride, for pride rests upon the justified love of yourself and nothing else. You make yourself no better by surrounding yourself with things, even beautiful things, and it certainly adds nothing to you simply to fatten your portfolio.

The possession of wealth is, however, not inconsistent with pride. The danger lies simply in making it your goal, when that should be personal excellence, that is, personal superiority with respect to some virtue or strength of your own that is eminently desirable. Such strength consists of creative power of one kind or another. A proud person is someone who can rightly claim to do something worthwhile, something that exhibits his or her human nature in a way that is a profound credit to that nature. We are all of us human, but those among us who are able to somehow glorify what is human in us are not common. This is, in fact, a redundancy, for the good and the common are necessarily opposed and mutually exclusive.

Thus the only way wealth can be a destroyer of pride is by becoming a lure, by diverting you from what is important, yourself, to what is not, to externals. So the proud can also be wealthy, without shame. But remember that the poor can also be proud, without shame. What matters, to a proud person, is how wealth is used.

The conspicuous display of wealth, let us note at once, is an unmistakable sign of vulgarity for three overwhelming reasons. First, if you are rich *and show it*, then this announces at once that it matters to you what others think of you. People who are genuinely proud care only about what they think of themselves, not how others happen to judge them. The proud set their own standards of excellence, and then live by them. To be proud is to be your own severest judge, to care how you appear in your own eyes, not in the eyes of others. Second, the display of wealth shows at once that your values lie not in yourself, but in things that have little to do with you and which do not, in any case, contribute anything to your own goodness or personal superiority And third, the only motive one could have for wishing to display wealth is the incitement of envy in common people, that is, those who are impressed not by things of true worth, but by things that are merely expensive. For a genuinely proud person to take satisfaction in the envy of others would be unthinkable, the more so if that envy is aroused by mere possessions.

Thus the proud eschew such things as expensive cars, clothing far in excess of need, dwellings and furnishing that are intended for display, as though one's home were a kind of gallery. A deeply proud woman dresses simply and tastefully, not expensively, and would not think of bedecking herself in jewels. A proud man drives an ordinary car, and cares nothing that it is old. People like this, the proud, are not noticed on the street, and have no interest whatsoever in drawing attention to themselves, especially by means of display. None of this is, of course, inconsistent with owning beautiful things, and a proud person, perhaps more than others, delights in things that are beautiful. But they need not be costly to be beautiful, and they need not be shown off to be loved.

SLAVERY

Epictetus, the Roman Stoic philosopher, said that if you want to know whether someone is a slave, do not ask whether he was bought or sold, or who his parents were; but if you hear him say "Master!" from his heart and with feeling, then call him a slave, "though he wears the purple hem," that is, even if he is of royal birth. Such a person, he said, is a "willing slave."

The point of Epictetus's observation is timeless. We have, in the conventional sense, abolished slavery, but most of us have not emancipated ourselves; the worst of it is, we do not want to. We are, in the Stoic's apt description, *willing* slaves. But slaves, nonetheless.

A slave is someone who cannot set his own goals and live his own life, but exists to fulfill the aims of someone else. That, and not abstract ownership, is the essence of slavery. Spouses, in the rare perfect or near perfect unions that sometimes result from total love, usually think of themselves as belonging to each other, fully, yet no one is enslaved by this. On the contrary, each contributes to the other's fulfillment. If, on the other hand, you submerge your will and your needs to those of others, then you are a slave. And even if the world praises you for this, for your unselfish dedication and service to others, and even if you inwardly congratulate yourself, you are still a slave—a willing slave.

The need to control is one of the commonest, and least worthy, aspects of human nature. Parents sometimes want not only to guide, strengthen, and build up their children, but to control them even into their adult lives. They have a certain ideal of what they want their children to be—how they want them to think, act, and determine their goals. So without consideration of whether that ideal matches those of their children, or whether these children might find fulfillment in becoming something quite radically different from their parents, the parents try, by all sorts of subtle threats and inducements, to foist on their children their own aspirations. This is sometimes true even when the aspiration of a son, for example is clearly more noble than that of a parent—when, for example, he seeks fulfillment in writing, perhaps in poetry, with little chance of recognition, and the parent had hoped he would follow in his successful footsteps in the world of business.

Equally familiar is the need many husbands have to be in control. They take it for granted that it is their role to decide how money is spent, where the family will live—indeed, to make all major decisions. Their wives thus become, to a greater or lesser extent, slaves and, in case they concur in the arrangement, willing slaves. The passive wife, who sometimes remains silent as her husband holds forth, and whose deference extends even to the smallest things, is all too common.

Male domination and control within families is very familiar, but there is another that is much more insidious and often eagerly embraced by vast numbers and, perhaps, even by most: control through institutions. Every government, for example, has vast powers of control, but in societies that are relatively free this control is not widely resented because, up to a point, it is absolutely necessary if there is to be any social life at all. A government, for example, through its legal institutions restricts and punishes criminal behavior, and one can hardly deny the necessity of this. Sometimes, however, by inflaming the passions of patriotism, governmental control goes much farther, enlisting willing people in causes that are only superficially fulfilling to them and often destructive of genuinely worthy ideals. Thus, by simply unfurling flags and, sometimes, accompanying patriotic rituals with stirring music, governmental forces can induce people to salute and declare allegiances, sometimes even at the expense of things that any rational person would deem far more basic and often nobler.

A more insidious instrument of control, and a very common one, is religion, especially religious groupings that emphasize doctrine. Here the transparent aim is to control and—this word is not too strong—to enslave. The fact that those enslaved absorb this control willingly and even eagerly does not mean they are not thereby enslaved. It shows only that they are, in Epictetus's apt description, *willing* slaves. They do the bidding of another—but do it willingly, their capacity for setting their own ideal of self-fulfillment having been replaced by ideals that are simply given to them.

This is why some churches lay such stress on doctrine, even doctrine that is, to rational understanding, absurd. It is not that it is particularly important to declare one's *belief* in certain often bizarre claims—for what difference can that make, *per se?* That anyone should declare his belief in the occurrence of certain strange events of long ago can, by itself, have no more significance than declaring one's belief that there is life on the planet Mars. But if vast numbers can be induced to affirm such beliefs, to the accompaniment of rituals familiar since childhood, then a church is given a powerful instrument for the control not only of behavior but of thoughts, attitudes, values, and ideals. The multitudes kneel, and with that, the capacity to create for themselves an ideal of personal excellence, quite different from what religion offers, is suffocated. And it is for this reason that doctrinal churches seek to reach children at a very early age, enrolling them in their own schools, for example, and attempting to enforce the practice of saying prayers even in public schools. Their aim is not to ensure that their children will say prayers— for that could easily be accomplished at home, before their children go off to school, for example. The aim is rather to extend their control to the children even of secular families. Why else would they care whether or not these children utter prayers that are more or less meaningless to them?

The point of these observations is not, of course, that all religious people are slaves to the churches. It is, rather, that in an important sense many are, and the important point to emphasize once again is that of the *willing* slave. You are a willing slave to the extent that you voluntarily do the bidding of others, quite regardless of whether their will coincides in its ideals with yours or, rather, what your ideal of excellence would have been had it been left entirely to you to create it for yourself. Thus it is no accident that the devoted adherents of the most doctrinaire churches, namely, those that describe themselves as fundamentalist, are almost never found among those who have distinguished themselves in art, literature, or any other areas where individual creativity are essential. Indeed, those who have bent their knee to this kind of religion, which places enormous emphasis on the requirement to believe the absurd, are almost never found even among the directors and executive officers of great corporations or the partnerships of law firms where, again, individual creative and often unorthodox thinking and planning are essential. Slaves, even willing slaves, have no place on those paths that can lead to great and sometimes lasting achievement, for the paths themselves are the creations of those who have forged them. To the extent that you embark upon a path handed to you ready-made, you have excluded from yourself, however praiseworthy you may be in the eyes of those who have led you that way, any possibility of achieving an excellence that can be called your own. And this means that you have forfeited any chance for personal excellence. You will have to derive your satisfactions from the applause of others, and this may—indeed, probably will—lead you to applaud yourself, though you really have no right to do so. Pride is the justified love of yourself, and this can never be derived merely from the approval of others, however exalted these may be. Pride can rest only upon what you do for yourself, not what you do at the bidding of others. Epictetus was right: If you say "Master!" from the heart and with feeling—which today would mean, if you kneel, bow, or defer even to someone of immense stature and power—then you are a slave even though, perhaps, a rich and blessed slave. Freedom is measured not by what you own, and not by any visible glory that you can claim, but solely by your heeding your own will with respect to what is important to you.

A mechanism of control that is even more far-reaching than doctrinal religion, though not as destructive of personal ideals, is custom, sometimes aptly referred to as a "dead hand." This expression correctly suggests, by the metaphor of a hand, that custom is an instrument of control, and the hand is referred to as "dead" because the roots of custom lie deep in the past, with generations long since dead.

The reason custom is so far-reaching is that you cannot, up to a certain point, emancipate yourself from it. Whether you kneel to this or that doctrine, or even bow to the trappings of the state, is at least to some extent up to you, so not everyone is the same with respect to these. You cannot, however, escape *every* requirement of custom; at least, you cannot do this without becoming an animal. Customs are the basic glue of any culture and, indeed, of civilized life itself.

Nor, as this implies, are all customs enslaving. A rational person easily sees the necessity of the most basic ones. Thus, the custom of our culture requires us to be true to our word, to honor promises and commitments, and to pay our debts even when we could perhaps escape penalty by not doing so, to be faithful to spouses—and, in a word, to honor what we have come to regard as the principles of decency. We do not lie or cheat, not because we would be punished under the criminal law if we did—for laws are often nonexistent or ineffective here, in our day-to-day dealing with others—but because the elementary principles of decency, known to all, would be violated. And those principles are the inheritance of our culture, that is, they are customary.

Are they rational? Some are, some are not. No one could rationally prove to you that you should honor your word, even in circumstances in which it would seem clearly advantageous for you not to, but a rational person nevertheless recognizes its importance. Indeed, if you are proud, you have the best reason there could be for veracity, for you see that it would be a *debasement of yourself* to lie, whatever the external rewards might be. If you are proud you love yourself—perhaps more clearly expressed by saying you love your *self*—above everything else, and you cannot therefore suffer its debasement for any external good whatsoever.

Aristotle was therefore entirely right when, in response to the purely philosophical question of how virtue can be taught, he said that the young are made virtuous by sheer habit, but for an educated adult it is a matter of rational choice. Children are gradually molded to decency, through the inculcation, by their parents, of good habits. But then in time they see for themselves that the behavior, heretofore purely habitual, is worthy of reasonable choice. A grown man can, indeed, *choose to lie*, thereby perhaps enriching himself, but he is a fool if he does. For if he were wise he would see, with rational clarity, that he was sacrificing the greater for the lesser good. No person who is proud can take the least satisfaction in the debasement or corruption of the self, whatever may be the rewards.

But not all custom is worth respecting. Much of it is useless and even, in some cases, stupid, yet it lives on through sheer inertia. And this is where the concept of the willing slave is especially important. People not only adhere to useless custom, but sometimes eagerly embrace it and are distrustful and scornful of those who do not. To respect rules that are necessary for civilized life, and therefore necessary for the realization of whatever ideal you set for yourself, is one thing; but to adhere to rules just because one has been taught to, or just because, in Aristotle's apt analysis, one has become habituated to them, is the clearest case of willing slavery. To say of someone who does this that he or she is slavish in deference to even the smallest customs is to use exactly the right word. It *is* slavish, and made no less so by being voluntary or willing.

Consider, again, what it would mean to say that you are a proud person. It means that you are the creator of an ideal, of an excellence that is unique to you; that is in every sense your own, and not some prefabricated ideal handed down to you by any priesthood or by your culture. And you not only create that ideal of what you are going to be, but you achieve it. You have copied no one—it is your own creation. You have sought the applause of no one but yourself, or at least, of yourself primarily. And, because this is true, you have gained a love of self that is justified. You really have become, and have made yourself, what you aspired to be.

But what is the chance of that happening if you take all of your rules from others, whether these be priests or simply the whole of your culture? As you have your own ideal and excellence, you have, beyond a certain point, your own rules. Rules of custom that are useless to you, and which have no rational basis other than their being endorsed by everyone else, are of no use to you.

To do otherwise is to be, in the literal sense of the word, slavish, and the slavishness is made the more contemptible by being willing. Thus there are people who seem unable to take a step without adherence to whatever rule, however trivial, governs that step. If they write a letter, they think if must follow a preordained format. Its salutation will be the expected one, and its content, in both substance and form, will hold no surprises, no hint of individuality. Their mode of dress is that of those around them. Nothing is done by these people that would ever make them stand out from others. Deciding what to do, from moment to moment, means, for them, noting what others do, and then doing much the same. It is as though they were fearful of calling attention to themselves, fearful of being different. Yet the proud are, of necessity, different. Those who exclude the possibility of difference, of being glaringly unique, by letting habit and custom guide their every step, are inevitably boring to those who have managed to rise above all this. Even their conversation follows the straight and narrow of customary rule. Candor and original thought are avoided, while the banal, the unquestionably acceptable, flourishes.

That is the picture of the conventional man, and the picture doesn't change much from one of these to another. He dresses like others, speaks like others, does just about everything the way others do. He thus earns the reputation of being all right, without severe fault, worthy of the general approval and, derivatively, of his own approval—for, as in everything else, his approval follows that of the crowd. And he is dull, and ordinary, exactly like those around him, never getting into any serious trouble or embarrassment and, it should be added, never achieving much of anything that has not already been done thousands of times by others.

We shall always be in the debt of Epictetus who, expressing the profoundest ideals of the culture he had inherited from the Greeks, gave us the concept of the willing slave, so perfectly applicable to the multitudinous lovers of what is customary; who are, seemingly by their own choice, the ordinary and the dull.

FALSE PRIDE

Pride is vulnerable to many corruptions, and this is made worse by the fact that its corruptions are often mistaken for the real thing. Pride is thus like many other human virtues, such as charity and love, precious qualities that easily degenerate into other things which are nevertheless still called by the same names. Thus charity, from the Latin *caritas*, was originally thought of as a loving quality of the heart. Now it has become almost synonymous with the giving of money to deserving organizations. Similarly, love has many illegitimate offspring, ranging from possessiveness to the indulgence of lust.

The commonest form of false pride is simple egoism or vanity. It is, for example, not uncommon to think of persons who have achieved high status of one kind or another as expressing pride when they create dramatic but superfluous reminders of this. Thus university and college presidents like to have portraits of themselves, always in academic garb, displayed in some place where the maximum number of people, visitors especially, will see them; they sometimes arrange to have buildings named for them. What for? What does such ostentation do for the college itself or

97

for its educational goals? Similarly, governors, almost as soon as they take office, have every sign identifying a state highway or bridge carry their names. Anyone crossing the border into a state is notified not only that he is crossing that border, but who governs there. In addition, the visitor is very likely to be told who is the commissioner of highways, as though this could be vital information. A bridge over New York's Hudson River, bearing the lovely name Tappen Zee, gets renamed for someone, virtually unknown, who by accident served as the governor for only one year. Such displays of one's name, created at great expense to tax payers, serve no use whatsoever except to nourish the vanity of the possessors of those names. There is even a university—perhaps several—which blatantly offers to sell such displays. In return for a relatively modest donation one can have his or her name affixed to a seat in the chapel, or to a library cubicle. For a substantially larger donation—the figures are clearly spelled out—you can get your name above a laboratory. And for truly impressive "gifts" a building will be named for you, and your name will survive there for generations, long after you have been totally forgotten. It is a kind of fake immortality. Your name lives on, to be sure, but not for anything you have actually achieved. It is a straightforward deal: the college gets some cash, you indulge your vanity. Nothing permanent is achieved, except an inscription of a name which, very soon, could be anyone's name, so far as those who see it are concerned.

What is lost sight of here is the true sense of pride. We see here a vain and even stupid attempt to impress one's stature *upon others*. But if you are a truly proud person you care little about what others may think of you; you certainly see the worthlessness of your mere *name's* perpetuation. The inscription of his or her name on a bridge, highway, building, or whatever has no more meaning to a proud person than its inscription on a tombstone. If you are proud you care about yourself, and your sense of your own worth rests, not on what name you are called by, but on what you actually achieve. Whether some greater or smaller herd of unknown persons is aware of those achievements is of little value to you. And it is certainly of no value whatever that those persons are reminded, by the appearance of your name here or there, of some presumed status you have achieved. They do not care. And neither should you.

In contrast to the fake pride just illustrated, which is so familiar, consider the following true story. A man amasses a great and growing fortune through personal achievement of a high level. From time to time his calls upon the president of his beloved alma mater and hands him an envelope, always containing some check or certificate or instrument of great value, and says simply, "Here is something for the college." Over the course of time these gifts amount to many millions of dollars. It is no secret that he does this, but at the same time, he forbids publicity of it, and would never permit any official acknowledgment or ceremony in which he would be the center of attention. Nor does he ever suggest the inscription of his name anyplace. This is a true expression of pride. This man does not need the applause of others to gauge his own justified worth. This modest man glows with pride, immeasurably precious, but it is an inward glow, which others can only glimpse.

PRIDE AND VERACITY

Truth has a simple but important property that is insufficiently appreciated by persons driven more by vanity and conceit than by genuine pride. It is expressed by saying that all truth is consistent with itself, while even the smallest untruth is at odds with everything. No true statement, whether momentous or utterly trivial, whether uttered today or a thousand years ago, has ever been contradicted by another. The entire body of truth, which would fill a thousand encyclopedias, constitutes a great web of self-consistency The minutest untruth, if inserted into this vast web, stands out like a great thorn, a conspicuous and ugly blot on what is otherwise a simple, pure, and beautiful mosaic of truth.

This is why lies are ultimately self-defeating. They stand in contrast to a vast network of truth which is self-sustaining. You can turn your back on a truth, you can pretend it is not there, but it is, and it is immovable, and can never be undone by anything. It is true, and will always be true. And it will forever fit, with perfect ease, into the vast web consisting of everything else that is true.

The web of truth is therefore indestructible. The most powerful machinery of deception that anyone can contrive cannot dislodge even the smallest part of it. The web of mendacity, on the other hand, is so fragile that if even one of its tenuous strands is disrupted the entire edifice is likely to collapse.

It has been said, correctly, that no one has a good enough memory to lie. If you affirm an untruth, then you must bear it in mind and, what is harder, make your every subsequent utterance consistent with that untruth—which will involve the endless fabrication of more falsehood, and superhuman memory to sustain it. You have to remember what it is that you said, and from then on, check everything you say against it, for otherwise you will find yourself saying something that is true and, alas! not compatible with your lie. If, on the other hand, your every utterance is true, then you need no special gifts of memory at all. You need only to continue to say what is true without checking what you say against anything you have ever said before, and you can be sure that all the things you assert will hang together.

Most people are at least dimly aware of this danger of affirming an outright lie; the danger, that is, of sooner or later stumbling and exposing it. This is, of course, the power of the cross-examination practiced by trial lawyers. It is very easy to tell the truth that dislodges the lie that the attorney wants to expose. All he has to do is ask questions. The witness, if he or she has told even the smallest untruth, has to remember it and fabricate whatever new lies will be consistent with the first one. This in time proves impossible, for no one's memory is good enough to do that.

But quite apart from the rigors of formal cross-examination, it is terribly easy to be caught lying, even in the most casual contexts, and terribly hard not to be caught. Truths, even when not elicited, slip easily from the tongue, and every one of them threatens to expose the lie.

And what is the consequence of this? It is that you will never be entirely believed again, even when you are telling the truth. To be discovered in a single untruth, even a seemingly innocuous one, even in a simple exaggeration, casts doubt on your credibility forever. A thousand truths will never undo the tarnish inflicted by that one untruth, for every one of them will be received with a grain of skepticism. "This person lied to me once," is the unspoken thought; "perhaps these are just more lies." Nothing can entirely cleanse one of the fault thus imputed. Your single lie infects your credibility forever. And if you then declare, with passion and sincerity, "Ah yes, I did bend the truth there a bit, but I shall never do it again," you will not be entirely believed. The stain is permanent. If, on the other hand, you prize truth, even small and seemingly insignificant truth, you speak easily and with total confidence in any situation. You have no fear of even the most severe cross-examination, knowing that nothing you will say can possibly trip you up, for it will automatically fit with everything else you say.

This kind of self-confidence is perfectly apparent in truthful people. In an interview, for example, they speak effortlessly and comfortably on whatever subject arises, not pretending to know what they do not know, but responding fully and easily on matters they know something about. Their candor is evident not only their speech, but in their entire demeanor. They are, as one says, *believable*. Persons who, on the other hand, have a fear of the truth—the fear, for example, that certain things, if known, would cast them in an unfavorable light—these people are guarded, their responses are minimal, and it is soon obvious that they are not entirely believable. This is, of course, the basis for the widespread distrust of political figures.

Someone who lies, or, indeed, merely has a tendency to exaggerate or "embellish" the truth, runs an additional risk that is not sufficiently appreciated. It arises from the fact that we all speak not merely with our lips and tongues, but with our bodies, our facial expressions, even our eyes. Everyone, even a child, comes readily to understand this "body language," and the beauty of it is that it is virtually impossible to lie in this language. When we are speaking we usually do not know what messages our bodies—

our expressions, primarily—are sending. When our lips are lying the rest of us usually is not, and the inconsistency leaps out. Thus someone telling an outright lie is apt not to realize that he or she is looking off to one side, not openly into the face of the hearer; but the person hearing this lie from the lips sees the doubt cast by the other's expression. The eyes especially convey messages, and this is doubtless why, in any conversation, we look into the eyes of the speaker and not, as one would otherwise expect, at the speaker's mouth. What is expressed by the eyes is always believable, whereas what flows from the mouth can be controlled and distorted. When both agree—that is, when the language of the body and the words from the lips agree—we are confident of what we are hearing.

Inveterate liars are, mercifully, not common. The odds are too heavily against them. Mendacity is in fact a poor formula for survival. What is common, however, is the "embellishment" of truth. This is indeed a euphemism, because exaggeration is in fact lying, and it shares all the perils of lying. The person who exaggerates the truth—that is, embellishes it with what are perhaps small lies—sooner or later trips up just as surely as the total fabricator of falsehood and with the same consequences. These people are very quickly seen to be lying, and doubt is thus cast upon everything they say forever after. Thus, you exaggerate something just once, and it becomes apparent that you have done so. Then, the next time you say something having some sort of dramatic content, something absolutely true and more than usually interesting, anyone hearing you at once wonders: Is this person exaggerating again? Whatever interesting content your account might have possessed is thus lost. And the sad part of this is that even if your account is true in every detail and particular, it still will be doubted. So you lose, for sure, and twice over, for your otherwise interesting *and true* account is robbed of interest, *and*, by your previous exaggeration, you expose yourself as someone who does not treasure the exact truth of things.

For example: Someone relates to an informal social gathering his travel by car over a very busy highway under conditions of severe fog, and a resulting pileup of vehicles which, luckily, did not involve him. He says, "and we counted sixteen trucks and cars piled up or in ditches." Three or four weeks later his wife, alluding to the same experience, says, "and we counted eleven cars and trucks piled up or in the ditch." One of these two, you instantly see, has less than a perfect regard for truth. It is not merely that the two had somewhat different impressions of what they saw, for both say that they *counted*. The actual number got inflated in the mind of one of them, who has thus, unbeknown to himself, exposed himself as untruthful. From this trivial exaggeration he now bears forever the mark of someone who exaggerates, and every future utterance of his will be seen in that light.

Here is another example. My good friend describes an enjoyable tea he had been invited to at the convent near his university. The occasion was made the more pleasant by the liberal and, indeed, feminist leaning of his hostess, the Mother Superior. At one point, according to the account given to me, my friend remarked to her that there was little likelihood that women would be ordained to the priesthood during the lifetime of the present pope, to which she responded: "Oh well, maybe there will be another Agca" (this being the man who had, a few years earlier, tried to assassinate the pope). Having said this, she immediately raised her fingers to her lips and blurted, "Oh dear, I shouldn't have said that, should I?"

A charming little anecdote, the more so for being quite astonishing.

Several years later this same friend again described this occasion, but this time the account ended: "Oh well, we can always pray, can't we?"

Again, an untruth has been disclosed—not a hideous one, to be sure, but one that is still ugly for its being untrue. And the person giving this account tripped over his own *truth*, and showed himself to be someone capable of exaggeration, which means, in fact, someone with an imperfect love of truth and fact.

Thus far we have spoken primarily of the impact *upon others* of mendacity, even the common kind that amounts only to exaggeration. For this, too, must be borne in mind, that even small and seemingly insignificant lapses from truth, the kind that are called exaggerations, are in fact lies, albeit small ones. But a lie comes no closer to being true by being a small one, and exaggeration is, in fact, mendacity. But what needs to be emphasized, more than the effect upon others, is the effect upon oneself. If you are proud, then you love yourself for what you are, not for what you appear to others to be. Hence, even if mendacity were to succeed, even if not one of your small exaggerations were ever detected—which is in fact quite impossible—you still could not be genuinely proud if you indulged in them. You could perhaps congratulate yourself on your lively anecdotes, you might even take some satisfaction in a victory that rested upon a lie or deception, in the unlikely event that this should happen; but one thing you could not do is elevate your own sense of self-worth or personal excellence by such means. For you would, if you were honest with yourself, be forced to try combining personal excellence with mendacity, which is a contradiction in terms. Perhaps there could be such a thing as a good liar, but you cannot possibly think of yourself as being good as a person and also a liar, of whatever degree. On the other hand, while no one was ever made good as a person merely by veracity, anyone who is thus good, and who can accordingly be proud, will most certainly count veracity among his virtues. The proud love truth and fact, whether great or small, and despise even the minutest distortions of fact. The arrogant may find little fault with untruths, particularly their own—but this only illustrates, once again, the difference between arrogance and pride.

AN IDEA WHOSE TIME
HAS COME—AGAIN

Classical Athens is correctly regarded as having been the cradle of Western civilization. Even a superficial knowledge of the achievements of that age, in a minute corner of the world, inspires one with awe. It was there that the rational approach to the world and life was born, and with it, Western science. Most of this was the work of hardly more than a dozen thinkers, among whom three stand out—Socrates, Plato, and Aristotle. The great intellectual movements that arose primarily from the reflections of these three are without parallel. It was the rationalism of the Greeks that for centuries posed the greatest challenge to the claims of the Church, until finally the scholastic philosophers felt obliged to try incorporating that rationalism into their systems. The tension between faith and reason remained, however, and survives still as a never-ending battle between religion and science. Throughout history civilizations have, with few exceptions, turned to priesthoods for guidance in the great questions concerning human nature and the world, but the philosophers of antiquity elevated thought and reason to that exclusive role. They were not, of course, without their gods, but they did not look to the gods for guidance and, unlike other cultures, the Greeks did not even have an established priesthood. And when this great light of civilization was virtually extinguished by the rise and spread of religion, plunging the Western world into the darkness which gives those ages their name, it was the recovery of this Greek spirit, the spirit of reason and creativity, that lifted civilization into its rebirth, or literal renaissance, and which has inspired what is best in Western civilization ever since.

Athenians of the fifth and fourth centuries B.C.E. had a view of human nature which seemed to them quite obvious. They thought of human nature as being clearly superior to the rest of living creation, and of themselves as being obviously better than other peoples they encountered, for whom they coined the word *barbarians*. Human superiority rests upon our power to think and create. This seemed to them obvious. And on this, too, rested their own superiority to the barbarians whom they viewed with contempt. The achievements of Athenian civilization—in art, literature, philosophy, and the birth of science—were daily before their eyes. We today do not sufficiently appreciate that our own edifices of civilization in the arts, literature, the rational thinking epitomized by philosophy, and science are all traceable to this origin. Our religions came from elsewhere and have, ever since, been at war, in one degree or another, with our Athenian heritage. That war goes on, and probably always will. It is, essentially, a conflict between two approaches to life and the world, one of them seeking light through thought and reason and emphasizing human creativity, and the other promising light through faith and a reliance upon authoritative books, as interpreted by a vast priesthood.

The pagan philosophers of antiquity, particularly Socrates, Plato, and Aristotle, of course shared this view of human and, more particularly, Athenian superiority, but they went a bit farther by giving philosophical expression to it. This idea is probably best expressed in Aristotle's writings. It has never been shown to be incorrect. On the contrary, it is enormously plausible, almost obvious, to anyone who thinks about it. But it is an idea that has been essentially forgotten, rather than refuted. It ran smack up against the religious view of human nature, epitomized in primitive Christianity, and even now it is difficult to get this idea clearly before us without its being suffocated by notions we have inherited from religion.

The idea can be most succinctly expressed as the claim that, first, human beings are, as such, superior to—that is, better than—other creatures and, second, some human beings are superior to—that is, better than—others. It was the second of these claims that ran afoul of religion, for religion taught that the least among us is every bit as good and worthy as the greatest, that no one can in any significant sense be better than anyone else. The religious explanation of human goodness was that we all borrow our worth from a god, having been, in fact, created by that god, and in that god's image. The Athenian view, on the contrary, was that our goodness rests upon our powers of thought, reason, and creativity, all of which were considered to be one and the same. In other words, our worth and superiority result from the fact that we have intellectual capacities found nowhere else, a fact that is perhaps misleadingly expressed by saying that we "have minds." But, as is obvious, not all people possess such capacities in equal measure. Some are wise, creative, and resourceful while others are less so, and some hardly at all. And from this it of course follows that, by the measure of worth before us, some persons are superior to or, literally, better than others, mostly because they have *made* themselves such. The most promising mind imaginable achieves nothing if left by its owner to decay.

Aristotle, like his predecessors, gave philosophical expression to this idea by invoking the idea of *function*. This concept is of course still very important. It would be hard to get through a single day without invoking it at some level or other, although scientists sometimes express a disdain for it as an explanatory principle. Be that as it may, Aristotle noted that virtually everything can be described in terms of its function. It is the function of a hammer to drive nails, of a knife to cut, of a boat to transport over water, and so on. Human beings can also usually be described, often essentially, in terms of their functions. Thus, it is the function of a physician to heal; of a novelist to create fiction; of a carpenter to build; of parents to protect, guide and teach their children; of a warrior to fight, and so on. Such statements are, in their banality, uncontroversial and obvious.

Aristotle further noted, quite incontrovertibly, that the concept of function has an important role in biology. Thus, it is the function of the eye to see, of the teeth to chew, and so on. Physicians even today have no difficulty speaking this way, as when they describe the function of the kidneys, the heart, or whatever. Indeed, it would be quite impossible to understand human biology without constantly invoking this concept of function.

And then Aristotle asked the big question: Is it plausible to suppose that everything, or virtually everything of any significance, has a function, and that yet a human being has none? Can it make sense to suppose that you, as a father, have a function, but that as a man you have none? Or that you, as a poet, have a function, but that as a woman you have none? And this amounts to asking: What are you here for? What are you supposed to be doing? If you are a surgeon approaching an operating table, the answers to these questions would be perfectly obvious. But now, disregarding whatever else you may be, and considering only the obvious fact that you are a person, can we not ask the same questions?

Here the skeptic is tempted to say *no*! This is getting too metaphysical. I, as a person, have no special function. It is just an idle and misleading question.

But let us not be hasty. Before leaping to that conclusion, let us ask how we determine the various functions of things.

To ask what is the function of some artifact—a hammer, knife, or whatever—is merely to ask to what use it is typically put, or what end or purpose it normally fulfills. Thus, a knife is used for cutting, a boat for transporting goods or people over water, and so on. Inanimate things like this have, of course, no ends or purposes of their own, but are instead used by people in pursuit of their ends or goals. Thus knowing what some inanimate thing is used for, we can, in an informative way, say what it is; not knowing this, we clearly have no idea what the thing in question is. If you are shown some totally unfamiliar fabricated object from a strange culture, you are apt to have no idea what it is, even though you could, by examining it closely, give a precise description of it in minute detail. But after learning that the object is used in that culture to, let us suppose, remove the seeds from some fiber to make clothing, then you do know what it is. You know its function, the end or purpose to which it is put.

If, next, you turn to living things, particularly those of a fairly "high" or complex kind, you are confronted with beings that have ends of their own, and you can understand their structure in terms of these and vice versa. Thus, you will understand, in an informative way, the structure of an owl as enabling it, for example, to fly noiselessly; or of a falcon, to fly very swiftly; or of a bat, to capture food in flight in darkness, and so on.

So, in general, you can say of the different kinds of creatures of the earth, that there is some mode of existence that each pursues, and you can, in an enlightening way, understand their structures in light of these ends. You understand why a bat, for example, is structured the way it is when you understand the kind of existence it pursues or, to say the same thing, when you understand how it functions.

If we turn now to human beings we shall see that the same considerations apply. Just as you can examine a bat and see the connection between its structure and how the bat can be expected to function, so also can you do this with a human being. For every kind of organism there is some thing or complex of things that sets it apart from every other kind, and in terms of this you can understand what that organism is and how it functions, that is, what it is supposed to do. Moreover, without knowing the latter, you will not be able to understand the former, any more than you can understand a human artifact independently of its function.

What, then, distinguishes a human being from every other creature? It is clearly the capacity to originate, plan, imagine, and carry out complex feats—in a word, to think or, more precisely, to create new things. And this is our function, this is what we are here for. To assert this is not, as has been so often supposed, to imply anything with respect to religion. It is not to say that we have been *put* here by some god to fulfill some end or goal. It is simply to note something that is obvious concerning human nature—that we, alone in creation, are capable of thought and reason to a high degree and, because of this, we can create new things. This is incontestable. It does not, of course, logically *follow* that this is what we ought to be doing; but if we permit ourselves the useful notion of function in our understanding of other things, including living things, then it is difficult to see why we should suddenly deny the applicability of such an idea in the understanding of human nature.

Aristotle, and the ancients generally, went a step further than all this in assuming that things can be evaluated as good or bad in terms of how *well* they fulfill their function. And of course this is obviously correct, up to a point. Thus, it is the function of a physician to heal, and we do not hesitate to distinguish between a good and a bad physician on the basis of how skilled or unskilled each is at this art. And so with everything else. Given the function of anything whatever, you can say at once whether a given specimen of that thing is *good* or *bad* in terms of how well it fulfills that function. And the implication of this, with respect to human nature, is so obvious that it hardly needs stating. Indeed, the ancients regarded it as too obvious to require defense. Some people are better than others, not just as physicians, sculptors, warriors, or whatnot, but *as persons*. And who are those persons who are good? Clearly, those who think, reason, and create—something we would express today by saying, those who use their "minds."

This way of viewing human nature, and of evaluating any of its specimens, is not esoteric, arcane, or invalid. It is perfectly plausible, simply carrying over to the understanding of human nature a mode of understanding that we do not hesitate to apply in other realms. Hostility to it arises primarily from a misinterpretation of the ideas of good and bad. Whether or not you are rational and creative implies nothing whatever concerning your morality, in the ordinary or customary sense. It implies nothing concerning your benevolence. What can be concluded from the degree and manner in which you use your creative and intellectual powers is the degree to which you are, or or not, superior *as a person* to those around you. However much you may have been taught to resist such a suggestion of personal superiority or inferiority, and to assail any line of thinking that might imply it, you should instead consider it seriously enough to ask whether there is really anything wrong with an aspiration to fulfill to the utmost that which distinguishes you as a person in the first place. The forces of custom that would batter you down to a level of equality with every fool and simpleton of the earth are hardly more deserving of honor than the insights of the wise, which enable you without shame to set for yourself a goal of personal excellence and devote yourself to achieving it.

WHAT ARE WE HERE FOR?

Most creatures exist only to perpetuate their own kind. Whatever other impulses they may have, such as self-preservation, which is a constant one, the perpetuation of their kind comes first. It is the ultimate reason for their toil and suffering. Some birds travel half the globe just to nest; giant turtles cover enormous lengths of ocean to lay their eggs at a fixed spot; salmon do the same and then, arriving at the approach to their spawning ground, struggle through powerful currents and over waterfalls just to fulfill that one aim. The general picture is the same throughout living nature. To exist, at least long enough to ensure that the species will continue, is the constant theme.

One result of this is that, with respect to all living things other than human, the creatures of the earth have no history. They have evolved, to be sure, over eons of time; but still they come and go leaving nothing behind except more of the same. The robins, squirrels, and ducks you see today are no different from those you observed as a child. They are born, do exactly what all others before them did, beget offspring, and are gone. Their lives are but endless cycles of sameness. Nothing new comes into being as a

113

consequence of anything they do. What they bring about has been done numberless times before, and will continue on forever, unchanged. The robin that takes wing today could have lived a thousand years ago without any noticeable difference.

We are different, in that we *do* have a history. A man born today could hardly have lived out his life a millennium ago without finding any difference. That was an entirely different world, and the vast changes that have occurred in the interim have been wrought by human beings. Our purpose, therefore, is not merely to perpetuate our kind, to ensure a succession of generations that are all alike. We, or at least some of us, make a difference through our living and through our goals and achievements.

This is but another way of saying that we, alone among all the creatures of the earth, are creative or, at least, we have the capacity to create. Totally new things emerge from our imagination and effort. No mere animal could ever create a poem, or music, nor could one ever form some plan for the future, some project never realized or even envisaged before, and then carry it out. The behavior of animals that sometimes suggests anything of this sort resembles human creativity only superficially. Birds sing, and some animals display striking beauty, but they are only doing what their kind have always done. Nothing is thereby created. But a person can envisage something totally novel, perhaps something great, perhaps only trivial, and then, through original thought and design, bring it into being. What is thus wrought might be something that is awesome to generations yet to come— a symphony, perhaps, or a great work of literature, or an invention that alters human existence forever. Or it might be something quite unspectacular and hardly noticed, such as the perfection of oneself as a great teacher, or a parent of extraordinary skill. Sometimes people become deeply involved in things for which there is no chance of their ever gaining fame. That does not matter. Fame and recognition are not the goals of creativity. You create something in order to bring about the realization of a dream, even though it may be of little interest to anyone but yourself. The point simply is that human beings, alone in creation, have the capacity to *create*. Nothing else does. And that is why human beings alone have a history. They make history—some in great and dramatic ways, others in small and unnoticed ways.

All this points to a kind of imperative, minimally expressed as: Do something. Better expressed, it says: Create something. To do otherwise is simply to waste your precious life. Do not, as Epictetus expressed it, rest upon your dead kinship with the beasts. All they do is eat, sleep, reproduce, then die and decay. For a person to do no better than that is in effect to lapse into a mere animal nature.

All this is so obvious that it would hardly need saying if it were not that so many people—perhaps even most—do lapse into that dead kinship with the beasts and do not even see anything wrong with it. They go through life with hardly an original thought; gravitate from one pleasure or amusement to another; gain a livelihood doing what someone else has assigned; flee boredom as best they can; marry and beget children; and then, without having made the slightest difference of any unique significance, die and decay like any animal.

The point is, you can do better. You can set for yourself a goal that goes beyond all this, something which, but for you, would never come into being at all, and then you can achieve it. If you are greatly gifted, and lucky, it might be something that will be long remembered, something that might even become an object of awe that will inspire wonder in future generations and amazement that any mortal person could execute such a creation. And if you are greatly gifted and not so lucky, then what you bring about will perhaps be something no less grand even though less noticed—a poem or book perhaps, whose merit is seen by few besides you. And if you lack this kind of genius, as of course most people do, then there nevertheless is something that you can become obsessed with, something you can do incomparably well, something that will absorb your energies and your creative thought and give worth to you as a person. And the imperative is, simply, to find it and do it. The alternative is to be, in every significant sense, an animal. Thus you can join the ranks of the proud, or you can, at the end of your long life, look back at a great stretch of nothingness, at a succession of pleasures gained, perhaps some pains and misfortunes avoided, of days and years spent to no real purpose. And if that should turn out to have been your lot, then all that can be said is that you had your chance, and you blew it. If shame is the opposite of pride, then we can surely say that shame is the appropriate response to a life thus squandered.

WEALTH

Although wealth is, to the discredit of human nature, one of the commonest stimulants to vanity and ostentatious display, it is no proper foundation for pride. You can only take pride in *yourself*, that is, in what you *are*. You cannot derive pride from *things*, however vast and coveted, that bear only an accidental connection to you. And pride, it must be remembered, is not merely the love of oneself—for even the least significant people have this—but the *justified* love of oneself, which is something that relatively few can properly claim. Thus to speak of taking pride in your possessions, or even in the skill and acumen you have displayed in amassing them, is to speak incoherently, for the skill has been wasted on something that contributes nothing to your true worth, whatever it may do for your power or status. To devote yourself to the accumulation of wealth, beyond the point of ensuring a leisurely and carefree life, is, quite simply, to waste your precious time, time that could have been spent making something of yourself. The ancient pagan moralists, from Socrates on, all saw this with perfect clarity, quite properly referring to possessions as "externals." The word carries the desired connotation

117

of things other than oneself, and points indirectly at the latter, oneself, as what is important.

Possessions are a perfect example of what does not fit the rule that if something is good, then more is better. It is clear that if we owned nothing we would lack an essential ingredient of civilized life; but the pursuit of wealth for its own sake, or even for the sake of other "externals" such as power, fame, or the capacity to incite envy, is a kind of disease. It is a distraction from what counts. It is like a boy entrusted to guard and protect something holy who, instead, expends his energy polishing rocks, until he entirely loses sight of his true mission. You are given one life to live and one thing to guard and protect, which is your true self. The religious sometimes speak of this as the soul, but the real meaning of this has long since been corrupted by priests and theologians with their own agendas. The truth, evident to anyone willing to think, is that you can make your life a work of art, quite literally glorifying yourself, or you can bungle the job in numberless ways, one of them being to become diverted to the love of possessions. You can, in short, quite literally abandon yourself and, worst of all, not realize what you have done. It happens all the time and is, in fact, a fate difficult to avoid.

This does not mean that possessions, or even great wealth, are things that are bad, the way such things as sickness, hunger, and loneliness are bad. It means only that you should not devote yourself exclusively to the pursuit of them, for you already possess, in yourself, something vastly more precious. The price, therefore, of going after wealth, even if you should succeed, is too high. You lose more than you have any chance of getting. Let me offer some illustrations.

Consider Henry David Thoreau, who went off to the woods and built himself a simple cabin near a pond, there to dwell alone for a year or longer. He had much to do. He spent his valuable time thinking, observing the nature in which he was immersed, reading, reflecting, and cultivating his bean patch. One day

Thoreau chanced upon an interesting and attractive stone, picked it up, and took it to his cabin, as anyone might. But in time he noticed that it became dusty and would require dusting, to display its pretty markings—so he threw it out in disgust. Even though the care of that object was minimal—an occasional dusting, the work of a moment—Thoreau had better things to do.

Would it have made any difference if, while dwelling in his cabin, alone with his thoughts and reflections, Thoreau had learned that he had suddenly and unexpectedly become rich—through an inheritance or something of this sort? Not at all. He would not have returned it, or given it away, but he would have given it little thought. His days would have passed exactly as before: thinking, reading, reflecting, and cultivating his bean patch. Thoreau had not been *reduced* to this solitary and simple life, but had created it for himself as something important to him at that juncture in his life and, when he finally abandoned his cabin and returned to town to his regular associations, he felt that he had been richly rewarded. Possessions, beyond what was needed for day-to-day life and comfort, had nothing to do with it. What concerned Thoreau was what he did with himself. As Socrates would have expressed it, he was busy all that time, "tending his soul."

Epictetus, the Roman Stoic, told his students a little story which, in its simplicity, illustrates this same point. We shall modify the story a little here in order to put it in a contemporary setting.

A man, Epictetus said, comes upon schoolchildren in a playground, and tosses candies, gum drops, and pennies into the air for them. The children all scramble to grab everything they can, stuffing their mouths and pockets, pushing each other and fighting, getting scratched up and dirty, and then go off grasping what they have been able to seize. They all behave, in short, like the children they are, without dignity or pride.

Now, Epictetus adds, suppose the governor is giving out goodies—judgeships, chairmanships of agencies, positions of power and status. See the children among us scramble for them; see them lick the governor's boots in hopes that something will be tossed their way; see how they abandon pride and dignity in their eagerness to belittle each other in the governor's eyes, inventing tales of wrongdoing, fighting for the tidbits the governor hands out.

The point of the story is clear. You are something of vast worth. Guard that worth. Do not throw it away by emulating an ignorant child, in a misguided eagerness to grab something that, in comparison to what you are, is of small worth, however gaudy and tempting.

But then Epictetus adds a most interesting twist to his story. He poses the question: What if a candy bar drops in your lap? Take it, he says, for a candy bar is worth just so much.

Thus, wealth or high office are not worthless things simply to be scorned. *If* you never attain them, it does not matter, for you already have what is important—yourself, and the ideal of yourself that you aspire to. But if, on the other hand, such things simply fall to you—drop into your lap, so to speak, unsought—then they are not to be scorned as evils.

But perhaps the best story from antiquity, illustrating the nature of true pride, is that told of Diogenes, the beloved cynic, who spent his time finding novel and striking ways to convey to his fellow Athenians the folly of their pursuits. Diogenes took to extremes the Socratic dictum that the mind or soul, the inner person, is all that matters, and that therefore the "tendance" of this, as Socrates and Plato expressed it, is what the wise should devote themselves to. Diogenes' sole aim in life was to perfect his thoughts and feelings, keeping his precious soul uncontaminated by the worldly things that so constantly tempt the foolish. He had no possessions, believing these to be stimulants of greed, and never allowed himself to be drawn to any worldly allure.

To understand a pun that is central to the little story, one must know that the Greek word for "dog" (kuōn, kunos) resembled the word "cynic" and, because of their scorn for property, fine clothes, pleasant dwellings, and so on, the Athenians who knew nothing of the Cynic philosophy imagined, erroneously, that the Cynics had taken their name from the fact that they chose to live like dogs. In truth, of course, they lived as they did in order to dramatize their scorn for worldly things, and to draw attention to what they deemed to be of true and incomparable worth, namely, the inner self.

So the story is told of Diogenes the Cynic that one day, as he was lying outside his tub, which was his shelter, enjoying the sunshine, Alexander the Great rode up on his horse and announced: "I am Alexander, the great king," to which Diogenes, without moving or rising to salute, responded: "And I am Diogenes, the dog." The exchange continued:

"Well, are you not afraid of me?"

"Are you good or bad?"

"Good, of course."

"And why should anyone fear that which is good?"

Now Alexander was so struck by the aptness of this observation that he exclaimed: "Ask anything you want of me, and you shall have it!"

To which Diogenes responded: "Then kindly step out of my sunlight."

The point of this simple story is almost certain to be lost on any modern reader, because of the way the concept of goodness has evolved, but any Athenian would have understood it immediately. It perfectly illustrates the meaning of true pride, albeit with immense exaggeration, for it is Diogenes, and not Alexander, who is the proud one.

To see this, we must focus on the meaning of "good." To us, human goodness means benevolence; therefore, a "good" person is one who is kind and generous. To an Athenian, human goodness was personal excellence or superiority, and had only an accidental connection with one's relationships to others. And Diogenes has taken this concept of personal excellence to its logical conclusion, believing that it has nothing whatever to do with riches or power or any worldly good, but consists entirely of the goodness of "soul," that is, of the inner person, the superiority and excellence of one's thought and feeling. You rise above others by the perfection of this, not by the acquisition of power. And by this standard Diogenes was, of course, superior to Alexander, whose "goodness" was mostly a sham, a mere appearance, consisting of little more than worldly power. Diogenes, knowing himself to be the better man, felt justified disdain for this misguided king, whose pride rested on things of secondary worth. Diogenes' pride rested on something real and genuinely worth something. He had a love for himself which was justified by what he was, not by those externals that he happened to own or control. So Alexander, known to all as "the Great," comes off second best to the simple and impoverished Diogenes, who could with both pride and irony refer to himself as "the dog."

PRIDE AND ARROGANCE

People are apt to associate pride with arrogance, and to suppose that the latter is at least a normal expression of personal pride. In truth, the two are so different as to be mutually exclusive. Remember that Alexander the Great, encountering Diogenes, succeeded overwhelmingly in arrogance, but pride was reserved for Diogenes.

Perhaps the difference can better be seen with a more modern example, this being a minor episode in the presidency of Abraham Lincoln. The story is apparently true, and not only sheds light on the character of this great man but, for our purpose, beautifully illustrates the meaning of pride.

It is reported that a gentleman called on President Lincoln to solicit a federal appointment for himself. After discussing the matter briefly the president sent the man over to see William Seward, his secretary of state. When the man returned from that interview the president asked him what Seward had said. "He said that you are a damn fool," came the reply. Lincoln's response was: "Perhaps I am then. Seward is usually right."

One needs to see beyond the words here. Lincoln was not

being self-effacing or expressing humility, and was certainly not concurring in a judgment that he was a fool. His response was that of a profoundly proud man, and he knew it. Its very playfulness was the expression of Lincoln's seriousness. He was a man of sufficient strength that he could dismiss, with frivolity, what a lesser person would treat as an insult. An arrogant president would have flushed with rage at this apparent insubordination, would have summoned the cabinet member into his presence for a tongue lashing and to demand an apology. A truly great man, conscious of his own worth, feels no inclination to such behavior.

Arrogance is an expression not of pride, but of basic insecurity. One tends to be arrogant to just the extent that he or she is lacking in a sense of true self-worth. It is an attempt to prove, not just to others but to oneself, that one possesses power and, in that sense, superiority over others. A proud person needs no proof of his or her superiority, and certainly has no need to prove it to anyone else. It is precisely because President Lincoln knew his own worth, and how this compared with, for example, that of Seward, that he could dismiss Seward with a kind of whimsy that, to the naive, might look like self-abnegation. Anyone possessed of a true understanding of pride can see that pride as clearly in Lincoln's words as he can through the holes in Diogenes' rags.

THE VULGAR

Vulgarity is generally thought to be a way of talking characterized by the use of graphic terms never used in polite discourse. But that is a derivative meaning. Vulgarity (from the Latin *vulgus*, meaning crowd or throng) is commonness, and a vulgarian is simply a common person, someone lacking in wit, sensitivity, and education. Indeed, the vulgar were originally thought of simply as the illiterate, and were thus contrasted with the educated, whom they vastly outnumbered. The thoughts and opinions of "the vulgar" were accordingly those of common, ordinary people, therefore thoughts and opinions that were not based upon learning or trained judgment.

The distinction is still a good one, even though the egalitarianism now considered mandatory for everyone would forbid characterizing any large group as "the vulgar." That may indeed be good policy as far as promoting peace and the ideal of community, but it is unfortunate in that it prevents us from making an important distinction between two kinds of people.

The vulgar are the common. They do not all share the same opinions and tastes, but their opinions and tastes are all equally

125

groundless. In general, the vulgar believe what they want to believe, and either do not see or do not understand any evidence to the contrary, or else they deny its relevance. They generally take their beliefs and tastes from those around them, that is, from the larger class of the vulgar, often from no better source than some church. Asked, for example, whether they "believe in God" they all say yes, with one voice, even though the idea of an actual god plays no significant role at all in the day-to-day lives of most of them. They respond to such a question in the way they are expected to, in what is *the approved* way, or in whatever way feels good to them. And it is the same in other matters of impor-tance—democracy, human rights, human equality, human dig-nity, the supreme worth of the individual, and so on. All such ideas receive the endorsement of the vulgar, very few of whom could give any intelligible account of what is meant by them.

The vulgar cling to the governing beliefs, tastes, and atti-tudes that they imbibed in adolescence, and the decades that fol-low might as well never have been, so far as any influence on these people is concerned. The music they liked then they like still, their tastes having undergone no refinement at all. And so it is with everything. What they were once comfortable with they find comfortable still. While the world changes around them, they remain essentially unchanged.

Vulgarism is thus not a distinction of class, power, or wealth. The richest and most powerful among us are likely to be no less vulgar than the least. Nor can the vulgar be distinguished by a use of what has come to be thought of as vulgar language. Strictly speaking, vulgar language is simply language that is misused, lan-guage in which significant distinctions are never made—in short, language that is common, and which thus betrays its user as a common person. If, for example, you hear someone employing such nonwords as "preventative," "incidences," "solicitate," or the like, then you are almost certain to be listening to a vulgarian.

The contrast to the vulgarian is someone who is *un*common,

whose beliefs, tastes, and attitudes have been tested and refined through experience and education. Thus a person of refinement, in contrast to a vulgarian, is not merely someone whose speech is in keeping with refined standards, but someone whose whole inner life and outward behavior are a credit to the highest self-created standards. To test whether you are a vulgarian, you can simply measure yourself against common people, to see whether you are one of them. Or, preferably, you can measure yourself against the best, who are uncommon, to see whether you can stand among these. But to do that you must be able to recognize the best and be able to admit it if you do not measure up to them. That is what is hard, even impossible, for most people. The common, on the other hand, are easily recognized and, if you find that you share their qualities, you can console yourself with slogans about the virtues of common people, but you are still a vulgarian.

Suppose, for example, you are in a cheap restaurant, the windows of which glow with electric beer signs, and you see a group of men at the bar drinking beer, making idle and pointless comments, and mindlessly watching the television screen. Simply ask yourself: Am I essentially the same as one of these? And there you will have your answer. But if you are in truth a vulgarian, you will probably have some reason either not to ask the question at all, or to rationalize away an affirmative answer to it.

The musical director of a symphony orchestra rehearsing the musicians, who impatiently shouts at the violin section, "Can't you get this through your fucking heads?" is irascible and difficult, but she is not a vulgarian. What she is doing refutes that. On the other hand, a spellbinding evangelical clergyman playing to the prejudices and ignorance of a congregation, working them up to a fervor of piety with one groundless declamation after another, is a vulgarian, even though no offensive word ever creeps into his speech.

PRECIOUS TIME

It has been said that time is the only thing in the world that is irreplaceable, and there is an important truth in that. If you waste a day, it is lost forever—you cannot get it back to do something with it. Other things, you can; if you lose a fortune, you can sometimes regain it.

What, then, if you waste a lifetime? People do. Perhaps most do, in this sense: while their lives drift by through the conventional four stages, and they are moderately content and without real complaint throughout, they nevertheless go to their graves having done nothing with themselves, living from one day to the next, sleeping, waking, eating, toiling, begetting, and that's it. They are much the same at age seventy as they were at age twenty—with the same ideas and attitudes, the same limitations, having made no attempt to remove them and to learn something from what the years might teach. At the end, they have nothing to point to with pride beyond, perhaps, the fact that they have lived decent lives, doing more or less what was expected of them and leaving something for their children.

Of course there is nothing severely wrong with such a picture, except that virtually everyone has the capacity to do better. We

128

cannot all be great, stamping our achievements on the memories of generations to come, but virtually all of us have within ourselves creative power of some kind, and can achieve a nobility in our lives that may remain totally unknown to all but, perhaps, a very few. That others will take note of what we do is, in any case, of small importance, and certainly no measure of our worth. There are numberless undramatic ways of achieving an inner, unheralded greatness. While one person will achieve his or her own excellence in the arts, for example, and perhaps be applauded and envied by all, another will find it in something as familiar as exemplary parenting, or great teaching. There are countless roads to fulfillment, some of them spectacular but most of them not. The point is that they are roads to the fulfillment of oneself, the perfection of oneself through the pursuit of an ideal that is one's own, whether of interest to others or not.

It must, however, be an ideal and not something that one simply falls into without thought. And there is the rub. Many people simply take the days as they come, and count themselves successful if they manage to get through them, one after the other, in moderate comfort and without boredom. Indeed, many look upon time as merely something to *kill*. Their aim is primarily to keep themselves occupied or distracted, to give themselves something to do, lest time, in its eventless passage, should engulf them in boredom.

There was a man whose life and interests centered entirely around his role as a stockbroker, and the general pattern of his life was typical of many. He spent long days at his office on the telephone, executing orders to buy and sell, chain smoking all the while, and even having lunch at his desk. In an advancing market his sense of life quickened as he saw his commissions increase and his bank account improve, often dramatically. This is what he lived for. His evenings and weekends were spent passing the hours in passive entertainment, enjoying small and ephemeral pleasures, keeping boredom at bay until he could get back to his office, his cigarettes, and his telephone, until one day he coughed a trace of blood, which was his death warrant.

One can say of this man that he certainly committed no wrong; he lived a blameless life and even one that was, at some level, satisfying. But we can also say—and this is the horrible part of it—that in the end he had accomplished nothing, left nothing that he could point to with pride except, perhaps, his many years of faithful toil. Essentially his life was spent avoiding boredom, killing time—and, in the end, killing a lifetime. And the fact that his bank account, at the end, was a large one does nothing to alter this evaluation.

We read of another man who, at an early age, had gained worldwide notoriety as a deal maker and, in a series of spectacular deals over the course of only a few weeks, enriched himself by something in the neighborhood of seventy million dollars. As the finishing touches were being put upon this spectacular sequence he discovered that he had inoperable prostate cancer and, soon after, he was dead and quite forgotten by the multitude who, in their misguided sense of what is important, had envied him. Meanwhile, the precious days came and went, not for him but for the least known of people who had learned how to make them count. Instead of storing up gold, they were enhancing what Plato would have called the treasures of the soul. Avoiding the religious overtones of this, we can make the same point by saying that there are people who have learned not to waste their time in pointless accumulation, whether of gold, nuts, or jelly beans, but to use their precious days to enhance the only thing they possess that is truly precious, and that is, themselves. To set for yourself an ideal, not of what you want to own, but of what you want to be as a person—this, and only this, is the way to use your time to advantage to yourself.

Someone has said that you should live each day as if it were your last, but there cannot really be very much truth in this. Perhaps the thought behind it is that if you thought your life was about over, you would probably stay out of trouble and might even seize this last chance to do something good in the way of helping others. Maybe that is true, but you surely have, or should have, a more important concern than this. Instead of stopping at the idea of doing something for others, perhaps you should consider doing something for yourself—not in the way of satisfying some passing need or barging ahead with indifference to others, but rather, really doing something for your *self*, in the way of taking a step toward fulfilling your ideal of personal and individual excellence. Thus it would be better to say that you should live each day as though it were your first—that is, the beginning of the new person that you at last aspire to be. The time has come for you to face an unflattering self-appraisal and to ask not what you want to *do*, or even what you want to do the rest of your life, but rather, what you want to *be*. It is time to set aside the great concern you have always been taught to have for your responsibilities to others, and give thought to your responsibility to yourself. No one else but you can make you the kind of person you aspire to be, and you cannot either unless you give it thought and make it the focus of your energy. There is something of lasting worth that you can do, which is such that, unless you do it, it will never be done at all. Maybe it will be some masterpiece of art, or literature, but probably not; more likely it will be something of great worth noticed by no one but you, and maybe it will be the legacy of your character conferred upon your children. Whatever it is, there is more to live for than merely moving pleasantly from one day to the next, like a clock that is wound up and then slowly winds down and stops before being rewound the next day.

CANDOR

Proud men and women, so relatively (and sadly) few, are above all candid. Indeed, this follows from the very nature of pride. Such people need never pretend to be what they are not, for what they *are* is, unembellished, something of great worth—for otherwise, they could not be proud. The proud do not conceal their thoughts and feelings, for why should they? What they think and feel is already good and even, perhaps, sometimes noble, and need not be concealed from anyone. Thus the proud are not devious or evasive. They respond to questions in a natural unguarded way, for they have nothing in them to conceal. Their conversation flows naturally and consistently. They have no need to try to appear to be anything but precisely what they are. Proud people do not pretend to know what they do not know, do not try to cover their mistakes, and readily and easily accept correction. You are tempted to do otherwise only when you are more concerned with how you appear in the eyes of others than with how you do in your own eyes—in other words, only when you lose sight of your pride. You know when you have blundered, and you know those things about which you are ignorant. This self-knowledge, however painful, is not made any different by another person's false perception of you. So even if you succeed in misleading others—which, incidentally, is very rare—you will never succeed in misleading yourself. If you have done something stupid, and this is somehow completely concealed forever from the world, you will still know that you have done something stupid. Your aim, then, is not so much to conceal it, since you cannot conceal it from the one person who counts—yourself—but rather, to learn from it. You never need to have much fear of what others think of you, assuming that your blunders do not sink to the level of crimes. If you have learned from them, you will have little to fear from what you will henceforth think of yourself.

Suppose, for example, that you have cheated. To be sure, no one would want this degrading fact known to others, but the real price you pay is forever knowing it yourself. It cannot possibly be reconciled with your sense of your own self-worth. So the reason for not cheating is not that you might be caught. You are already caught, by yourself, and the price you pay is already much too high, because you pay with yourself.

Or suppose you deceive someone for personal gain, and it works—your victim is indeed deceived, and you gain by it. But now measure what you have gained together with what you have lost. You have lost your pride because you have lost the only valid foundation for it, which is your own worth, as seen not by others but by you. And now you should honestly ask, was it worth it? How could it be worth it?

This is part of the beauty and comfort of pride—that you can be your genuine self. You need not weigh or be guarded in your speech, which instead flows comfortably and consistently, being the expression of thoughts in which you can feel no shame. The proud move about with total ease. They fear no questions or scrutiny. They do not tremble lest someone ask the dreaded question or see the shameful deed, for they have already put every question to themselves and can see any shameful deed for exactly what it is, ugly and shameful, and thus are in no danger of committing it. Only those who sense, perhaps accurately, that their own inner worth is not great, who place higher value on things other than their own personal excellence—only these are tempted to clothe themselves with deceptions and make-believe and to cover over the reality of themselves with appearances more acceptable. The proud have no need to distinguish, with respect to themselves, between what they are and what they appear to be. These are for them one and the same.

PRIDE AND RULES

A proud person creates his or her own rules, but we must be careful not to read into this implications that are not there. It does not mean that a proud person is disregardful of others, or that this person is heedless of the basic principles on which civil society rests. Moreover, while the proud live by their own rules, they are also their own judges—*and very severe ones*. This means that the proud set very high standards for themselves. Such persons are not shaken by the disapproval of others, although they do care deeply about self-approval. The real failure is failure not in the eyes of others, but in one's own eyes. This is an essential mark of pride.

It follows from this that the rules and customs of others, even those of one's own culture or group, are weighed, every one of them. Is this, one asks, a rule for me? The fact that something is taken seriously and done faithfully by everyone else is by itself no reason at all why you should do it. Most people, for instance, take the flag seriously and adhere to fastidious rules concerning the treatment and display of it. This is not true in other cultures. All countries have flags, but the sanctity of the flag as a national symbol seems to be uniquely American. Now this fact—that everyone, or nearly everyone, is deeply ceremonious in the treatment of this symbol and scowls severe disapproval at anyone who is not—is certainly by itself not the least reason why you should uphold these practices. To claim otherwise would amount to saying that what others think of you is what is important—more important, indeed, than what you think of yourself—and this can never be a mark of pride. You may derive comfort from the smiles of others, you may feel more secure in their approval of you, but this is not pride. It comes close to being the opposite.

To pursue this example, what a proud person asks is not: What is expected of me here? But rather: What is this symbol a symbol of? And is that something that ought to be honored? Is the flag, for example, a symbol of militarism and war? Or is it, instead, a symbol of the values embodied in the Constitution and its Bill of Rights? These are the relevant questions. What others think and do is not relevant.

The same applies, of course, to other quasi-sacred things and the practices that have grown up around them, such as churches, certain holidays like Christmas, and so on. The proud may indeed take church seriously, or again, they may not, but if one takes church and the observances connected with it seriously just because everyone else does, this is not pride but the surrender of it. The same is true of semi-religious symbols like Christmas. Many persons treat indifference to his holiday, or the refusal to participate in the rituals connected with it—the music, decorations, special symbols, and so on—as manifestations of something akin to bad character. But it is of course no such thing. What one needs to ask, concerning any such near-universal practice, is simply: What does it mean for me? What it means for others is irrelevant, nor need you care how others may feel about the way you answer this question.

The point, though it would seem obvious by now, must be stressed once more, perhaps written in stone: What matters is what you think of yourself. What others think of you does not, as such, matter at all, if you want to stand among the proud.

At this point it is worth recalling again the example of Diogenes the Cynic. What Diogenes was trying to teach his fellow Athenians by his seemingly whimsical antics was impossible for all but a few to understand, and people today might find it even harder. You must dwell on the image of Diogenes in rags, lying outside the tub that was his shelter, confronted by the great Alexander in his royal regalia, and realize that in this image it is Diogenes who is the proud, not Alexander. Diogenes' pride is not a pretense. It is totally genuine. Alexander's pride is derivative, and rests entirely on externals and appearances, underneath which there may be no trace of it at all. Diogenes appears to us here as nothing but a beggar, utterly disregardful of himself, and we are apt to ask incredulously: Is this what you have in mind by a proud person? The answer is: Yes, precisely. But until you can see that this is indeed correct, then you cannot understand the true nature of pride. Diogenes understood it perfectly.

SPEECH

A person with an untrained, slovenly, and childish mind cannot possibly have a sense of personal excellence, for it is the refinement and precision of thought and sensitivity of feeling that, more than anything else, sets the proud apart from everyone else. To be a worthwhile human being, you must be more than just another human being. The latter exist in abundance; the former, though not rare, are in the minority. To be among these is more important than wealth or power or any other external good, for it is what you *are* and not merely what you have.

Probably no single thing marks you so accurately as the quality of your speech. However refined may be your dress and grooming, or whatever else may be instantly noted, a single ill-constructed sentence or verbal misuse gives you away instantly. If your thinking is childish and irrational, then whatever stunning impression you may make in any other way, your speech will instantly betray this quality of your mind. A single ill-formed remark or absurd or illogical combination of words stamps you at once as a vulgarian. Anyone sees the folly of turning to you for anything resembling wisdom or acumen or even reliable judgment.

To see this, imagine two men much the same in appearance standing side by side, and fill out the images in ways that equally favor both. Let us suppose them to be of impressive stature and bearing, in the prime of life and, to all appearances, prosperous and self-assured. Add such additional positive attributes as you wish, keeping the two about the same, in your imagination, with respect to all these. But now suppose each to utter a single, simple remark, having the same meaning in each case, one of them saying, "She and I work for the same company," and the other saying, "Her and I work for the same company." The second person is now instantly stamped as a vulgarian, and nothing will remove that stigma. Give him every attribute of strength and power that you wish, everything that would mark him as above the ordinary lot, he nevertheless remains a common person. He may indeed love himself—most people do—but that love is not justified, for he still has the mind of a child, insensitive to even the plainest solecism. How you speak is a perfect barometer of the way you think, and thus, of your worth as a person. If your speech is incoherent, illogical, irrational, or confused, then so is your thinking. What you say will rarely be worth hearing and will be so judged by anyone of genuine pride. Your opinions will be dismissed in advance before you have uttered them, for having once heard some irrational combination of words from your mouth, a person of intelligence will assume that all your thinking is similarly infected, and that appraisal of you will be a correct one.

By correct speech is not meant florid or arcane vocabulary, or complex or convoluted combinations of words. Speaking correctly means little more than speaking accurately and clearly. Words are chosen for their aptness, not for what you imagine to be their impressiveness. For example, a *house* is correctly referred to as a house, not as a home, the latter having the wider meaning of a house that is lived in. And people *live* there; nothing is made better by saying they *reside* there. A retarded child is retarded, and the description is not improved by saying merely that the child is in some sense *special*. Similarly, an adult moron is in truth a moron, and no precision is gained by speaking of such a person as merely *intellectually challenged*. Words like these are euphemisms, and people who are not greatly concerned about precision and accuracy in their thinking turn to them only because the words somehow *feel* better. Such corruptions of language are the result of treating egalitarianism as an ideology rather than simply as wise public policy. We are, by this ideology, expected to deny clear and obvious defects and faults, and to speak as though there just cannot be any differences in personal worth, in spite of fact.

While this is not the place for a treatise on correct English usage, it is not difficult to say how it is achieved. You need only to develop a sensitivity to language and a determination to use it correctly. Redundancies, for example, are instantly noticed, for you have taught yourself to hear them. Metaphorically, a red flag springs up in your head if you hear someone say "divert away from," "another alternative," "again reiterated," and so on. Most linguistic misuse is a result of trying to make one's speech more interesting than it actually is. Thus someone says, "He literally threw out the baby with the bath," which is an absurd remark, or "It was heart-rendering," or "there's nothing worse" than, say, losing your wallet and all its contents in a foreign land. Nothing is made more interesting by overstatement or misused intensifiers. The purpose of speech is to express facts, thoughts, and feelings correctly and accurately, and usually with as few words as possible.

A proud person who slips into incorrect speech does not mind being corrected. The deeper shame, by far, would be to repeat the error over and over, in blissful ignorance of what any person of refined thought and speech instantly recognizes. If you have thought all this time that "enervate" has approximately the same meaning as "energize," or have been saying "nucular" when you meant "nuclear," then is it not time for someone to straighten you out? Illogical or otherwise incorrect use of words is an irritant to the ear of anyone who has cultivated the art of thinking logically, precisely, and accurately. There is certainly far more to being proud than speaking correctly, but failure here is inexcusable. The English language is the richest on earth, and a wonderful vehicle for the expression of thought. It must not be abused. The cost of misuse is great, not so much to the hearer but to the person misusing it. Hearing language being used pretentiously, incoherently, or with redundancy, contradiction, or absurd euphemism is like finding flies in your gourmet food. And just as it is worse still to fail to notice the flies that are there, so also is someone to be pitied who, day after day, exhibits the same linguistic incompetence, does not know it, and would resent your attempt to correct it.

PRIDE AND
MARITAL DISSOLUTION

Probably nothing tests pride as severely as the dissolution of a marriage. Every impulse antithetical to pride takes over—fear, greed, jealousy, paranoia, and a general relapse into childishness. The forces working against pride and self-esteem in such a situation are so strong that few can survive them and still retain the calm and confident self-appraisal that pride requires. Attorneys who handle divorce cases assure us that in no other kind of litigation do bitterness and enmity rise to such intensity.

About half of all marriages fail completely, and of those that do not a great many, perhaps even most, survive only in the sense that the partners remain in the same household, often with only minimal affection for each other and sometimes in a state of ongoing disdain or hostility. Love often dies in a marriage long before any visible rupture appears, so that the partners "stay married," but only in a legal and formal sense. And, indeed, it is doubtful whether any human institution is so loaded with the possibilities of ongoing misery. Some people remain married and joyously in love, for life, but this is an ideal that is rarely achieved. Most marriages fall within the larger spectrum ranging from dull, loveless, barely tolerable, and miserable to totally impossible. It is these last, the impossible, that result in dissolution and divorce. Most of the others, though in varying degrees bad, do not reach this level of badness.

It is beyond our purpose to diagnose or offer therapies for failing marriages. Rather, we are concerned only with the retention of pride in the face of forces that beset a marriage that has utterly failed.

The first and most basic requirement is to resist, by every means, the impulses that are nourished and inflamed by marital separation, especially paranoia and resentment. Marital dissolution fosters these impulses like nothing else, and it is also the strongest nourishment for resentment. Faced with the certainty of divorce you feel hideously vulnerable: You see property, sometimes lots of it, suddenly threatened, and when small children are involved you see the precious bonds of affection similarly imperilled. And when on top of this you see a spouse, whose love you expected to last forever, withdrawing and becoming a foe, a source of overwhelming insecurities—indeed, someone empowered to make real some of the things you most dread, such as the loss of your children—then resentment becomes overwhelming. And it is, needless to say, profoundly exacerbated by the presence of a third person in the background. These things are so familiar, even to those who have not personally experienced them, that they need only be alluded to here.

What, then, is appropriate for a proud person in the face of threats and forces like these?

The very first step, and perhaps the hardest, is to avoid a confrontational attitude. When one feels threatened and attacked, the most natural response is counterthreat and counterattack in the attempt to ward off the evils that threaten. But this always fails. Threats, whether in this or any other situation, are *always* met with counterthreats. No one ever wins. This is especially true in those cases of marital dissolution in which fear, bitterness, and resentment guide the steps of both parties. *Both lose.*

The avoidance of confrontational attitudes means, first of all, the retention of a calm demeanor and, indeed, civility and friendliness. Every semblance of threat or attack must be met with a smile and a serene inner calm. Do not let yourself rise to—or, rather, be dragged down to—the level of personal antagonism.

The reason for this first step is in fact very clear to anyone who values personal pride. It rests upon your perception that *you*, and not your property or other externals, are what is important. Property, once lost, can often be regained or replaced, but self-esteem seldom can. Once compromised, it is usually damaged forever. Thus you remind yourself that you really *do not care* what happens to the things that you own, even though these may be the fruit of your life's work and, perhaps, of an impressive value. What matters to you is what has always mattered, if you are a proud person, and that is what you *are*.

None of this means, of course, that a proud person simply stands by as a willing victim of whatever may happen. You do what needs to be done to protect what is important to you, but always in a spirit of serenity and calm and, indeed, if possible, of magnanimity. These are what are essential to what is really important to you, namely, the kind of person you aspire to be—someone who is, in the ancient sense of the term, good and who stands out from others in this respect.

The impulse to paranoia, the feeling of being threatened by someone possibly capable of inflicting great harm, is thus met by the realization that, whatever may happen to the things you possess, no harm can thus befall *you*. The sun will rise and set as before, the hours and days will be allotted to you the same as before, and, whatever may befall, you will still have all that you need to be the person you are and the person you aspire to be. This is what is precious. All the other things are "externals." Nor can anyone, except you, damage the affection between you and your children. They will continue to bask in your love and, if you are proud and above the pettiness that invades almost every marital dissolution, you will forever enjoy their love and esteem. Children grow up and eventually place their own assessment on everything, including their parents, and these assessments are usually deadly accurate. And they are determined not by what any court has said or by the contents of any decrees, but by what a parent actually is.

The other thing that a proud person must rise above is resentment. Nourishing wounds—sometimes mistakenly described as wounds to one's pride—and trying to inflict them in reprisal is always debasing. However well founded your resentment, you must never express it but, on the contrary, give expression only to the opposite. This is of course not easy to do, but a genuinely proud person manages it.

Few things are as provocative of moral judgment as marital dissolution. The temptation to blame is overwhelming and, if a third person is involved, blame and condemnation are directed at this person, who is seen as a home wrecker. But no outsider ever destroys a good marriage. Extramarital involvement is always a symptom of a marriage in trouble, never the cause. Hence, to direct blame and judgment at the outsider is not only unfair but also stupid, for it draws attention away from the real problem. The same should be said concerning the blame and judgment that spouses direct at each other, usually fortified by partisans of the one or the other. It not only is fruitless, it also amounts to focusing on matters that are quite unreal and thus distracts one from the problems that are very real indeed. And, needless to say, it exacerbates bad feelings, precisely when mutual respect and understanding are most desperately needed.

The points at issue here can perhaps best be seen by an imaginative illustration. Let us suppose that your husband or wife has betrayed you by deception and infidelity and, after every mean-spirited act imaginable, has finally left you for someone else.

The reactions that such a situation produce are overwhelming. First of all, there is the sense of betrayal. Someone who has solemnly promised affection, love, and esteem until death, and has

usually done so in circumstances of great ceremony and with overtones of religious commitment, now breaks that promise. Second, there is the sense of abandonment. You have been dumped,
cast aside—even these descriptions seem inadequate to the situation. Third, there is the feeling that you have been robbed.
Something that was clearly yours forever has simply been taken
away and is now held by another person. Fourth, there is an overwhelming sense of jealousy, for nothing evokes this with such
strength as this kind of triangular relationship. Fifth, paranoia
sets in, for you see things precious to you, and essential to your
happiness and well-being, threatened—property, children, everything. Everything your estranged spouse says and does poses a
threat to your possession of these, and they can all be taken from
you by judicial decree. Sixth, there are sure to be feelings of inad-
equacy and even guilt. Something must be *wrong* with you,
morally or otherwise, for these things to be happening. Seventh,
you are likely to feel disgraced, or at least to some degree a failure
in the eyes of all those who know you. This feeling is not, to be
sure, the problem it once was when divorce was a rare occurrence
and the shame attending it far greater, but it still occurs. And,
finally, there are overwhelming feelings of anger and resentment.

That is quite an inventory of bad feelings, and it is no wonder that persons enduring a marital separation are often at their
wit's end and driven to extremes of instability.

If you are a proud and rational person, however, you have
powerful resources to counter all these evils. In the first place, you
know that it does not matter how other people view your situation, even if they should be unanimous in pointing the finger of
shame and guilt at you. It does not matter who they say is to
blame, who they say is treated shabbily, or whatever. Their opinions and attitudes are of no concern to you. All that matters, if
you are proud, is what *you* think, for you are the sole legitimate
judge of yourself. So you can look closely at yourself and decide
whether what you find meets your own severe standards of

approval. If not, then do something about it, and that is enough. If you feel betrayed, then you should feel bad for the betrayer, not for yourself, for no betrayal of affection can damage you as a person, provided you are a proud one. Perhaps you cannot help feeling abandoned, but this does not mean that nothing is left for you. A proud and resourceful person does not feel that he or she has no resources save those that are bestowed by others. So instead of thinking of abandonment, think instead that someone who shared your life no longer does—that is the whole of it. It is not an easy way to look at things, but it can be done, up to a point, and it is vastly better than self-pity. And the sense of being robbed need not overwhelm you, for no one can take from you what really matters to you, namely, your self, your pride, and the strengths or virtues that this rests upon. Feelings of paranoia can be banished by the same reflection. You need feel no fear of losing something that is totally within your own power. Property can by compromised, but you do not measure your worth by this anyway. And jealousy is, of course, an emotion that by its nature is appropriate only for children and fools. Finally, you cannot feel disgraced in the eyes of others if, as a matter of principle, you have little concern for how you appear in the eyes of others.

Marital dissolution creates strains that no one can handle with ease, particularly when the rejected marital partner is still deeply in love with the other, but there can be little doubt that a genuinely proud person will deal with it better, and with far less injury all around, than one who is weak and conventional, yielding not only to every destructive passion from within but to destructive external forces as well.

But now, having gone this far, see whether you can take one more step—a very large one, to be sure, but one that is sometimes within the power of a proud person, and totally beyond anyone who is not proud. This is the step, beyond pride, to magnanimity. It can be illustrated as follows.

Suppose now that you are a wife, abandoned in favor of another woman. (The illustration would, of course, work just as well the other way around.) If you allude to this woman at all—and there is no reason why you should not—then speak *well* of her. This will of course be in opposition to your strongest feelings, but, more effectively than anything else, it will demonstrate, not just to others but, more important, to yourself, your superiority to her and, indeed, to everyone who is at all involved in this. And, carrying the illustration one step further, suppose you encounter this third person at some gathering or other, perhaps in the company of your estranged husband. Your impulse will of course be to turn your back. Instead of that, speak to her confidently and pleasantly, and remark to her that your estranged husband is a fine person, and you know she will bring him the kind of happiness he deserves. Not an easy thing to do! But worth it. And, if the likelihood of face-to-face encounter is remote, you can even compose a note to this effect. The effect of such behavior, to which only a magnanimous person can rise, can be overwhelming, and the effect upon the proud person herself, in nourishing a pride that rises to personal greatness, is totally positive. It is not easy, but it can be done, and it is worth it. But you have to have the pride that is necessary to carry it off, for otherwise you will succeed only in making a fool of yourself. This sort of thing cannot be done as an act. It has to be an expression of genuine personal excellence.

PART TWO

PRIDE AND THE RULE
OF MANNERS

INTRODUCTION

What have manners to do with personal pride? The two supplement each other, in a way that makes both essential to a coherent philosophy of living. They are not otherwise connected. A proud person can be bereft of fine manners, and a simple, self-abnegating person can be possessed of them, although this is perhaps less common.

Pride is, essentially, a matter of how you think of, and how you treat, yourself, while manners have to do with how you think of and treat others. The two ideas are thus quite different, and yet both have to do with your relationships to persons—to yourself, in the first case, and to others in the second.

It is part of our customary ethics, derived from religion, that we should cultivate humility, not pride, and that the love that the proud have for themselves should instead be directed to others. Thus the ideal of a good person is, by this tradition, the self-effacing person who loves everyone.

The first part of this notion, humility, is the very opposite of the ideal that has been set forth here. The appropriate object of your love is precisely yourself, but with the qualification that this love must be justified by what you are. And as for the love that, according to the religious tradition, we are supposed to have for everyone except ourselves, this turns out to be an absurdity. You cannot love the whole human race. You cannot love persons unknown to you, for you do not know what they are, beyond the bare fact that they are human.

This is, of course, according to the teaching of religion, sufficient; that is, it is enough to know that persons, otherwise unknown to you, are human, for this makes them veritable images of God. From such a starting point it is easy to derive the notion that every human being, of whatever limitations, is possessed of a quality sometimes referred to as human dignity. This strange notion has found a place even in the thinking of philosophers who imagine that they have rejected any religious foundation for ethics and base their claims only on reason and experience. The fact that neither reason nor experience discloses any such quality in human nature does not seem to matter to them.

Of course there is such a thing as human dignity, but it is not common. It is displayed by the proud, and is thus relatively rare. It is not the possession of everyone, and does not result simply from being born. The concept of human dignity becomes empty if you are prohibited at the outset from finding anywhere throughout the human race anyone who lacks it.

The exhortation to love everyone, even strangers and enemies, amounts to the urging of a *policy*. It is not really a commandment of love, for that would stretch the concept to absurdity. It is, rather, an exhortation to act, as a matter of policy, *as if* you loved everyone.

Perhaps it would be conducive to peace if more people tried to act that way, but the point remains that this is no genuine love. To clothe what amounts to nothing more than a policy or mode of behavior in the language of love is not only a hypocrisy, but a mischievous one. It leads you to think that the ideal of love is fulfilled simply by acting a certain way—a way of acting that, with respect to utter strangers, is based upon no noble feelings at all.

Still, we need a guide to our relationships with others if we are to live full and rewarding lives. A proud person is possessed of something very precious, in the creative achievements that are the basis for his self-love, but this is not enough for a complete life. We are not hermits. We live with others, and we constantly need them. The proud love themselves, and cannot in any meaningful sense love everyone else. So there is needed some guide to our relationships to others, and this will be a guide to what is here unpretentiously called *manners*.

We shall set forth a rule of manners, which turns out to be a rule of the utmost simplicity, and then illustrate it with a variety of examples more or less arbitrarily chosen. These examples are for the most part banal, drawn from the day-to-day experiences that are familiar to everyone. Most human relationships, outside the family circle, are superficial and undramatic, but they are nevertheless important. What follows is therefore not a guide to ethics and duty. No rules are offered for resolving life's greater problems. What is offered, instead, is a simple introduction to fine manners. It is meant only to illustrate a very simple rule, which is all anyone really needs in his or her daily encounters with people, and to indicate the blessings that follow from being guided by it.

PRIDE AND MANNERS

Our age has largely lost track of the ideal of fine manners. Indeed, few know what the words even mean. People confuse manners with mere etiquette or, sometimes, with a kind of self-conscious mode of behavior, as when someone is described as "mannered." Fine manners can also become entangled with the concept of ethics.

What we have in mind here by manners is a certain clear ideal of civilized life that goes far beyond mannered behavior as well as etiquette, and is only loosely connected with ethics.

In describing this or that person as "mannered" we are sometimes calling attention to nothing more than how that person chooses to act with a view to conveying a certain impression. Thus the erstwhile poet acts in the way he imagines poets should act, perhaps imitating the mannerisms of some celebrated poet. Meanwhile a celebrity or near celebrity may act in the way many people expect celebrities to act—posturing, perhaps waxing witty. The self-styled man of the world acts in a still different way, and so on. All these self-conscious modes of behaving, however, have nothing to do with genuine manners.

Nor, in speaking of manners, are we referring to mere etiquette. Etiquette has solely to do with what one says or does in this or that situation—how guests are seated at a formal dinner, how one addresses an archbishop, decorum at a wedding, and so on, endlessly. Etiquette, in short, is behavior in accordance with a vast and complex system of rules, and large books are devoted to the elaboration of those rules. Many of the rules are arbitrary and concerned with only the least significant aspects of social life. What, for example, is correct behavior with regard to exiting an elevator? Should female people exit first? Or those already near the door? It hardly matters, and yet it is nice to have some kind of rule. Or how do you address a letter to persons whose names are unknown—the editors of a magazine, for example? Again, there are various possibilities; but it is desirable, even sometimes quite important, to know the "right" way. It is to questions like these that books of etiquette are devoted.

The concept of manners is vastly more important than that of etiquette. A person can be faultless in the observance of the latter and yet fail abysmally with respect to the former. And while the rules of etiquette are numberless, good manners are governed by but one rule—a rule that is easily enunciated, yet difficult to comprehend and enormously difficult to live by, due simply to the obstacles created by human psychology. Any nitwit can become expert in etiquette simply by taking the matter very seriously, learning its rules and carrying them into practice. None but a profoundly thoughtful person, on the other hand, who has both a deep understanding both of self and the needs of others, can possess truly fine manners. Indeed, these become for such a person one of the foundations of life, and those capable of rising to them are relatively few. An unthinking, silly, or stupid person can never become well mannered, nor can the most serious, thoughtful, and intellectual person achieve this level of living without first setting it forth as a deliberate ideal. The obstacles lie within one's own psychology, and are for that reason not easily overcome.

This would seem to lift manners to the level of morality or ethics, but here, too, there is a fundamental difference. The most important questions of ethics are usually those regarding choices between sometimes difficult alternatives—whether, for example, it is "right" to terminate a pregnancy or how to treat the very old or terminally ill. Such questions are often difficult, indeed impossible, to answer, and the overwhelming desire of moralists to obtain some sort of rational approach to them spawns all-encompassing rules, the "thou shalts" and "thou shalt nots" intended to give people guidance in areas of difficult decision. The cultivation of fine manners contributes very little to the resolution of such problems, and yet the two are not entirely unconnected. It would be impossible, for example, for anyone of even the most basic manners to be cruel, just as it would be a violation of ethics. But while ethics cannot exist apart from rules, or what are known as ethical principles, fine manners rest upon but one rule.

That rule, in all its seeming banality is: *Be considerate*. How very simple that seems. But it is in fact impossible to apply it without understanding the most basic needs of people, and this is an understanding which few have. Almost anyone, to be sure, will concur when those basic needs are described, but this is a merely intellectual assent. It is all quite forgotten when the occasion for considerateness is at hand. What happens then is that your own needs engulf your thoughts and motives, and the other people around you become, in effect, foreign objects, beings of whom you are visually and otherwise aware, but whose significance quickly becomes that of what their effect upon *you* is going to be.

Anyone, we have noted, can be mannered in the sense of displaying the kind of self-conscious behavior that is intended to impress others, but the possession of fine manners is reserved to relatively few. No special intelligence, sensitivity, or understanding is needed for mere mannered behavior. Indeed, it is a reliable sign of the limitation of these qualities. When you see mannered behavior you perceive at once that the person displaying it is of limited sensitivity and understanding. It is also a sure indication that this person is incapable of sustained and consistent good manners.

This does not mean that mannered behavior is exceptional or perhaps aberrant. On the contrary, it is so common that one might suppose it to be embedded in human nature. To be mannered is common. To possess beautiful manners is rare and precious. The two cannot coexist, and the latter is usually overwhelmed by the former.

To illustrate this, imagine a gathering of vacationing strangers. We shall suppose they have been brought together at a ranch in the desert, where it is the custom for guests to go horseback riding through the morning, relax in various ways, with reading or games or whatever through the afternoon, and then all dine together in the evening. Before dinner they all gather in a pleasant setting for cocktails and to get acquainted. The guests come and go, most of them for brief stays, so such friendships as are made are of brief duration, and constantly changing as guests arrive and leave.

The circumstances ensure that these are likely to be people of some standing and significance, for the ranch is quite remote and costly, and not everyone would find the kind of activities available there especially enjoyable.

What, then, will be in the minds of the guests as they gather for their evening cocktails and dinner, thrown into close proximity to each other and needing to make conversation? Each wonders, first of all, about the others: Who are they? What is their status? Do they control wealth or wield power? And each, above all, wonders where he or she stands in relation to the rest, since all are, needless to say, eager to stand out.

Thus, one lets it come out, with as much subtlety as possible, that he knows the governor, alluding to him casually by nickname and mentioning, at every opportunity, the governor's closest associates, thus conveying the impression that he is one of these. In truth he is quite unknown to the governor or any of these associates, but was simply assigned by his company to lobby for a bill under consideration by the legislature, and in the course of that activity saw the governor once, briefly. Another of the guests is discovered to be a congressman, and within a few minutes—as few as possible—his encounters with the president, alluded to by first name, slip into the conversation. A third turns out to be an actress whose name is not known to the others, though names that are well known to them are all quickly brought up. And so on. Name dropping is the rule. Allusion to things associated with wealth and power—certain cars, yacht races, prestigious communities, distant travels, and so on—enliven the talk. The guests posture; not conspicuously, perhaps, for this would give it all away, but they posture, nonetheless, with affected casualness and self-conscious laughter, especially at their own wit.

The picture is fairly clear. And what is its most conspicuous feature? That no one there really cares at all for anyone else in the room, other than to impress them. The friendliness and camaraderie are feigned. The talk goes forth from mouths and finds its way into ears, not to be absorbed by any mind, but only to serve as stimulus for what can be said next. The people are, as obliquely as possible, only talking about themselves, and indeed, talking only to themselves. Their interest in the others is vicarious; they have no real interest in any of the needs, desires, thoughts, and aspirations of anyone else, but only in where they themselves stand, or can be made to stand, in relation to them.

This is mannered behavior, *par excellence*. The rules of etiquette are all scrupulously observed—no one belches, utters vulgarisms, or the like. The principles of civility are fairly well adhered to—there is not much interruption of speech, talk does not become very loud nor laughter too raucous. And of course no moral or ethical principle is in the remotest danger of being violated. It is, in short, at a common and recognized level, a perfectly civilized gathering of people.

But the thing to note is that there is in this picture not the least hint of fine manners.

Now imagine that one of the guests has little to say. He observes and listens to the others, and responds appropriately when this is expected, but volunteers little of his own, with the result that after the better part of an hour no one knows much of anything about him. The jigsaw puzzle is complete, everyone having found his or her envied place within it, with the exception of this one piece. So the question is finally put to this quiet one, with casualness and politeness: "And what sort of work do you do, sir?" To which the reply comes: "I work for a university." And that is it. No more questions are asked, as that would be prying, though curiosity is greatly aroused, since the vague answer given admits of a rich array of possibilities. Had he chosen, this somewhat mystifying guest might have said, in all truth, that he was the president of one of the world's great universities—*but he didn't*. And manners like this are as rare as they are beautiful.

Notice, next, that had everyone in this gathering displayed the same modesty, then genuine conversation would have been possible. Things worth hearing would have had a chance of getting said; discussion of things of some interest and possibly even importance might have ensued; minds, and not just egos, might have been animated. In short, the verbal stimuli could have given birth to those most precious of human creations, namely, thoughts and ideas, instead of proceeding directly from the eardrum to the muscles of the tongue.

And the other thing to note in this picture is that, while the buoyant egos in the group are perfectly apparent, only one of those portrayed is genuinely proud. He does not need the approbation of others, certainly not of strangers, to reinforce his sense of self-worth. His own love of himself is sufficient and, most important, it is justified. He thinks that he is a considerable cut above others, or that he is, in the strictest sense, better than most, and he is right. The cocktail conversation he listens to casts no doubt on this but, on the contrary, tends to confirm it.

WHY DO WE NEED
A RULE OF MANNERS?

Pride and manners are two quite distinct things, the first having to do with how you view yourself, and the second with how you view and treat others. It would probably be perfectly possible to be proud and quite bereft of manners: You could love yourself, that love being justified by what you in fact are, and still be contemptuous of others and their feelings. This would, however, clearly be a fault. You cannot, contrary to what is often taught, base pride simply on how you treat others; still, no matter what your strengths, virtues, and achievements, an inability to relate comfortably to others is still a glaring fault.

The proud are supremely self-confident and totally at ease, no matter where they are or whom they are with. The reason is obvious: they are good and they know it. They need no reminders, nor do they need to impress it upon others, for self-esteem is always better than the esteem or even adulation of others. Those who are always trying to impress others with their worth thereby show that their self-esteem falls short, that it needs to be supplemented by the favorable view of others. A person of worth does not need to call attention to it, and is therefore at ease and not self-conscious. Persons of worth have no need to be constantly guarding their speech or trying to make a favorable impression. They do not drop names or call attention to themselves. And this sublime casualness and ease enable them to achieve perfect manners without effort, because putting themselves in the background they enable themselves to become aware of the needs and feelings of others—the very first step toward true manners.

Rules of etiquette enable you to get through special situations without blunder. They are thus needed only sometimes. But the rule of manners is what enables you to get through life, and it is thus needed always, or at least whenever you are in any kind of interaction with others. And that rule again is: Be considerate. No one has ever gone wrong by adhering to it. It never fails. While others stumble about in new situations, not knowing quite what to do other than to respond impulsively or defensively, a proud and rational person responds with considerateness, and thereby has an unfailing guide.

What do you say to someone who's dying? To someone who has suffered great loss or disgrace? To someone who has spectacularly triumphed? To someone who has treated you in a demeaning way? You do not need rules for these very diverse situations. You need but one.

Thus, you encounter someone who has been seriously disgraced—has perhaps just been released from prison for embezzlement or a similar offense. Do you pretend not to see him, to avoid an embarrassing encounter? This is what most people would do, because they do not know the rule of manners. But that rule suggests, instead, that you put your arm on his shoulder and find something good to say to him, express regret for what happened instead of pretending it didn't, and reassure him that your esteem for him has not been lessened—this sort of thing. This combination of candor and reassurance is what is required, just because it is, obviously, what is considerate. If you have any doubt of this, then imagine yourself to have been thus disgraced and consider what sort of treatment you would find redeeming.

The following simple, even banal, account that was given to me by a friend illustrates the beauty of our simple rule.

> When I was informed that the assessment on my house had been raised by seventeen thousand dollars I was at first irate. I knew that the house would never sell for this higher figure, if put on the market, and meanwhile, my tax liability would be pegged to that figure. So I made an appointment with the assessor, to try to induce her to reconsider. I arrived to find that she had all her figures and documents before her and was thoroughly prepared to defend her assessment. So we went over everything, and I complimented her on her thoroughness, and thanked her for her time. I clearly had no chance of getting a reduction. But a few days later I wrote, calling her attention to a factor favoring me that she might have overlooked, and at the same time I thanked her for the courtesy she had shown and for her sense of public service. That would appear to be the end of it, and I put it all out of my mind, but a few months later I received a new notice of a change of assessment, which reduced it by seventeen thousand dollars. I do not know that my note, and the casual politeness with which I treated her, was responsible for this. Certainly nothing improper was done, and I have no doubt that the new figure was the correct one. But I cannot help thinking that had I been confrontational, challenged her judgment and fairness, perhaps threatened to enlist an attorney to straighten her out, then that new assessment would never have appeared in my mail.

The foregoing story illustrates something else about our rule, which is that actions tend to be met with appropriate reactions. If you attack, expect a counterattack. If you insult, expect to be insulted. A tug of war may be won, but always at a price, usually more than the victory was worth.

Of course a counterthreat or attack and not considerateness is the natural response to what you see as a threat or mistreatment. The reason for this is that it makes you feel strong and in control; on the contrary, to confront bellicosity with a smile makes you feel helpless and defenseless. Lawyers, whose profession rests upon and nourishes confrontation, often play upon this aspect of human nature. Thus, you feel injured or violated in one way or another and bring a lawsuit. Your attorney expresses your complaint in the strongest and most frightening language possible, and you begin already to feel victorious, just reading it. What you probably do not know, though the lawyer does, is that some lawyer on the other side will bring a countersuit using language just as strong. Even though the countersuit may be groundless, you are going to have to fight it, and this will be costly—in time, money, and emotional stress. The contest will become joined, the battlefield will become defined, compromise will be made impossible and, more likely than not, there will be no winner. And all this futility will have resulted, very likely, from nothing more than the natural human tendency to protect oneself by fighting back.

In truth, the most effective weapon in personal encounters in not a weapon at all. It consists of a calm, self-assured demeanor, a soft voice and a smile. You do not, by this approach—which is nothing more than applying the rule of considerateness—yield or surrender anything. What you do, instead, is to disarm your attacker. An assault, whether physical or verbal or else through the formal and decorous means of a lawsuit, is seen as an attack upon your adversary's self-worth, and it is met with a counterattack upon yours. Considerateness, on the other hand, is seen as a reinforcement of the other person's sense of self-worth and, as such, it has the power of an enormous but gentle lever. It always works. Bellicosity never does.

THE RULE OF CONSIDERATENESS

The proud need but one essential rule of conduct: to be considerate. Adhering always to this guide, you need no other beyond those you choose or invent for yourself, for the proud do, indeed, with this one exception, live by their own rules.

The rule of considerateness is not what defines you as proud. Fools and simpletons can be considerate and often are. What distinguishes the proud is their achievements, for it is these that set them apart, and actual achievement is the only proper basis for justified self-love or pride. If you think of some of our exemplars of the proud person, you are thinking of people who, by virtue of the very different gifts and powers they possessed, achieved something of lasting worth. This is all that unites them.

Thus, the rule of considerateness has no necessary connection with pride, but is a practical rule of manners. It guides you unerringly in your relationships to all other persons, whether they be friends, kin, or total strangers. And the special reason that it befits the proud is that it is not only consistent with the justified self-love that distinguishes these, but enhances it. Arrogance, rudeness, and the disregard of others' needs and feelings should have no place in the conduct of the proud. They suggest, instead, the kind of insecurity and uncertainty of one's own worth that a proud person never displays. There is no better image of a proud person than one who, having achieved a certain greatness through his ability, strength, and courage, goes far out of his or her way to give others a chance to at least do the same.

One thinks, for example, of a man who, having amassed a great fortune through his resourcefulness and intelligence, went before a school of disadvantaged young people who lacked hope for any great lives, and promised to pay the college costs of every single one who would do what was necessary to gain entrance into college. He was not only true to his word in providing these large sums, but he gave, day after day, for years, his valuable time to helping these students through his individual counseling and encouragement. He became something of a father to them all. Now one cannot say of that man merely that he made himself look good in the eyes of all who knew what he had done, for this is worth very little. Nor is it of the greatest significance that he won the gratitude of all those who, at such great cost, he had helped, even though we can suppose that he did. What is most important is that he could take a very close look at himself, could measure himself against his own demanding standard of self-worth, and be perfectly satisfied with what he found. He had, in other words, not merely a love for others, justified or not, but a justified love for himself, which is the definition of pride. What he could find in himself was a loving and considerate man but, more than that, a noble one.

THE IDIOCY OF SILENCE

When people do not know what to say they typically say nothing. This is a good rule, for there are few situations in which silence is not good. There is one kind of situation, however, in which silence simply betrays one's ineptness, and that is a situation of great loss, through bereavement, marital separation, and similar reversals of fortune.

So awkward do people feel in the presence of someone terminally ill that they avoid that person, even when it is someone for whom they would normally profess friendship. They do not know what to say, so they avoid having to say anything. It is as if they thought of death as abnormal, something to be kept out of sight and out of mind and, in any event, unmentionable. The ineptness is similar in cases of bereavement. Not knowing what to say to someone who has suffered the profound loss of a loved one, people fall back upon pompous and meaningless formulae, like "conveying condolences" and so on—expressions to which no one can attach the least meaning, resorted to only to get one through an awkward situation.

What *do* you say to the dying or the bereaved? Can it really be the role of someone who is intelligent and proud to say nothing, or to reach for some formula that can only be seen as changing the subject?

The idiocy of the inept is betrayed even more clearly in situations of loss that are common and perhaps less devastating than death. What, for example, do you say to someone whose wife has left him? How do you deal with the pain that shows in his face? Or what about someone whose business has failed? Or, perhaps most difficult of all, someone whose life has been touched by scandal?

The rule of considerateness guides us unerringly in every such situation, but it is a guide that works only for the proud. People who are inept, unsure of themselves, and concerned more with how they look to others than how they appear to themselves only betray their weaknesses in this kind of "awkward" or "delicate" situation, as they likely call it. A proud person finds nothing awkward or delicate here at all.

Consider, now, some of the situations involving profound loss that arise, sooner or later, in everyone's life, and the manner of dealing with them.

Death and Dying

Suppose someone you know well, who is perhaps not a close personal friend but one whom you admire, is discovered, in the prime of his life, to have inoperable cancer. Recovery is perhaps not totally out of the question, but it is extremely unlikely, and this is known to him and to everyone. Now he is home with his devoted family, in pain some of the time and always faced with the overwhelming reality of his condition. He is too young to die but fairly sure that he will, and soon. He will fight his disease with courage and hope, but not with false hopes. Lifelong projects will almost certainly be left unfinished. His children will grow up without him, and he will not taste the joys of their achievements. His wife will be left alone.

What should you do?

The worst choice is to send him a "get well" card. It is the clearest mark of stupidity and does nothing for its recipient except, perhaps, depress him still more. It only spares you the need to go see him, and to be forced to find something worthwhile to say; it also gives you the false feeling that you have done something and perhaps even met some sort of social obligation. The hypocrisy is transparent. You know as well as he that he is unlikely to get better, an overwhelming fact that the card breezily tries to dismiss. You have not only exposed yourself as a fool, but done it at the expense of someone suffering deeply.

Probably the next worse choice is to try to cheer the patient up a bit by talking of inconsequential things—the weather, the doings of mutual acquaintances, anything to get his mind off things. And you tell him he's looking good, you hope he'll be back on his feet pretty soon, this sort of thing.

You do not cheer your friend up by indulging in pretense. To speak as though he will get well as a matter of course is a painful dissimulation. He knows better, and he knows that you know better, too. All you have accomplished by this foolishness is to get yourself through an uncomfortable few minutes until you are out of there and going about your business again. Your taking the time and trouble, over and above licking a postage stamp, makes you feel that you have done something, but the net effect is the same. Besides doing nothing for your friend, you manage by this clumsy but conventional behavior to conceal from yourself your own idiocy.

Suppose, finally, that you are simply honest and sincere. Instead of going through motions, blindly or in keeping with some imagined rule of behavior, you can be what a proud and honest person quite effortlessly is, all the time. Thus, you call upon this man, making sure in advance, however, that he wants to see you. Do not presume this. Ask his wife or someone whether, perhaps, he might just prefer to be left alone. Most people facing death do not want to engage in pointless chatter—which is, however, something you are not going to do.

Thus, you can ask him how it's going. He'll understand what you mean. And you have been thinking of him—lots of people have. He is struggling against great odds—you do not need to say that, but the point is not to pretend otherwise. You understand the gravity of his condition, his fears, perhaps, his pain and his dread. These are not the things you necessarily talk about, but the point is that you do not avoid them or cover them over with falsehood. Your friend knows the truth, as do you. If this is somehow mutually acknowledged then your concern for him will be seen to be genuine, and will therefore be meaningful. All this being clear, you can then talk meaningfully of other things—not trivialities that serve only as distractions from an awkward silence in an awkward situation, such as weather and the events of the day, but what is on his mind: his wife and children, the future of his business, possibly even his feeling about death. These are things he is sure to have been thinking about a lot. They are apt to be thoughts that are deeply oppressive to him, or at least serious and important. Sharing them makes them far less onerous. But they cannot be shared with anyone who prefers the idiocy of silence or the stupidity of distracting chatter.

What is the rule here? It is nothing but the rule of the proud —considerateness. Simply ask yourself how, if you were dying, you would want others to treat you. With silence? With a pointless going through motions and shallow chatter, meant primarily to cover up their own discomfort? Or with the openness of someone who in fact feels the love and friendship that he or she professes, the honesty and sincerity of the proud.

If, for example, this is a close friend, someone you genuinely admire, now is surely the time to convey this fact, to recall some of his achievements and some of his actions and tell him what they meant to you. If there are things you can do for his family, tell what they are. Part of the dread of death is the sense of things left undone, and the assurance that they will be done is precious at a time like this. Let him know that his memory is going to be kept alive, especially for his children. Resourceful people do not care to live just for the sake of being alive. They live to some purpose, and a genuinely significant person lives for the fulfillment of important aims, sometimes even great and noble ones. Such a person accepts death with equanimity in the knowledge that these goals will survive him and be fulfilled. It is the role of his friends to assure him that they will.

Confronting our own death is probably the hardest thing we ever do. The sense of loneliness and dread must then be overwhelming. Probably nothing can so thoroughly cleanse one of every mean and self-regarding feeling. However, this does not mean that death should be approached solemnly or gravely, but only that it be treated seriously and honestly. Sometimes a proud person who has loved life, and is embarked on large and engrossing projects, finds all of these suddenly frustrated by the threat and near certainty of death. Not only must the things which gave life much of its meaning be left unfinished, but even the hope for the continuance of life is soon extinguished. He does not want anyone to treat this overwhelming reality as though it were not there, or to try distracting him from it by trivia. Nor, on the other hand, does he want pity. What is called for is simple candor, to see things exactly as they are. A dying person is in a situation that must somehow be coped with, and yet it cannot be dealt with the way anything else is dealt with. You can try to overcome ordinary reversals, even overwhelming ones, and sometimes succeed, but there is no way to overcome death. It sweeps everything away. It is the task of a proud person to cope with that somehow; meantime it is the work of friends to enable him to, or at least not distract him from it with hypocrisy, pretense, and lies.

Bereavement

Personal loss is different from most other kinds in that nothing can compensate for it. Fortunes that are lost can sometimes be regained, and so it is with most of life's goods—the loss of reputation, health, whatever. But when someone you love is forever taken from you by death the pain is acute because the void cannot be filled. Probably nothing quite matches the suffering that results from the death of one's child, especially when you have raised and nourished that child long enough to have accumulated a great store of memories. These do not die with the child, but are likely in fact to become more vivid, as you strive to preserve everything you can of the dead child. And while these memories are treasures, they are also reminders of the emptiness that will always be there.

People understand all this, and in general they know how to treat the victims of personal loss, the bereaved. Hardly anyone tries to distract that person with empty chatter or insincere talk. We know how to console, more or less. But the point should still be made, that one should not pretend that the loss is not there, or that it is not an enormous one. It must instead be addressed. Let the victim of it know that you know the depth of his or her suffering, and that it is irreparable. There is, for example, nothing the least untoward about saying outright that it must be awful to have one's wife or husband or child forever taken away by death. It is surely a hurt that will never heal. These things are true, so face them. It is not appropriate to minimize them by offering phony assurances that things will soon get better, or to offer reminders of the blessings, real or imagined, that remain. When you hurt deeply you have no interest in having shallow people coming around to try to make you think you do not. People who do this are only trying to cover over their own awkwardness.

Marital Separation

It is strange that hardly anyone knows how to deal with separation and divorce, in spite of the fact that usually one or the other partner of a failed marriage has been profoundly hurt. People treat this, as they do death, as something not to be talked about.

We are not speaking here of the resentments that emerge from the destruction of a marriage. These are usually acute, and often rise to sheer hatred. People are at no loss for words when these find their normal expression. They join in the vilification of the detested former partner. This, of course, does no good at all; on the contrary, it exacerbates the evils already present, but it is not our purpose here to make that fairly obvious point. It will suffice to say that a proud and intelligent person simply does not become a party to this. He has no interest in contributing to the bad feelings, but instead saves his energy for more significant things.

What we *are* talking about is the pain that the destruction of a marriage causes in one or both partners. It is apt to be the pain of loneliness and, almost certainly, the pain of rejection or abandonment. Someone feels cast aside, worthless in the eyes of someone once, and perhaps still, profoundly loved. It is a unique suffering, quite unlike others because of this element of felt rejection. You are not abandoned by the death of someone dear, ground down by the failure of your great schemes or projects, crushed by the destruction of your reputation, or left to contemplate your mortality. But when someone who has promised to love you forever, and who has in fact given you that love for years—when this person then finally withdraws it, and casts you aside, you suffer in ways unlike any other.

Everyone knows this, and you would expect they would act appropriately, but they almost universally do not. Instead, they lapse into the idiocy of silence. The whole thing is treated as though it were an embarrassment, about which the less said the better. Or worse, they exude false cheer. If they are partying they exhort you to join in. Or they conspicuously cast about for nice things to say—about your blessings, your wonderful children, what a great person you are—this sort of thing. They act, in short, as though what is called for is to cheer you up. In fact, they are simply made uncomfortable by your obvious misery, have no idea what to do or what to say, and go off in these inappropriate directions simply to cover their own embarrassment. They are, in short, thinking only of themselves.

What is appropriate here? As always, the rule of considerateness supplies the unfailing guide. How would you wish to be treated in such a situation? Certainly you would not, if you were deeply lonely and hurt, want people treating you as though you did not exist, or were as mute and unfeeling as a piece of furniture. Silence is not what is called for. Nor would you want those around you goading you to false cheer, pretending that you were not lonely and hurting, just to save *them* the discomfort of seeing that you are.

If you have a friend whose husband has left her, and who is likely to be suffering the pain of loss or rejection, then seek her out, and talk to her about *that*. Give her a chance to say how she feels, to express the pain and bitterness and, without feeding the resentment that will also be there, let her know that it matters to you, that you care. There is, of course, not much more you can do, but you *can* do this. It is not enough simply to ask, "How are you? How are you doing?"—polite and empty questions to which the habitual answer is always, "Fine—and how are you?" These questions must be asked not automatically but in a way that indicates that you really mean them, that you really want to know. Ask them in a way that will permit of a truthful answer, which is apt to be, "I'm miserable." And then deal with that answer sympathetically and honestly.

Scandal

Otherwise good people sometimes fall into deep error involving deception of great magnitude. And sometimes they are caught in it and their reputations are destroyed forever. It is a dreadful thing to happen to anyone, and made more dreadful by the fact that the damage is irreparable. When someone has committed some great wrong, or even a small but clear one, then he or she will never again be thought of by anyone without instant association with that wrong.

Consider this example. A man of great energy and resourcefulness rises to a high office in a university—becomes one of its vice presidents, let us suppose. He moves in the best circles and wields considerable power and influence, giving direction to the policies of that institution. Then he is discovered to have diverted some of the university's finances to his own use—furnishing his house, buying a car, something of that sort. He should have known better, and did, but it seemed to him a small thing and, above all, he thought it would be unnoticed and that it was perhaps fairly common anyway. In short, he slipped and got caught. We can even suppose that the theft was relatively small—a few thousand dollars out of a budget of millions. But it was unmistakable—a couple of small invoices, for example, were faked and the embezzlement was traced directly to him. He is charged, admits to the theft since the proof is clear, and sentenced to a brief jail term and then to a longer period of public service. And, needless to say, he is disgraced for the rest of his life.

Now this man, let us suppose, was your friend, someone you were accustomed to lunching with from time to time; you knew his family, had been several times in his house and he in yours. Now one day you happen to run into him on the street. He averts his eyes in shame and pretends not to see you. His mortification has been too great, he cannot risk whatever might happen by encountering you and has reason to think it would not be pleasant.

What one must bear in mind here is that this man's disgrace is ineradicable. He will take his shattered reputation to his grave. Anyone who ever knew him will, upon the mere mention of his name, instantly associate him with that act. His mortification is everlasting. One can usually overcome to some extent the loss suffered by abandonment, the grief over the death of a loved one, or indeed almost any loss, but not this one. If you speak of this man as "paying for his crime" by serving out the judicial sentence then you fail to see what is going on. The payment goes on forever, and it is heavy.

So what do you do now, unexpectedly encountering this one-time friend turned criminal and ex-convict?

You speak to him with friendship in your voice. You ask him whether he has a few minutes for a cup of coffee, and if he says he does not, suggest another time, a specific one, to get together for coffee or whatever. Talk to him. Do not pretend that what happened did not happen. You can say sincerely that you are sorry and saddened by what he did, but that despite that, he is still a wonderful person and friend in your eyes; that it is too bad his great talents and abilities must now be untapped—for that is indeed true. And in spite of all he has suffered, there is still a good life for him—an entirely new life, certainly, but still a good one with his family, new undertakings, and so on. Power and influence of the kind he once enjoyed are not essential to personal happiness. Often those who are happiest have none of this at all, pursuing obscure but fulfilling paths of their own.

Clearly, this is the course for a proud, thoughtful, and intelligent person to take. But very few take this course. Not knowing what to do in such circumstances, they do and say nothing. They lapse into the idiocy of silence.

To see the propriety and wisdom behind the candor that is urged here, you need to do no more than put yourself in that man's position and thereby imagine yourself to have been caught red-handed at something you, too, have done and gotten away with. None of us is guiltless. We can all painfully recall things we have done, or at least come close to doing, which, if detected, would have destroyed our reputations or compromised us in others' eyes. So ask yourself: What if it had been you, and not he, who had gotten caught? How would you now want to be treated? In short, apply the rule that covers every case of manners that one can think of, the simple rule of considerateness. The proud cannot disregard this rule; it is the key to fulfillment in your relationships with everyone. Silence is no substitute for it. Silence, under these and other circumstances we have considered, is the escape hatch for the weak and foolish. There is no need for any intelligent person to find himself among these.

THE POWER OF APOLOGY

The most powerful expression in our language is "I am sorry," with emphasis upon the second word rather than the third, in situations where apology or regret for one's own behavior toward another is urgently called for. The effect is instant and telling. The person to whom it is directed is disarmed, the resentment evaporates. Nor is it in any sense a mark of capitulation or defeat to utter this expression. On the contrary, it is the proud who utter it readily and sincerely as a natural response and without reflection on who is really at fault.

Think, for example, of the trivial incidents and offenses that arise almost daily You bump into someone in a store. Or accidentally trip her. Or knock bundles from her hands. Or scrape a fender in the parking lot. Or accidentally sever the connection during a telephone conversation—things of this sort. No fist fights are about to break out, of course, but nevertheless momentary irritation or even mild resentment erupts. They are cured instantly and totally by the words "I am sorry," and by them one exhibits pride not humility. It is only those somewhat lacking in self-esteem who attempt to cover up such minor offenses. Nor does it matter who was at fault. If someone bumps into you, then let it be *you* who is first to say, "I'm sorry"; if the response—which is most unlikely—is one of irritation, then you can in your mind dismiss the offender as a vulgarian.

And here we should note the difference between saying "I'm sorry" and "Excuse me." The latter is not an apology, not an expression of regret, but a request. To bump into someone and *then* say "excuse me," is totally inappropriate—the request comes after the fact. And the tone is wrong. It sounds as though you consider yourself to have done something that is quite okay and are now asking someone simply to disregard it.

To see the power of apology in relatively trivial situations, imagine one that is typical of those that constantly occur. You are stopped at an intersection, the car ahead of you begins to move forward, and you follow. But as you look to the side for any oncoming car, the one ahead of you suddenly stops and you bump into it. No real damage is done, but the driver gets out in a towering anger, hurling epithets and abuse.

Whose fault? His, perhaps, perhaps not. But you have a choice. You can rise—or stoop—to the rancorous tone that he has set, returning abuse and belligerency. Or you can utter the most powerful words at your command: "I *am* sorry." Such a response is not easy in these circumstances, except for the proud. A genuinely proud person finds no difficulty in this response, simply because he or she is above this kind of verbal wrangling with a stranger. It is to such a person a small thing, and to magnify it with anger would be the response of a small mind. By these words, moreover, the other person is disarmed, silenced. He or she has nothing to say beyond simply repeating what has already been said to no effect. Bellicosity has come up against a stone wall, and he is now reduced to mere muttering. You can offer to pay, then and there, for any damage, which is either nonexistent or negligible, and let him then minutely inspect the vehicle in search of it, displaying once again the triviality of his mind and spirit. Having retained your equanimity, you go on your way as though nothing of significance has happened, which is indeed the correct appraisal in the case of someone like yourself, who has more important things than this to dwell on.

Only the small-minded, as we have noted, withhold apology for the minor, accidental irritations they cause. The apology "I'm sorry" rises instantly and habitually to the lips of a proud person who is above defensiveness over something so trivial. Nothing was ever made worse by the utterance of these words, and the effect is almost without exception to smooth things over so that all can get on with what they were doing. To cause offense or irritation, however inadvertent and trivial, and say nothing or, worse, minimize or try to remove your own role in causing it, is one of the surest marks of the self-centered, weak, or small-minded.

If this is so with respect to small things, it is emphatically and obviously true of things that matter, things that cause deep and justified resentment. For example, to overlook or bypass someone in matters in which that person quite properly expects to participate is to treat him or her as unimportant, and calls for a sincere apology. Suppose, for instance, you convoke a meeting of colleagues or co-workers to deal with a matter of interest to them all; but there is one person who would understandably expect to be included whom you nonetheless omit, because you personally dislike her, or have a low opinion of her judgment. She is profoundly offended, and angrily confronts you. Now you have a choice. You can justify excluding her, suggesting that it was for this or that reason not really her business, or you thought it was not of interest to her. Or you can simply say, "I am truly sorry." The latter reply, and this alone, works. However justified and appropriate the omission may appear to you and perhaps others, it cannot appear so to her. No one admits to incompetence or inferiority under such conditions, no matter how manifest it may be.

So the general rule is: You cannot give offense, whether small or great, and whether intended or not, and just walk away from it, leaving the irritation or, sometimes, genuine injury to fester in resentment. "I'm sorry" is the balm that wipes away the hurt and, it must be emphasized, proves clearly your own decency and justified self-love. You are above the trivial and also possessed of sufficient esteem for yourself to admit error and even apparent stupidity. It takes someone who is *not* stupid, and knows it, to say, "how stupid of me." The nobility of a genuinely proud person is perfectly apparent and easily withstands the admission of error.

THE SENSE OF SELF-WORTH

Every normal human being, in reasonably normal circumstances, is totally governed by a sense of self-worth. All other things that are valued derive their worth from this. People aspire to fame, power, and wealth, and to the boundless approval and often envy of others, but this is only because they think of their precious selves as being at the center of all these. Possessions beyond a certain point have no use whatsoever except as ornamentation to oneself. There can be no difference whatsoever between being rich and very rich so far as the satisfaction of needs is concerned, *except* for the deep need to enhance one's sense of self-worth. People take joy in their beauty when they have it, or in their strength or wit, just because they derive deep satisfaction from thinking of themselves as the possessors of these virtues. It is their individual worth that matters, and these other things matter only as they contribute to this.

This is well known to everyone of a diplomatic turn, and is indeed the heart of diplomacy at every level. If you wish to influence someone, then somehow make that person feel good about himself and success is likely to follow. And conversely, nothing so effectively dooms you to enmity than to undercut, even in some trivial way, someone's self-worth.

For example, imagine a woman whose job at a travel agency is at about the lowest level of responsibility. She wants to work her way up eventually to the position of office manager, where she will enjoy both a generous and ever increasing salary and the esteem of others. If you suppose that the path to this goal will be the perfection of her skills in the business, together with such obvious prerequisites as neat grooming and courtesy, then you overlook a basic psychological fact. What is equally important is how she appears in the estimation of those—the present manager, for instance—who will control her promotion. And this, in turn, will depend largely on how she manages to make them feel about themselves. If the present manager feels admired by this subordinate, even in matters having nothing to do with the business, then the upward climb will be smooth and steady, whereas if the opposite is the case—if the manager feels but slightly put down by the other even in trivial matters, and even if this occurs only once, it can become an insuperable obstacle to the latter's aspiration.

Thus, the subordinate responds appreciatively to the manager's wit. Or genuinely admires her taste in dress. Or is impressed by her grasp and command of the kind of detail that is involved in such work. It does not matter what it is, so long as it tends to nourish the other's sense of self-worth. It is people like this who have, almost by instinct, the diplomatic sense, for whom life is made easy.

If, on the other hand, this subordinate utters, *just once*, a deprecatory remark reflecting on her manager's self-esteem, that remark will become lodged in the memory and feelings of the other forever. No words, kindness, or deeds by the offender will ever eradicate it. If the two were to part, even on the friendliest of terms, and then encounter each other twenty years later, that slight, that affront to the sense of self-worth would the first thing to arise in the thought and feelings of its victim. It would not be mentioned, of course, and would perhaps be instantly suppressed as being of only trivial significance, but still it would be there, ready to be felt again. Genuine friendship would very likely be rendered impossible—and all for nothing more than the most incidental comment. It matters neither that what was said had not the slightest bearing on anything of importance, such as the business both are engaged in, nor that the comment was perfectly true. All that matters is that someone was led to feel diminished in worth.

To illustrate this point with the simplest examples: An aspiring young stage manager mentions to his supervisor that the latter smells bad, or perhaps only that his breath is bad. Will that remark ever be forgotten? Will the fact that it is utterly true soften its impact?

A woman comes home from a meeting which she has chaired feeling very good about how she handled it all. Under her guiding hand, difficult issues were disposed of smoothly and effectively. Irritations were never allowed to explode into rancor. And in the end praise was lavished on her by all present. So with considerable pride she gives her husband an account of the evening, only to receive from him the scornful comment: "Ah, yes! You do need your little moments, don't you?"

Here again is a seemingly trivial puncturing of someone's self-worth, but it will absolutely never be forgotten. The remark, casually made, will, even thirty years later, survive the husband's death, tarnishing the widow's memory of him.

A man surveying the many paintings on display at an art show strikes up a conversation with a woman there, and each rejoices in the newly found company of the other, exchanging knowledgeable and sometimes witty comments on the works being shown and on other things as well. He then remarks on how dreadful, how artless, how quite without esthetic merit he found one of the paintings. He does not know, and never learns, that this painting was her creation. Will she ever wish to see him again? Or, what will be her first thought if she does run into him again, perhaps years later? The injury inflicted by him will never heal, even if she should someday decide that his judgment of that piece was essentially correct.

All these banal anecdotes illustrate something that is quite well known. Certainly no one needs instruction on how to hurt other people's feelings. But the all-pervasive sense of self-worth that underlies this, and its overwhelming importance in all human relationships, is insufficiently appreciated. It is so pervasive that, like the air we breathe, it receives little attention. We are acutely sensitive to what hurts *us*, but often quite unaware of the effects, especially the lasting ones, of what we say to others. Certainly no husband who cherishes his wife's affection would make a trivial and pointless remark if he realized that the wound thus inflicted, however slight, would never heal. Though he can have forgotten it in a day, she never does, for it touches upon the most precious thing in her life and seems to diminish it.

All this does not mean, of course, that we should always remain silent with respect to what others may not wish to hear. To adopt this sort of policy would be to reduce all human relationships to shallowness. Casual relationships are, of course, such by their very nature. There is usually no depth in the relationships you establish at work or in your regular comings and goings, with people about whom you know little except for their names and what, superficially, they do. With respect to such relationships unfailing tact and diplomacy is the inflexible rule. To put such a person down, perhaps gently, gives a brief personal satisfaction, the more so if that person is boastful, boring, arrogant, or otherwise unpleasant to be around. But it is also gratuitous. It is a violation of manners, and achieves nothing at all beyond that momentary satisfaction which might, indeed, be delicious to someone of small mind or limited feeling. It has no place at all in the feelings of someone who is proud and blessed with fine manners. Someone who thinks well of himself has no need for invidious comparison with lesser people. To make yourself look good by making someone look bad, however subtly or indeed justifiably, has no place in the manners of a proud person, for a simple reason. Someone who is proud cares nothing for whether his or her virtues and strengths are appreciated by others. The only concern of the proud is how they appear to themselves. If you are proud, you do not need to diminish another or to invite attention to another's limitation, however obliquely or even correctly. Your own self-appraisal is all that matters—always provided, of course, that it is accurate and correct. As we've said, the fool who imagines himself wise is a fool twice over—for being a fool, first of all, and then, for fooling himself.

Your treatment of those you know only casually must thus never depart from the rule of restraint in what is said. Nothing at all is gained by wounding the feelings of casual associates, even if what is said is true. The brief sense of exhilaration resulting from a fleeting feeling of superiority is specious and even worthless to the proud, who need no comparison with lesser persons. Sarcasm and pointed jokes, even conjoined with wit, have no place here, and the fact that remarks of such character can evoke giggles does not justify them. A person who is clumsy certainly requires no reminder of it, nor is a graceful person made the least bit more graceful by being compared with one who is not. The same can be said for someone whose thoughts come slowly, who does not easily catch on, who in short lacks wit. What is the point of reminding him of this? And so it is with all the common human shortcomings. They should, in all casual relationships, simply be ignored. Not only are such shortcomings never removed by calling attention to them, but no strength or virtue is ever nourished by that means. The only fruit of such behavior is friction and resentment, often of small magnitude but just as often virtually ineradicable.

What about close associates, however? What about genuine friendships or relationships of abiding love? Should you here follow so scrupulously the rule of restraint, never saying anything that will hurt, but instead limiting your words only to what will make others feel good about themselves?

Hardly, for to heed such a policy not only does not foster love and friendship, it renders them impossible. Between lovers and friends candor must be the rule, because such a relationship is impossible without trust, and trust is impossible without confidence that what is spoken between friends is inflexibly true.

THE VISIT

Friends and relatives occasionally plan visits to each other, sometimes for an hour or two, sometimes for days. These are not always welcomed, and often merely tolerated for the sake of civility, particularly when they involve persons related only by marriage. The impending visit of the mother-in-law is notoriously dreaded. But even welcome visits can be miserably mishandled, and often needlessly.

The unpardonable offense—unpardonable because utterly needless and thoughtless—is to appear at the door of a friend unannounced for nothing more than a visit. This is thoughtless even when your intention is to stay only an hour or two. But to arrive with a suitcase is unthinkable to anyone with even a minimal sense of manners. However fond of each other friends may be, however much they may delight in each other's company and wish there were more of it, no one wishes to be taken by surprise. People have schedules of varying rigidity. But even those whose lives are casual, whose responsibilities are minimal, and who love company always have something in mind for the day. They may be glad to forego this with pleasure at the prospect of your company, even putting these things off for a considerable time; but why should they not resent the lack of some forewarning? Telephones are always at hand. You may think your friend would like nothing better than to see you, and you may be quite right. But then again you may be quite mistaken. As dear a friend as that person may be, there are very likely to be several things he or she would at the moment like better than having you call. And the one thing that is certain is that your suddenly appearing, when you might have given notice that you were going to, will be an irritation. It is simply the plainest violation of the rule of considerateness—not a gross violation, but needless and thoughtless. With the exception of children, whose behavior is more or less random from one moment to the next, no one wants a friend just to "pop in." If such a surprise is unavoidable, it should at least be accompanied by some sort of apology, and you must make certain it is welcome. You cannot assume this.

Even the most unthinking person would rarely call upon the closest of friends for an extended time without any forewarning, but there are people who, strangely enough, think it acceptable to give no hint of how long they are planning to stay. This is perhaps not as bad as arriving unannounced, but it is almost as bad and just as clear a violation of manners.

Imagine this. Persons you dearly love, in whose company you rejoice, people you have perhaps not seen for some time, have arranged to come see you. Good. This can be filled out in any pleasant or even exciting way you like—lots of talk, recalling of old times, trips to places enjoyed by all, music and plays perhaps. But now suppose you have no clear idea how long the visit will be. Will they be staying for a day or two? Or will it be a week? They have given no hint. You are reluctant to ask them, for this might make it appear that you want the visit to be short, which is not your intention.

Why did they not say? Why, when they announced their plan in the first place, and determined that the visit would be welcomed, did they not then and there say how long they would like to stay? And why did they not ask, in addition, how that would fit in with your plans?

Strangely, the reason seems to be that they imagined this would cast the wrong light on things. They want the supposition to be, on all sides, that being together is such an enjoyment for all that the longer it can be, the better. But that is clearly pretense. People *do* want to know what to expect. Plans must be made, meals prepared and planned ahead, schedules rearranged, appointments kept or canceled. For you to suppose that such things as these can all be simply disregarded on the vain assumption that the opportunity to enjoy your company outweighs them all, is not merely inconsiderate but an unpardonable conceit. It is a betrayal of an utter lack of manners, for it exposes your unawareness of the first and only principle of manners, which is to be considerate. You have failed to *consider* the effect of your vanity and thoughtlessness on the lives of your friends. It would be the most minimal undertaking for you simply to *inform* them of what you have in mind. Friends they may be, even precious friends, but friendship can never be strengthened by this kind of behavior. All that is promoted by it is a pretense of friendship, a kind of going through the motions without even a basic level of communication. People do want and need to know what to expect, even from those they love and trust most.

THE SOCIAL EVENING

Consider the place of the social evening in the lives of many people. What we have in mind here is not the typical *party*, which is usually a celebration of something or other, such as a birthday or the new year. A social evening consists of adults, usually couples without children, gathering by invitation at someone's house for cocktails and dinner. These typically rotate from house to house as participants loosely take turns inviting their friends.

The institution of the social evening has an important place in the lives of those who enjoy some measure of success in whatever they do. It is a perfect setting for the expansive ego, and vanities are much on display. Indeed, conversation is sometimes larded with it. To enter such a gathering, to have warranted the invitation, and to be noticed and perhaps even admired or, more exhilarating still, envied—this can be a heady thing.

Most persons in whose lives the social evening holds a significant place understand perfectly the requirements of etiquette. They do not even think of them. They know that you do not pick up your fork until the hostess does, that you normally do not sit next to your spouse at dinner, do not speak in loud tones, lounge in your chair in some slovenly manner, interrupt, gesticulate with cutlery, and so on.

And yet, astonishingly, most people do not in fact really know how to act in such a setting because they have not mastered *manners*, and this is the kind of situation that brings forth some of the very worst failings in this area. Such people lack manners because they have never much practiced the kind of restraint that this kind of situation requires, which amounts, at bottom, to the reigning in of the ego. The social evening being the perfect stimulus for the indulgence of vanity, those who have not disciplined themselves in the control of this badly fail the test of proud manners. The fact that they are apt to be well educated, successful, and worldly does not help and may, in fact, make things worse.

This is not at all to suggest that a social evening should be staid, somber, or boring. On the contrary, it is precisely the lapse of manners that is certain to make it dull. There is a great difference between being serious and being solemn, between laughing and guffawing, between sharp wit and the heavy joke, between gaiety and drunken reveling, and indeed between pride and vanity. The proud cultivate the first of these pairs, not the second.

What most often degrades a social evening is someone, almost always male, who talks too much and too loudly. Things others say are picked up by him only as stimuli for more talk. He is not interested in the content of anything that is said beyond its suggesting some fresh stream of words for his own mouth. Such talk is mostly about the talker himself, his interests, achievements, observations, and things closely connected with him such as his family, business, possessions, and so on. Whatever may be his learning, status, and worldly success, he is a vulgarian, for he has not taken the first step toward genuine pride. The aim of all his talk is not to inform, entertain, or amuse, not even to stimulate conversation or the exchange of ideas and feelings. Its sole aim is to impress. To him, it is as though he were surrounded not by persons, even persons who are interesting and clever, but merely by ears, his role then being to pour words into those open ears. And too often, alas, the possessors of those ears respond by talk of the same kind. Indeed, an observant person sometimes finds, in this hubbub of talk, little more than pairs of people matching egos by pouring words over each other, each feigning interest in what the other says but, in truth, hearing very little except what comes from their own mouths. It is worth remembering the reflection of the ancient Stoic who said that nature gave us two ears but only one mouth, that we might listen more and talk less.

What, then, does a genuinely proud and considerate person do in such circumstances? The question is particularly worth facing for the host or hostess. If you are the host, then you have presumably invited people *for their enjoyment*, not primarily for your own, and you will consider the occasion to have been successful only to the extent that you have enabled your guests to look good.

But suppose, instead, that you have been invited for cocktails and dinner. The setting will be pleasant, and the guests will include a newspaper editor, perhaps, as well as a judge, an artist of standing, a writer, and maybe a couple of academics—in short, some educated, sophisticated, and successful people.

Now consider the requirements of pride, which are, first, that you have a *justified* love of yourself, meaning that you in fact, and not in mere appearance, measure up to the fairly severe standards of personal excellence that you set for yourself; second, that, having this, you do not need the admiration, much less the envy, of others, for what you think of yourself is far more important to you than what anyone else may think; and third, you will be guided in every encounter by the rule of considerateness.

Thus, you arrive approximately on time—not early, so as to find your host and hostess scrambling with last-minute preparations, but also not late. The notion that one should never be on time or the first to arrive for such things is the invention of the frivolous. You should be fairly on time, and there is nothing the least wrong with being the first there.

And the other requirements of civility and etiquette are met as a matter of course—the appropriate compliments on appearances and preparations, good-natured pleasantries, and so on.

Now comes the requirement of manners, the need actually to be the person of pride that you constantly set as your goal. This requires that, above all, you do *not* try to impress the others, that you restrain any impulse to call attention to yourself, that you devote your energy now to listening rather than talking. Do not talk about your work; instead, ask others about theirs. Do not talk about your children, but again, ask about theirs. And while others hold forth in self-referential comment, be content to remain more or less silent, the more so if it is evident that those around you are too absorbed in themselves to hear whatever you might say anyway. Attentive silence is sometimes dreadfully effective, and though it seldom elevates the level of interpersonal discourse, it rarely degrades it. What you hear, in keeping your ears open and your mouth shut, may hardly be worth hearing; but you must remember that what you would say, were you to fall into the pattern of those around you, would hardly be worth hearing either—if, indeed, it were to be heard at all.

The final admonition is: When it is time to leave, leave. It is vastly better to leave too soon, well before anyone else does, than too late. Above all, do not make motions to leave, or declare your intentions to and then tarry. Guests sometimes—indeed, usually—have the mistaken notion they will be conveying the impression that they are having so much fun that they are finding it difficult to go. No. Such vacillation only irritates your host and hostess. You said you had to go—*so go*. The party is over, and they have things to do. Someone who has been more or less a bore all evening hardly redeems himself by dragging the evening out beyond the point that he himself has announced as time to go. But if you have not been a garrulous bore all evening, then do not spoil things by becoming one at the last minute, dragging out your reluctant farewell. Thank your hosts, and go while you are still ahead.

HIGHWAY MANNERS

Probably nothing has contributed more to the debasement of manners than the automobile. Drivers treat their vehicles as if they were tanks, within which they are invulnerable. The sound of a horn from behind is treated as an insult and responded to with an obscene gesture. If someone makes a clumsy turn, momentarily disrupting another driver, the latter bursts forth in sputtering and insults, sometimes shouting these to the offender. There are drivers whose entire course through heavy traffic or otherwise difficult conditions is accompanied by abusive commentary on the driving skills of those around them.

The best that can be said about such behavior is that it is relatively harmless. Most people care little about how they are treated by utter strangers, only momentarily encountered then out of sight forever. When altercations actually break out between drivers they almost never go beyond verbal abuse, soon and easily forgotten.

But notice what such behavior says about the person who displays it. He—or, perhaps less often, she—betrays himself as a child. Children quarrel, and their very frustration is met with outcry and name calling. Can't a grownup do better?

A proud person, to be sure, cares little about the opinions of others, and yet it is a sorry display for such a person to virtually declare: "Look, I am but a child, I never grew up, never learned to control my childish impulses, and when I am behind the shield of my car you see my true nature."

Bellicosity, the bearing of fangs and claws in the face of trivial threat or simple frustration, is the response of an animal. It has no place in the behavior of the proud. And besides this, if you are proud you must still be the judge of yourself. So note to yourself the next time some trivial frustration on the road produces an outburst: "Here am I, a fool, behaving like an animal." Your behavior is a mirror of yourself, and you should not be reluctant to look into it. Rude and childish behavior on the highway, which is so common, does not befit even the commonest person, and has no place whatsoever in the conduct of a proud one.

Moreover, while it is of secondary importance, it is worth considering that the person at whom you hurl some abusive remark from your car might turn out to be someone you know—your clergyman, let us suppose, or your employer. Or suppose it should be someone to whom you are soon after introduced at a social gathering. This would be poetic justice. That person would forever think of you not as a bold and articulate person who stands up for his rights, but quite simply as a fool. And the judgment would be correct.

It is also worth bearing in mind that the person who sounds a horn at your slow pace or delay may in fact be on an urgent mission—a passenger may be gravely ill, or the driver may be suddenly stricken on the highway or trying to keep an important appointment. We should not assume, as we sputter at some stranger through our car window, that this person's standards are as shabby as our own.

ADDRESSING ADULT STRANGERS

The rule of considerateness, together with an awareness of the importance of everyone's sense of self-worth, provide a good guide to the manner in which strangers should be addressed. No fixed rules for this are needed, except for persons holding special titles or roles, such as bishops, senators, judges, and so on; and even in these cases special forms of address are rarely needed except in formal correspondence and on certain occasions.

You should be particularly careful about using first names, sometimes with the mistaken idea that this will convey a sense of friendliness. There are two groups that are notorious for addressing adult strangers barely known to them by their first names, namely, car salesmen and physicians. Car salesmen attempt by this kind of affability to suggest friendship, even in the absence of any basis for it, and therefore, trust, even addressing by their first names people many years senior to themselves. Physicians may be similarly motivated, but they also sometimes imagine that, as physicians, they enjoy a special status in society and are thereby entitled to regard lay persons as if they were children.

In any case, the effect of being spoken to by a stranger who addresses you by your first name is likely to be a feeling of belittlement, the more so if the person speaking to you would probably be astonished if you were to address him that way. How many physicians, for example, would be delighted to have patients barely known to them address *them* by their first names? Far from suggesting any kind of affability or equality a physician suggests, by this feigned friendliness, a kind of personal superiority which is in all likelihood not there at all, except in his or her own imagination.

Unless there are clear considerations to the contrary, the right way to address anyone only slightly known to you is with "Mr.," "Mrs." or "Ms." Obvious exceptions are people very young, where the use of a first name is genuinely a token of friendship, and those who have introduced themselves by their first names, as waiters and waitresses, for example, often do. Clerks similarly sometimes wear an identifying name tag bearing only the first name. There is seldom any difficulty in knowing what is called for here. But what is to be particularly avoided is the assumption that because someone is an employee, for example, or the employee of someone you customarily address by a first name, then that employee should be similarly addressed. Though your close friend may address that employee by his or her first name, it by no means entitles you to do so.

For instance, you call upon your attorney, a long-time friend, who introduces his new secretary—"This is Linda Scott, our new secretary." Say "Miss Scott," if she appears unmarried, or "Ms." if this is unclear.

It is very hard to go wrong with this rule, which will usually hold even for those whose role is in some sense a menial one. Service station mechanics, file clerks, window washers, painters, plumbers' assistants—such persons will almost never find it strange to be spoken to in a manner of formal address, the way you would speak to the most well-positioned stranger. And above all, where first-name usage would seem to confirm menial status it must be scrupulously avoided. Consider, from the other's standpoint, how it feels for you to appear to be saying: "Ah! Since you are only a such-and-such, then I can call you Suzie, even though I have never laid eyes on you before."

It was a once fixed custom for a woman, upon marrying, to drop her surname and assume that of her husband, whereupon the "Miss" of previous use suddenly became "Mrs." No corresponding change was made in addressing the husband. "Mr." he was before, and that is what he remained. Now women in growing numbers see this as an expression of gender bias, and even as implying subordination or subservience to the husband. And indeed, the question does seem both elementary and unanswerable: Why should she abandon the name she has had from birth and suddenly assume his name, when no corresponding change is called for from him? Marriage does indeed alter a woman's status in significant ways, but it alters a man's status no less. So the solution would seem to be for both to retain the surnames under which they have always been known.

This, however, renders "Miss" and "Mrs." inapplicable or, at the very least, misleading. The use of "Miss" conveys, falsely, that the person referred to is unmarried, and use of "Mrs." with the maiden name no longer has its intended referent, referring instead to her *mother*. Upon marrying, a woman hitherto known as Miss Smith surely ceases to be Miss Smith, but she most assuredly does not become Mrs. Smith. Hence the need for "Ms." This is a form of address applying to any female person regardless of marital status, as "Mr." applies to any adult male.

The expression "Ms." thus fills a gap in linguistic usage. Without it we would simply have no way of referring to married women who have retained their surnames. But, more important, this expression enables us to speak of, and to, women without their marital status entering into consideration, driving home the important point that whether or not a given women happens to have a husband is not the most important thing about her. The expression is thus a way of recognizing a female person as a person in her own right, and not merely as an appendage to her husband.

All three expressions, "Miss," Mrs.," and "Ms.," thus have uses as forms of address, and how they are used is simply a matter of judgment. A young and plainly unmarried girl should be addressed as "Miss," if not by a familiar first name, and a very elderly woman would rarely if ever be addressed as "Ms." There are no fixed rules here. It is, however, invariably safe and correct to say and write "Ms." in addressing female persons who are between these extremes of age, and it is also extremely convenient, relieving you of any concern for what their marital status might be.

Some people have the erroneous notion that addressing a man as "sir" is somehow demeaning, especially in the case of a man clearly younger than oneself or evidently of a lesser professional or social status. This is almost never true. You will rarely go wrong using this form of address, especially when speaking to men who are either total strangers, or, in any case, not close friends.

Almost any male who is a total stranger to whom you have need to speak, should be addressed as "sir"—when asking the time of day, for example, or directions, anything of this sort. And it makes not the slightest difference what your relative status appears to be. No matter what may be your power, wealth, or status, if you address an utter stranger you should use this expression, even when his own status can be assumed to be subordinate to yours. Thus you will not go wrong using this expression in an airport, for example, when asking airline employees about departure or arrival times, flight numbers, the location of lounges, and so on. By such usage you convey that you regard the person thus addressed as a significant person. It is an expression of politeness that goes far in facilitating, and making pleasant, interpersonal contacts, particularly among strangers.

Consider, for example, the simplest kind of situation: Someone utterly unknown to you walks off, leaving behind a book where he was sitting. Here is the choice before you: You can say, "Hey, Mister, you left your book there." Or you can say, "Is that your book, sir?" The choice should be obvious. And it matters not in the least that the person so addressed may show, by his eccentric garb or otherwise, that he cares little for the opinions of others. He will not resent your courtesy.

As we move now from contacts between strangers to those between associates, discretion is needed. Close associates use first names, so no problems arise; but what of occasional contacts between persons when relative status is in some sense clearly defined, as in the case of employers and employees, or within hierarchies such as universities, hospitals, courts, and the like?

Here it works best to accept whatever hierarchical arrangement is in place, however artificial it may be. This spares you the need to assesses the relative status of those you interact with. For example, if you are a professor, of whatever standing, you should address the male president of the university, or any male dean, as "sir," even though that person may be half your age and, indeed, even if you have for him a hearty disdain which is perhaps well known. You do not thereby compromise your pride in the least but, on the contrary, you convey the fact that it rests upon something more substantial than any mere form of address.

There is one form of address that requires special attention because it is so widely, almost universally, misunderstood and, indeed, sometimes abused. This is the term "doctor." The misunderstanding of this expression, often by physicians themselves, results largely from linguistic accident, together with the somewhat special role that physicians have. The word "doctor" is often taken to be synonymous with "physician," and is even used in the plural, which is, strictly speaking, not grammatical.

The term *doctor* means literally *teacher*, and is related to such words as doctrine and dogma (that which is taught), docile (teachable), and so on. The *master* of a given art, such as medicine or law, was once so called because he or she was deemed sufficiently trained to practice that art. Thus has arisen the expression "Master of Arts," still in use in our universities. The doctor of a given subject, on the other hand, was someone deemed sufficiently expert in that subject to teach it, and was for this reason a doctor (that is, teacher) *of* whatever the subject was, i.e., a doctor of philosophy, of medicine, of laws, of theology, whatever. These were the teachers within those areas and not normally the practitioners of the arts in question.

The word "doctor" has, however, a certain resemblance to other words which do, in fact, stand for an activity or art. Thus, a sculptor sculpts, an assessor assesses, a painter paints, an administrator administers, and so on; but a doctor does *not* doct. There is no such activity. If this were an actual word, it would mean to teach.

It is because of such accidents as these that "doctor" has ceased to be merely a form of address and has become in addition, but quite incorrectly, a term applicable to persons holding a doctoral degree in medicine and engaged in the practice of some branch of medicine, including veterinary medicine.

Physicians are themselves largely responsible for this unfortunate and divisive usage, treating the term "doctor" not merely as a form of address, appropriately used in addressing anyone holding a doctoral degree in any subject, but as a kind of *title*. Thus physicians feel no embarrassment in appending "M.D." to their names even in contexts in which it is totally irrelevant; for example, on letters or other documents unrelated to medicine. It is thought to represent a special status and, indeed, it is unfortunately taken as such by lay persons. It is for this reason, too, that any listing of the faculty of a university where medicine is taught is likely to have the expression "M.D." appended to the name of every holder of a doctoral degree in medicine, even though every faculty member of that university is likely to hold a doctoral degree, and is thus, according to the original meaning of the term, qualified to hold a teaching position.

One implication of the correct understanding of these forms of address is that anyone holding a doctorate in any subject, whether it be medicine, education, theology, or whatever, should never refer to *himself* or *herself* as "Doctor" as if the term were a kind of title, except possibly under circumstances in which it would be important to the hearer to know this. People do not ordinarily refer to themselves by saying "I am Mr. Jones," "I am Miss Smith," and so on; no such forms of address are needed when you are not addressing anyone but only referring to yourself. Nor should the holder of any doctoral degree ever identify himself in print with such a form of address, because, again, it is only a form of address, not a title.

The use, and misuse, of forms of address have no far-reaching consequences, but are relevant to our theme for several reasons. One of these is that personal pride should rest upon what you are and what you achieve, and never on how you are addressed. If, as the holder of a doctoral degree, you take pride in being addressed as *Doctor* or, worse yet, if you ever refer to *yourself* by that expression, in speech or on printed stationery or whatever, you merely expose yourself as a vulgarian who not only does not understand the use of forms of address, but who bases pride upon the misuse of them. Pride is a virtue. Vanity and conceit are not. And it is a minimal expectation that a proud person will at least use language correctly and not merely in a way that flatters the ego.

PART THREE

HAPPINESS

INTRODUCTION

Thus far I have tried to portray a genuinely good life as being that of someone who is proud, considerate, and as a consequence of these qualities, fulfilled. Your pride can rest only upon what you are, and that has to be something which, in the ancient sense of the word, is good. Otherwise you have only groundless conceit. And the love for yourself that is part of such pride must be balanced by considerateness for others—indeed, for everyone—for otherwise you will find yourself isolated. There have been people, sometimes enormously creative people, who have thus isolated themselves without apparent regret. Their pride has been kept intact, but their lives have been incomplete with respect to happiness, simply because of their isolation and the needs thus left unfulfilled. Even those who can endure loneliness are never made better by it.

Happiness, it has been suggested, is a kind of ultimate fulfillment, of precisely the kind that is treasured by a proud person. It is the fulfillment of oneself as a person, and this means, as someone capable of creative activity. This is a power that we share only with the gods. Other creatures do things, but they create nothing.

Ultimately, what a genuinely successful person creates is his or her own life, which becomes itself a work of art.

This is, of course, not what our culture has taught us to think of as the good life. Two competing pictures of the good life are always before us, one of them emerging from the materialism that a secular culture everywhere spawns, and the other from our religious tradition.

Thus, the very expression "the good life" evokes a picture of opulence. It is an image of beautiful and costly dwellings, cars, and boats, expensive things—luxuries beyond measure. That a life thus lived is in no true sense a *good* life should by now be clear. It is in fact a total corruption of goodness as this is supposed to apply to human beings. The ancient idea of goodness, on the other hand, as consisting of virtue or (in its broad sense) strength, is a clear and useful one. It has sadly been eclipsed by corruptions such as this, but it survives in the writings of the ancient moralists. It has been a major part of my purpose to restore that idea and to encourage skeptical scrutiny of the corruptions that have tended to replace it, such as the one before us now—that a good life is nothing more than one of material abundance.

The very different idea that is nourished by our religious tradition is that a good life is one of service to others. There is perhaps nothing seriously wrong with this, except that the emphasis is misplaced. Your primary obligation is always to yourself. That is what you are mainly responsible for. No one else can bear that responsibility for you. You must, in other words, first serve yourself before you can make it your mission to serve everyone else.

But how do you serve yourself? What are you called upon to do? Not, surely, to indulge your passions and appetites, for that would not set you apart from any animal. Nor, surely, are you to spend your precious strength, energy, and time in the accumulation of things, for that would be a diversion of your efforts to externals, to the neglect of your self.

To serve yourself is to make the best of yourself that you can.

And, since you are a human being, this means, once again, to foster that in you which makes you uniquely human, namely, your creative intelligence. How you do this will be up to you. Perhaps it will lead to recognition or fame, but more likely not. Your goodness, or even greatness, may remain within you. What it will lead to, however, is something vastly more precious than fame or glory, and that is happiness or fulfillment. No one is born to happiness, nor has anyone ever received it as a gift from others. True happiness, or your fulfillment of yourself as a person, is something that you have to create for yourself. It is not easy to do, and it may take a lifetime; but not only is it worth it, it is, finally, the only thing that is worth struggling for.

THE ANCIENT IDEA
OF HAPPINESS

Underlying all the moral philosophy of the ancients were two questions: What is happiness? And how is it attained? Those are the questions to which we now turn.

Happiness has to be the basic concern of all ethics, for if human beings had no capacity for it and for its opposite, there would be no point in reflecting about ethics at all. This was so obvious to the ancients that it seemed to them to need no defense. All these classical moralists justified their systems, finally, by claiming that the ideals they portrayed were the ingredients of a happy life. Even Plato felt the need to justify the austere lives of the guardians of his republic by claiming that they were, notwithstanding appearances, happy; and he recognized as a possibly fatal criticism the suggestion that they were not. The Stoics, too, in spite of their unbending rectitude and the severity of their principles, maintained that their ideal life of reason and self-denial was the only genuinely happy one.

However much the ancient schools differed in their various conceptions of happiness, they were agreed about its importance. Their word for it, *eudaimonia*, is not even adequately translatable into English. It usually comes out, in translation, as "happiness," but not without loss. Something like "fulfillment" would in some ways be better, but we shall stay with happiness, keeping in mind its shortcomings.

Eudaimonia means, literally, possession by a good *daimon*, or spirit, and this in turn conveys the idea of extreme good fortune on the part of it possessor. One possessed of *eudaimonia* was thought of by the ancients as blessed beyond measure, as having won something of supreme worth and, at the same time, something very elusive and hence rare. Just what *eudaimonia* is was seldom clear, even in the minds of the greatest moralists, but there was no doubt at all of its importance and value. To discover the nature of this *eudaimonia* and the path of its attainment appeared to many great moralists of that age to be the main task of philosophy.

Most people claim they know what happiness is, which is unfortunate, for this prevents them from learning. You have no incentive to inquire into what you think you already know. In fact, however, there seem to be few things more infected with error and false notions than people's ideas of happiness. It is very common for people, in their ill-considered quest for personal happiness, to spend their lives pursuing some specious ideal—such as the accumulation of wealth—and then, having succeeded, to miss the happiness erroneously identified with it. Of course we are reluctant to come to terms with our own illusions, and few who have wasted their lives are willing to admit it even to themselves; but their failure is often quite obvious to others. We tend to be tolerant of error in this regard, for its only victims are the possessors of it. Another person's dashed expectations seldom threaten our own. And we are therefore content to suppose that if someone seems to be happy, perhaps he or she really is happy after all. But one can see how shallow this is by asking whether one would really wish to *be* that other person. It is hard to see why not, if that other person is believed to be truly happy. But we know, in fact, that such persons are not; they only seem so to themselves, largely because they are unwilling to admit their own folly.

It was from reflections such as these that ancient moralists were fond of quoting Solon, to the effect that no man should be deemed happy until he is dead (for example, Aristotle, *Nicomachean Ethics*, Bk. I, Ch. 10). This paradoxical remark seems to suggest that the dead are more happy than the living, but that is not what is meant at all. The point is, rather, that the search for happiness is the task of a lifetime and that it can elude one, even at the last moment. And indeed, it does elude most people, even those who think they are on the track of it.

HAPPINESS AND PLEASURE

I t is very common for modern philosophers and others, too, to confuse happiness with pleasure. John Stuart Mill even declared them to be one and the same. Others make the same mistake, sometimes speaking as if happiness were something which, like pleasures, can come and go or be artificially induced or evoked by stimulation. The ancients rarely did this. They were partly protected from this error by having such a word as *eudaimonia,* which is far richer in its connotations than either of our words *happiness* or *pleasure*. The identification of happiness with pleasure would have sounded odd to them, whereas to us it may not.

Familiar modes of discourse suggest to some that pleasure and happiness might be equated. For example, being happy and being pleased seem, at one level, to be about the same. Someone who is happy with something—his job, for instance—can also be described as pleased with it. And it is but a short step to equate being pleased with having feelings of pleasure.

Or again, it is perhaps quite impossible to imagine that someone might be happy while consistently and continuously exhibiting the symptoms of pain, or be thoroughly unhappy while continuously or repeatedly exhibiting the usual signs of pleasure. Thus do pleasure and happiness, or pain and unhappiness, seem clearly connected, not just causally but logically. And it is not hard to suppose that the connection might be one of identity or, in other words, that happiness and pleasure might just be two words for one and the same thing.

In fact, however, happiness and pleasure have little in common other than that both are sought, and both are sometimes loosely referred to by the same vocabulary.

Pleasures, for example, can often be located in this or that part of the body. This is even more obvious in the case of pains. But you cannot speak of the happiness felt in your back when it is being massaged, or of the unhappiness in your tooth or toe. Again, pleasures, like pains, come and go, and can be momentary; but one cannot momentarily be a happy person. One can momentarily exult or rejoice, to be sure, and while such states are typically ingredients of a happy existence, they are certainly not the same thing. Even persons who are quite plainly not happy can nevertheless feel occasional pleasures, just as those who are happy sometimes feel pain; and just as unhappy people once in a while exult or rejoice, so do genuinely happy people feel dejection and frustration.

Again, pleasures sometimes arise from bad sources, just as pains occasionally arise from good ones; but one can hardly speak of genuine happiness as being rooted in evil, or of unhappiness growing from what is wholesome and good. There would, for example, be something incongruous in describing someone as achieving genuine and lasting happiness from the contemplation of suffering, though there are persons who apparently derive pleasure from such sources and from others just as bad. And that reflection suggests another point of contrast, namely, that the term happiness is one of approbation, while pleasure is not, or at least not in the same way. Thus one can speak of happiness as an achievement, and admire those few people who manage to win it; but one hardly thinks of pleasures that way, not even those pleasures that are thought to be refined and even noble. It is at least moderately inspiring that someone born to a wretched existence should somehow die a happy person; but no comparable response is evoked by the thought of such a person dying with feelings of pleasure, even though this is, to be sure, preferable to its opposite. Happiness can even be thought of as the supreme good, as many philosophers have indeed described it; but it is hard to think of pleasures that way.

Furthermore, there are many different kinds of pleasures—eating, for instance, or music, or receiving praise. Pleasures are innumerable and varied. But there are not different kinds of happiness, and indeed, even the use of the word "happiness" in the plural is odd. No such anomaly attaches to speaking of many pleasures. One is happy or he is not, or he is more or less so; but one cannot move from one happiness to another that is quite unlike it, as one sometimes moves from pleasure to pleasure.

And from that observation it can be noted that happiness and pleasure are really quite different kinds of things to begin with. Pleasures are, in the strictest sense, feelings, just as pains are; but happiness, and similarly unhappiness, are opposite *states*, not feelings. One can, to be sure, feel happy or unhappy—but not the way one feels a pleasure or pain. Feeling unhappy is feeling oneself to be in a certain general state. Pleasures and pains, on the other hand, are typically, and often quite literally, things felt—the pain of a toothache or the pain of missing someone far away, for instance.

It should also be noted that small children, idiots, barbarians, and even animals are perfectly capable of experiencing pleasure and pain, but none of these can become happy in the sense in which the term is used here. One can, to be sure, speak correctly of a happy child, or a happy moron, but we need to attend carefully to what is being said in such cases. A happy child, for instance, is one who *fares well as a child,* in other words, one for whom the benign conditions of well-being are met. These include affection, the sense of trust and security, loving discipline, and so on. Under such conditions a child can, indeed, be a *happy child* in the sense of not being morose, disturbed, depressed, sullen, and so forth, which is a perfectly clear sense of happiness. But the child is not happy in the sense that is important to philosophy, that is, in the sense of having achieved fulfillment or having been blessed with the highest personal good. This is the kind of happiness that can only be hoped for in time in the case of a child. This happiness of a happy child, though real and important, consists of little more than feeling good, a feeling that is rooted in certain salubrious conditions of life. It is a good, but it is not the great good that is the object of life, the kind of good that normally takes the better part of a lifetime to attain.

The point is perhaps better made with the example of a happy moron. A person severely limited in those capacities that are so distinctively human can, like a child, feel happy. But that is about all his or her happiness is—a feeling. Such a person fares well, to be sure, but only as a moron, not as a person in the full sense of the term. The point can be seen very readily if, contemplating a happy moron, one puts the matter to oneself this way: Happiness is the ultimate personal good, and this person is obviously happy. Would I not, then, be willing to be just like that moron, if I could thereby enjoy the same happiness? Of course the answer for any normal person is a resounding negative. This shows not that happiness is not the ultimate personal good, but rather, that the happiness here illustrated is not the kind of happiness that anyone upholds as the highest good. Happiness, in this fuller sense, is much more than a simple state of euphoria. It is the fulfillment of a person as a human being and not as a child, or a moron, or whatever other limited person one might suggest.

We can surely conclude, then, that happiness and pleasure are not the same, and that the concept of happiness, unlike that of pleasure, is a profound and difficult one.

Yet it would be rash to dismiss pleasure as having nothing to do with genuine happiness. It would be truer to say that pleasure, along with other things, is an ingredient of happiness in the sense that no life that was utterly devoid of pleasures could ever be described as a fully happy one, however estimable it might be otherwise.

Pleasure, then, should be included within that vast and heterogeneous assortment of things that the ancients classed as *externals*. This apt term was applied to all those things of value to one's life, which result from accident or good fortune, or are bestowed by others. What others bestow, however, they can also withhold, and similarly, one can be cursed by chance as readily as one can be blessed. Externals, in short, do not depend upon oneself. They are largely or entirely beyond one's own control, and are for that very reason called externals.

And it is clear that persons cannot, for the most part, bestow pleasures upon themselves. They need other things and other persons as the source of them. This does not render pleasures bad, but it does make them largely a matter of luck. They belong in a very happy life but cannot be made the whole point of it. Genuine happiness, on the other hand, while it can be utterly ruined by chance—by dreaded illness, for example, or other disasters—nevertheless depends on oneself, in case it is ever won. Wisdom, or the choice of the right path to happiness, cannot guarantee that one will win happiness; but, on the other hand, one is certain to miss it without that wisdom.

It would thus be as narrow to identify happiness with pleasure as to identify it with any other external good, such as property, honor, youth, beauty, or whatever. External goods are goods, and while a happy life cannot be devoid of them all, neither can any sum of them, however great, add up to such a life.

HAPPINESS AND POSSESSIONS

It would be unnecessary even to consider the identification of happiness with the accumulation of wealth were it not that shallow people, who are very numerous, tend to make precisely that identification. The pursuit of happiness is simply assumed by many to be the quest for possessions, and the "good life" is thought by the same persons to be one of affluence.

The explanation for this, too, is not hard to find. Possessions, up to a certain point, are essential even to life. They are needed, beyond that point, for leisure; and while life is possible without leisure, happiness is not. There is, accordingly, a natural and wise inclination in everyone to possess things. If we add to this that all persons tend to be covetous and envious, then we have most of the explanation for the widespread greed for possessions, and of the identification of happiness with the feeding of that greed. Indeed, the accumulation and the display of wealth sometimes become important mainly as a means to inciting envy.

It should, however, be obvious to any thinking person that happiness cannot possibly be found in the sheer accumulation of possessions, even when they are used to purchase great power, or when they are philanthropically directed toward the public good, as sometimes happens. Such purchase of power and bestowal of wealth sometimes mitigate the ugliness of the greed lying behind them, but these cannot add up to happiness in anyone. And if happiness is the great goal in life, as it surely is, there are obscure, unknown people, of modest possessions, far more to be envied for what they have than even the very richest.

The pursuit of possessions beyond a certain point, far from constituting or even contributing to happiness, is an obstacle to it; for one has no chance of finding the right path to anything if he is resolutely determined to follow the wrong one, convinced that he is already doing things exactly right. The feeling of power that great wealth sometimes nourishes, and the envy that is incited in others, are both exhilarating, but neither can be regarded as an important ingredient of personal happiness. At best they add zest and challenge to one's life, effectively banishing boredom, but this is a poor substitute for happiness. Indeed, the lover of possessions, who indulges that love to the exclusion of things more important, can be compared to the glutton who indulges his love of food. For food, too, is necessary for life; but gluttony, far from constituting or even contributing to a good life, is utterly incompatible with it. To set that as one's ideal of life would be grotesque, and the clearest possible example of a wasted life. The successful pursuit of great wealth is no less grotesque and as certainly the waste of one's life. Most of those who would be repelled by gluttony, however, seem strangely blind to this comparison.

And this is really sad. For each of us does, indeed, have but one life to live, and if possible that life should be lived successfully. The chance of this happening is greatly diminished when the term "success" is applied to a kind of life which, from the standpoint of philosophy, is incompatible with success. That term should be reserved for the achievement of genuine happiness, and not for some popularly accepted illusion of happiness. If, to pursue the comparison once more, there were a race of people who exalted food without limit, indulged in gluttony, and envied corpulence as the mark of success in this pursuit, then we would say with certainty that theirs was a false and in fact disgusting ideal; nor would we change our judgment of them even if they declared with one voice that this was their happiness. The illusion of happiness is not happiness, nor is the feeling of happiness always a mark of its possession.

HONOR, FAME, AND GLORY

Aristotle thought that the appropriate reward for a proud man was honor, and this does, indeed, seem to be a more appropriate goal for such a person than pleasure. If you are honored for what you actually are, and that is in fact something noble, then such honor is well placed and you are, to some extent, justified in believing that you have achieved something worthwhile.

Still, such things as honor, fame, and glory, though certainly not despicable, do depend upon others and must therefore be classed as externals. One can seek honor, for example, and even honor that is deserved; but whether one obtains it will always depend upon the perceptions and values and, sometimes, the caprices of others. One cannot bestow honors upon oneself. People tend, moreover, to honor and applaud their own benefactors, or sometimes even people who merely make them feel very good, such as charismatic clergy and the like, rather than to honor noble character for its own sake. What they give then resembles the price of a purchase more than a gift. Thus a victorious general is honored, rather than a losing one, even though the latter might in fact have displayed more resourcefulness and courage than the former. Similarly, a person may become rich at the expense of others, then be honored for charitably returning part of his wealth to the very public he exploited.

Moreover, people sometimes honor and even glorify things that are neither honorable nor glorious, such as sheer power, even when it is selfishly used. Also, the masses of people are often eager to raise to great fame those whose uniqueness is some mere eccentricity; this is sometimes true of popular entertainers. Or it may be something of very little worth, as in the case of prize-fighters. People can, in fact, be swept off their feet by trifles and are willing to heap great honor and wealth upon the producers of such trifles, as in the case of professional athletes who represent no group and no ideal other than the outright sale of their skills.

Perhaps the fairest thing to say concerning the things we have been considering—wealth, honor, glory, and the like—is that, like pleasure, they often contribute to happiness but never add up to it. Personal excellence or even heroism are often parts of a lasting happiness, and the recognition of such qualities by others often adds to that happiness. But the real reward of personal excellence, of the kind that leads one to do, perhaps with almost superhuman effort and resourcefulness, what no one else has ever done, is simply the possession of that excellence itself. To be uniquely able to create an extraordinary piece of music of great merit, or a poem, or a story, or a philosophical treatise, or a painting, or a building, or to accomplish any feat of great significance requiring genius or exemplary courage—all such abilities are gifts in themselves that are not much embellished by the gifts added by others. What one finds satisfying are qualities belonging to oneself rather than things added. At the same time, it would be unrealistic to treat the recognition or acclaim of others as worthless. What we should say is that such honor and acclaim are sometimes a part of one's happiness, possibly even a necessary part; but they can never constitute the sum and substance of it.

WHAT HAPPINESS IS

The idea of happiness, we have suggested, contains the idea of *fulfillment*. It is also something of great and perhaps even ultimate value, and, except when destroyed by accident or disaster, it is enduring. It is not something that comes and goes from one hour to the next. We have also said that it is a state of being and not a mere feeling.

Happiness can be compared with something like health, to derive a useful analogy. For while there is such a thing as the feeling of health, no one imagines that health itself is no more than a feeling. To be healthy is to be in a certain state, the description of which we will consider shortly. And like happiness, it is very precious. Again, like happiness, health is something that is normally lasting; one is not momentarily healthy. Nor, like happiness, are there different kinds of health. One either possesses it or one does not. And for this reason the word "health," like the word "happiness," can only be used in the singular. Health, when one has it, is usually lost only through accident or disaster, not through choice; so again, the comparison with happiness is apt.

The one way in which the analogy of health to happiness

breaks down significantly is with respect to choice. Health is normal and natural; one can almost say that we are normally born with it. It is something chosen and worked for only under unusual circumstances and then only in a limited way, as in the case of someone who has lost his health and strives to recover it. Happiness, on the other hand, is certainly not a gift of nature; it is quite rare and is always the fruit of choice and effort exercised over a long period of time. Effort is needed to keep or regain health but not to win it in the first place, and in this respect it is quite unlike happiness.

Still, the analogy is useful, for health, like happiness, is a kind of fulfillment. And here it is very easy to see, in a general way, just what that fulfillment consists of. One is healthy when her body and all its parts function as they should. A diseased or unhealthy body is one that functions poorly. Similarly, a diseased or unhealthy heart, or lung, or whatever, is one whose function has been partially or wholly lost, so that a diseased heart and a malfunctioning one, for example, are exactly the same thing.

HAPPINESS AND THE
CONCEPT OF FUNCTION

The idea of health, we have noted, can best be understood and defined in terms of the idea of function; indeed, it is inseparable from that idea. And the point of making those seemingly banal observations is that, since the analogy between happiness and health appears so very close, we appear justified in supposing that happiness, too, might best be understood in term of function.

But function of what? If health consists simply of a properly functioning body, what is happiness? The idea of happiness is obviously larger than that of health because, although this has not been noted before, the former presupposes the latter. A person can be healthy and lack happiness but not the other way around. Someone lacking health, however courageous or otherwise estimable he or she may be, cannot be fully happy, unless one of those rare individuals who combines great inner strength with extraordinary creative power—as will be explained shortly.

This suggests that happiness is understandable as consisting of the proper functioning of a person as a whole. With this reflection it will be seen that we have come full circle back to the viewpoint of the ancient moralists who defined virtue in much the same way. We see, abstractly, the plausibility of the claim they so often made, that virtue and happiness are inseparable.

Let us now look a little more closely at happiness as thus conceived and then see whether this conception of it is borne out by actual experience.

The ancients quite rightly singled out the intellectual side of human nature as constituting our uniqueness. The exercise of this was, they thought, our proper function, and excellence in this exercise our special virtue. They called this part of our nature "reason"; but this meant for them more than simply the exercise of intelligence in discovering truth as well as in governing conduct. Socrates and Plato construed reason more narrowly, sometimes identifying it with dialectic, that is, with philosophical argumentation. Modern philosophers have, for the most part, unfortunately gone along with this narrow conception.

Let us then think of reason or intelligence in a broader sense, to include not merely the activity of reasoning (as exhibited, for example, in mathematics, law, and philosophy) but also observation and reflection and, above all, creative activity. This is certainly what distinguishes us from every other creature. Human beings are, by virtue of their intelligence, capable of *creating* things that are novel, unique, sometimes of great worth, and even, though rarely, of overwhelming value. One thinks, for example, of scientific theories or great works of art or literature, or profound philosophical treatises like Spinoza's *Ethics*, or the great and lasting music that emerges from the creative genius of one person. It is here, certainly, that we see what distinguishes us from all other living things and entitles us to think of ourselves as akin to the gods. Other creatures have no history and are virtually incapable of even the most trivial innovation or novelty. But it is not so with human beings. Their works rise and fall, to be replaced by others that no one could have foreseen. Human beings, in a word, think, reflect, and *create*. It is no wonder that we are referred to in Scripture as having been created "in the image of God," for this has traditionally been thought of as the primary attribute of God, namely, that God is the *creator*.

Aristotle thought of the pursuit of knowledge as the human virtue *par excellence*. It is significant that he thought of this not merely as something passive, a mere absorption of things seen to be true, but rather as an activity. And it is the nature of intellectual activity to be creative. To the extent that the mind is active, it is also creative; this is true even in the sciences and mathematics, where there is thought to be the least scope for novelty and innovation.

If we think of happiness as fulfillment, then it must consist of the fulfillment of ourselves as human beings, which means the exercise of our creative powers. For we are, among the creatures of the earth, the only ones possessed of such power. The idea of fulfillment, however, is without meaning apart from the idea of function. Therefore, as our bodies are fulfilled in health, so are our bodies and minds together fulfilled in creative activity. There are no real substitutes. The appearance of health, and the feelings associated with it, are often marks of that underlying state, but such things are not identical with it. The former can be present when the latter is not. And similarly, the appearance of happiness and the feeling of happiness are often marks of that precious state itself, but by no means to be confused with it. A person can appear happy and not be, and, what is less readily understood, can feel happy and not be. Children, idiots, and animals, as we have seen, sometimes feel good, indeed, characteristically do; but they cannot possibly be happy in the true sense of the term. There simply is nothing more to be said of them with respect to their happiness other than that they feel good.

Of course one might be tempted at this point to protest that if someone feels happy, what more can be wanted? Is it not quite enough to feel perfectly happy, without making much of the sources of that feeling? And why withhold the term "happiness" from anyone if that person is totally content with his own condition?

What more is wanted, of course, is the genuine thing. We see this readily enough if we imagine someone in whom the feelings of happiness are present but the proper fulfillment of function is not, as again in the case of someone severely retarded. Whatever may be that person's feelings of self-satisfaction and joy, no one capable of a genuinely intelligent and creative life could ever trade it for this other. Feelings of joy complement and add to the happiness that most persons are capable of, but they can never replace it.

WHAT IS CREATIVITY?

When we think of creativity, we are apt to construe it narrowly as the creation of things, sometimes even limiting it to things belonging to the arts. But this is arbitrary. Creative intelligence is exhibited by a dancer, by athletes, by a chess player, and indeed in virtually any activity guided by intelligence. In some respects the very paradigm of creative activity is the establishment of a brilliant position in a game of chess, even though what is created is of limited worth. Nor do such activities need to be the kind normally thought of as intellectual. For example, the exercise of skill in a profession, or in business, or even in such things as gardening and farming, or the rearing of a beautiful family, are all displays of creative intelligence. They can be done badly or well and are always done *best* when not by rule, rote, or imitation but with successful originality. Nor is it hard to see that, in referring to such commonplace activities as these, at the same time we touch upon some of the greatest and most lasting sources of human happiness.

Consider, for example, something commonplace and yet fairly unusual: giving birth to and rearing a beautiful family. There is, to be sure, nothing in the least creative about the mere begetting of children. It is something any fertile adult can do. But to raise them and turn them into successful, that is, well-functioning, happy adults requires great skill, intelligence, and creativity. We see this at once when we compare someone who has succeeded at this and ask what that person's happiness consists of, and how it compares with some of the specious substitutes for happiness that we have alluded to.

With respect to the first question, that is, what such a person's happiness consists of, we can easily see that it is not mere feeling. To be sure, the feelings of happiness are there, but they are based upon a state of being that is far more precious and enduring, namely, the lasting realization of what has been wrought. Feelings of reward, or of praise, or of the envy of others may be worth something; but if, for example, they rested upon nothing real, or upon actual error or misperception, they would be worth very little. There would be no real happiness behind them, only the feelings of happiness. With respect to the comparison of this person with someone whose happiness is perhaps spectacular but nonetheless specious, it is again not hard to see who is more blessed. Consider a man whose wealth, far in excess of his needs, has simply flowed to him without any creative effort on his part, as in the case of wealth that is inherited. This person cannot possibly have the happiness of even the most ordinary individual who has created something valuable and lasting, even if it is of a commonplace sort. To envision this, you need only put before your mind a clear image of both lives, and then ask not which one you envy, which one is more honored by the masses of people, which one shines with more glory, which is filled with more feelings of exhilaration, but simply: Which of these two persons is happier?

THE DEFEAT OF HAPPINESS

Happiness is often represented as something to be pursued, something that might be conquered; and quite rightly, for this calls attention to the fact that it can also be lost, or that one might fail altogether to find it. It by no means flows automatically to those who wait for it, even when all the conditions for it are right. It must be chosen and sought.

Of course, the clearest way in which happiness can be lost is by calamity, such as dreadful or life-destroying illness and things of this nature, which either cannot be foreseen or cannot be warded off when they are foreseen. The Stoics maintained that even catastrophic setbacks or illness could not destroy one's happiness, but this was an extreme and unbelievable position. It is true that happiness cannot be conferred upon one, but it can certainly be taken away, and under some circumstances it is idle to speak of pursuing it.

The other ways in which one can fail to become happy are, first, through ignorance of what happiness is, and hence an inability to distinguish genuine happiness from specious forms, and, second, from a lack of the creative intelligence necessary for its pursuit.

Thus, people who think happiness results from possessions, for example, have no chance of becoming happy, for they go in the wrong direction. They may succeed in their pursuit of wealth, but having done that, they find themselves using that wealth to pursue things equally specious, such as power over others or the envy of others, and other things totally unrelated to the kind of creative activity we have described; or else they find themselves going through the kinds of motions that have characterized their lives, superfluously adding wealth to what they already have in great excess. The mere doing of things, perhaps on a large scale, achieves no more happiness than the mere defeat of boredom— for which, incidentally, most people appear quite willing to settle. Sheer boredom is indeed a baneful state. To escape it is, to some extent, a blessing though a negative one. Hence the incessant activity on the part of some—things done for no purpose beyond making more money; or travel undertaken for new sights and sounds passively absorbed; or projects pursued, sometimes on a grand scale, just to impress others; or things purchased for the same purpose. This is how many people live, escaping boredom, keeping busy, being preoccupied with something from one day to the next, giving little thought to life or death. And this does achieve, for the moment, the banishment of boredom and loneliness; but that is as close to happiness as it gets. Meanwhile others who are wiser, having little of all this and almost never knowing boredom, go about life in their own way, creating from their own resources things original to themselves, quite unlike what others have done, things small, sometimes not small, sometimes even great and lasting, but every one of them something that is theirs and is the reflection of their own original power. Such people rejoice, perhaps unnoticed—and are happy.

The second way to fail is through the sheer lack of what is needed to succeed. For if genuine happiness is found through the exercise of creative intelligence, it is obvious that, without this, a person will have to be content with a specious kind of happiness, far less than the *eudaimonia* we have described. Many people, perhaps even most, belong in this category.

Thus there are those whose every day is very much like the one just lived. They are essentially people without personal biographies except for the events which are the product of the mere passage of time. In this they are like animals, each of whose lives is almost indistinguishable from others of its species, simply duplicating those of the generations before it. One sparrow does not differ from another. What it does, others have done and will do again, without creative improvement of any kind. Its life consists of what happens to it. People who are like this have a similar uniformity. They do much as their neighbors do and as their parents have done, creating virtually no values of their own, but absorbing the values of those around them. Their lives are lived as regularly as clockwork, and thought, which should be the source of projects and ideals, is hardly more than a byproduct of what they are doing, an almost useless accompaniment, like the ticking of a clock. You see these people everywhere, doing again today what they did yesterday, their ideas and feelings having about as little variation. It should be noted, however, that such people are by the ordinary standards that prevail *quite happy*—that is, they are of good cheer, greet each sunrise with fresh anticipation, have friends, and spend much of their time exchanging trifling remarks and pleasantries with others like themselves. They are, in a word, contented people who would declare with total sincerity, if asked, that they are perfectly happy, asking no more of the world than to escape poverty or illness, or anything else that might threaten their contentment.

But we must not be misled by this. What such people have are certain feelings of happiness—feelings only. These are not bad, not even really illusory, but they do fall far short of the meaning of happiness that the ancients tried to capture in the word *eudaimonia*. Such persons are not fulfilled but merely satisfied. They have the kind of contentment that is within the reach of anyone capable of suffering but who luckily manages to escape suffering. What they possess is not even distinctively personal or human. The measure of their happiness is nothing more than their lack of inclination to complain.

It is, to be sure, doubtful whether any normal person entirely fits this baneful description, but one can hardly fail to see that it expresses what is almost normal. Even the least creative among us are usually capable of something original, however innocuous it might be. But what is sad is that the kind of happiness that is within the reach only of human beings should be attained by so few of them. And what is sadder still is that those who have no clear idea of what happiness is, or worse, themselves lack the resources to capture it, do not care. It is, in some ways, almost as if they had not even been born.

It is no wonder that the ancients thought of happiness as a blessing of almost divine worth, as something rare, and something that can be ascribed to someone only after he is dead.

would be well - normal - again, there was nothing to worry about. My wife, Mili, went home to offer her gratitude to God. But was her offering premature?

During my medical career, I have always found that instinct plays a crucial role. And this time, once again, that instinct was correct. I was eating my hospital lunch and thinking of having a nap to free myself of worries when, around 3 pm, my surgeon rushed in. 'I showed your scans to my colleagues,' he said, 'and unfortunately, you will need emergency surgery. We don't have the facilities here either for the surgery or post-operative support, so you are being transferred to another hospital. Right now.' Two years later those words still ring in my ears. Wasn't this the same doctor who, a few hours earlier, had insisted everything was fine? Yet now I needed an Anterior Cervical Discectomy operation and fusion along with urgent cord decompression as emergency surgery.

In a scene that wouldn't have looked out of place on a TV drama, I was rushed by ambulance as an emergency transfer to Queen's Hospital, Romford, a neurosurgical institution. Accompanied by an anxious and tearful Mili, I was strapped to a cervical board during the bumpy, hour-and-a-half ride, facing upwards, staring at the roof of the ambulance, knowing my life was going to change and change dramatically, perhaps forever. Looking at my wife's worry-stricken face, I promised myself I'd stay positive, no matter what.

Positivity can play a big part in healing. Over the years I had said this to many of my patients, and now I was saying it to console myself.

When I arrived at the ward in Queen's, it was quite late. My little daughters, a home without their parents, were being looked after by our great neighbours and friends, Varun and Heena, who made dinner while Aidit and Sanna organized pizzas and took care of them overnight. It was quite tiring when we reached the ward eventually after the long journey and I was still strapped onto the board when the Nurses objected to Mili being there. 'We don't let any visitors stay overnight, she said. But I came in the ambulance and left my car in the other hospital, Mili replied. Bhaskar is having surgery early in the morning. I'm not leaving him, she reiterated with determination. I could feel the resignation in the nurse's voice, but she still stated' It's against the rules. At that point I jumped at the conversation, still immobilized, 'Sister, please, just for today, let her stay. She will be just on the chair. We have had a hard few days as you probably know. I know you are only doing your duty and being a doctor, and I appreciate it. My wife is worried, the kids are with neighbours. Won't you please let her stay overnight, she will go first thing in the morning, please? I guess I left her with little choice. She left the room and came back with a blanket and a cup of tea for Mili. Beneath the facade of sternness, she had a soft caring soul, something every nurse should have. She let Mili stay.

Within a few minutes, Mili fell asleep out of sheer fatigue. The room was just bright enough with some streetlight through the curtains. I looked at her face and a cascade of emotions filled me up. Ranging from gratitude for her being with me to disappointment with myself for the stress and anxiety I had caused her, for changing her life in exactly the way I never intended to. I loved her and hated myself. Mili met me and accepted me in the way I was, at the time when I was in one of the dire straits of my life. She got me out of the gutter (probably not the best word, as that gutter also taught me some rich life experiences). Our relationship has always been more spiritual than physical. After the incident, especially after the diagnosis of cancer, mostly have been focused on the well-being and education of our daughters. My last two years have been busy preparing Mili and my daughters to be able to sustain a wonderful and independent life in my absence.

My second, more extensive surgery took place the next morning. I do not remember much about it though, under anaesthesia, I kept babbling on. Perhaps this was because it was my birthday, my first (and hopefully last) birthday on an operating table. Afterwards, my friends, brother and mother-in-law brought me a cake and sang happy birthday to me around my bed. Allegedly I sang too - out of tune, as usual!

Only later, my birthday celebrations over, did I realize that the second operation had been too late. The damage was irrecoverable. I was left with a permanent disability, the consequences of which would affect not only my career but also my family. I now have reduced power in my legs, sensory ataxia (a condition where you can't feel where you are standing or stepping so causes loss of balance), loss of function of three fingers in my right dominant hand, severe and chronic neuropathic pain that feels like electric shocks passing through my body, reduced movement and pain in the neck and an inability to walk without an aid even for short distances.

Writing those words, and expressing my condition on the page, is still a surreal process. Did this happen to me? Will, I one day wake from this dreadful dream? Ah, if only. Somehow, I must deal with my pain and my limitations, yet how much easier this is with a fine heart and a functioning brain. I will never give up. I'm ready to take on the world again.

The Beginning

I was born in the remote but beautiful city of Guwahati, Northeast India, in the state of Assam, in 1975. We were not wealthy but rich in love and closeness, blessed with loving but strict, disciplined parents, who gave us the freedom to dream and the strength to pursue those dreams. They empowered in us, two brothers, the ambition to reach for the sky but to keep our feet on the ground. And dream I did, to be a good doctor. All I ever wanted to be was a doctor.

In those days of black-and-white television, medical dramas and documentaries were popular. I was so impressed with the white apron, the stethoscope hanging from the neck and the rush of adrenaline while treating trauma. The power of healing, to be able to make people feel better, was going to be more than a career, it was going to be my passion.

My childhood was fun, too. One of my earliest memories is my fifth birthday party when a close cousin put chewing gum in my hair. You're right, there's no way to remove it so I had a telling-off while the gum was cut out, as well as chunks of my hair!

In school, I was taught by some great teachers which was a blessing. Those teachers played a great part in whom I am today, leaving their imprint on me forever. I am full of gratitude to them and, over three decades later, we are still in touch. I feel their blessings every single day. Are there still such teachers?

Nalini Miss was my science teacher who looked after me as her son. She would always have extra time to answer my queries, however silly they were, and I did have a lot of questions, always. Anjana Miss was my English teacher, a beautiful lady who was my first teacher crush. We would eagerly look forward to her class just so we could see how she looked that day. In one of the tests, I misspelt the word 'beautiful'. She called me to the front of the classroom, told me off and made me write the correct spelling 10 times in front of everyone. It was so embarrassing. I have never forgotten that spelling! Moreover, thanks to her, I always make it a point to recheck every spelling before submitting any document.

I thought I was a good student, but one incident left me with consequences for life. There was a lot of healthy competition in the class where, for two consecutive years, I came third. Not surprisingly, I was happy and content with myself. Then one day, when the results were announced, my headteacher invited my father to meet him and I was also summoned. I thought I was going to receive a pat on the back, but instead, the headteacher said, 'You, Bhaskar, do you always intend to travel third class in your life, or do you have it in you to get into first class? I know you can do it, but do you want it? I don't think you do. I was lost for words. My head hung in shame. I had let my dad and my teachers down. I would not let that happen again. I promised that from then on, I would do my best to be a winner, nothing less. Life is about doing your best to win, and I knew I could. That embarrassing incident continues to inspire me whenever I feel down.

Looking back now on that incident, I think my headteacher did me a huge favour by taunting me. India is known as a country of a billion people, 300 million of which, at any one time, are school children. Unlike in the UK where education is about progress, in India education is not just a way to get ahead in life, it is a struggle for existence. To stand a chance of gaining entrance into a premier government-run institution, you must score in the high 90s. Even then there is no guarantee. Last year one of my nieces scored 95% in her A-Levels but still didn't get a place at her chosen college. The pressure is huge. To survive means being a winner. That tough competition toughened me up. Incentives also helped at times. I was in year 9, and most of the guys wore wristwatches and trousers now. They looked smart. Every chance someone got they will flaunt their watches. I needed one too, to show off. And I wanted one with a brown leather belt and a white dial. Can I have a watch, Dad? I asked as soon as he reached home from the office. 'Why?' he asked. 'The school clocks are not working?' Well, they are, I said. 'I just want to look

smart'. He put his hand on my shoulder and quietly said, '
You don't become smart by wearing a wristwatch, you
become smart by what you do'.

Of course, he was right. I asked what I need to do to
prove my smartness to which he said 'If I come first in
the whole year, I will get the watch I want. That was it.
Talk about a dog with a bone, I worked my socks out and
did come first that year and earned my first watch. A
proud moment for me and my dad.

What a contrast now that I never wear watches of any
kind now.

While this survival of the most competitive kind of
education has led to many Indians heading top
organizations globally, sadly, it has also led to suicides
and mental health conditions amongst those students
who couldn't do as well as they had hoped. Fortunately, I
was blessed with teachers and parents who kept me
focused, and I managed to get into the right colleges and
universities.

My teachers advised me to join the Indian Civil Service,
believing I would make a good administrator, but I
wasn't convinced. I couldn't see myself sitting in a
bureaucratic office giving orders or taking orders from
half-educated politicians. My mind was made up and,
with my parents' support, I decided to pursue medicine.
Nevertheless, I did have a backup plan. Engineering was

another subject I initially studied but thankfully I managed to secure a place in medical college.

My school fees were Rs 5 (5p) per month, followed by two years in a premier institution of its time - Cotton College - where monthly fees were Rs 10 (10p). The government medical college was Rs 25 (25p) per month. I made great friends during these years, lifelong friends who are still contributing to my life. We studied books written by professors from the UK and the US. Since these books were expensive and mostly unaffordable, we photocopied them page by page or borrowed them from the library. Those were the days! The internet was something we were only just beginning to hear about. Computers were big white boxes, televisions looked like kitchen cabinets and 'Google' was a new word.

'Come out, come out, there's been a big accident outside,' someone was screaming in the hostel corridor. It was our final year night at medical college and there was a rock concert. I, along with all my buddies was pretty much stone drunk by midnight but the night was still young, and we all wanted to drink more. After all, following years of studying, we'd soon be doctors. We'd taken a break from the concert to go to the boy's hostel to raid the rooms for any leftover drinks. At that time brands didn't matter; any alcohol was good enough. But, hearing the excited voices, I also went outside to see that a car had toppled over and looked pretty much like a broken cardboard box. It was quite a scene. The guys ran to the spot to see what had happened. I was too drunk to run so walked slowly without much bother. Then, lo and behold, I recognized the registration plate. That smashed car was mine! To be honest, it was my dad's new car that I had borrowed for the night. Good Lord, I had no clue what just happened as people looked at the car and then at me. I wasn't even anywhere near the vehicle, who on earth had driven it?

My very good friend Rupant, who is now a senior Neurosurgeon, while stone drunk, had, without my knowledge, taken the car keys from my pocket while I was busy with others raiding the rooms for alcohol, and decided to drive somewhere to buy more drinks for everyone. But he drove in the wrong direction and ended up hitting a lamppost and toppling the car, as if in a Hollywood action movie. Fortunately, he escaped with just a few scratches and bruises. The car wasn't as lucky though. By now the word had got around and the broken car almost became a shrine as more and more people gathered and made up their own stories, each raunchier than the other. Meanwhile, the shock sobered me up and soon I began to dread the morning and how to face my dad. Rupant however, went to sleep after getting some first aid. Sometimes alcohol helps you forget your worries, you know!

The next morning both our dads came to the hostel to inspect the damage. In front of more than 300 medical students, I got a tight slap from my dad while Rupant's dad apologized to my dad and reassured him that he would bear all costs for repairing the car. Both of us were told off badly by our dads while all the guys, from their balconies on three floors of the hostel, enjoyed the spectacle. Some even encouraged our dads to punish us more. Friends, eh? From that day onwards, the two of us became the butt of jokes for everyone, especially the girls. Even our professors would ask us to narrate the event and make fun of us. There was no way we had any chance of dating a girl at the university after that incident. I was just glad that Rupant became more infamous than me.

Still, I'm glad to say that the car was eventually repaired (although I was never allowed the keys again) and Rupert and I are still the best of friends. He is a great buddy any day.

Many memories later, I graduated from Guwahati Medical College. This was the moment I started to live my dream, over the next two decades devoting myself to my patients, tending not only to their medical needs but counselling them, too, building relationships, and understanding the importance of connecting on a personal level. Whatever my role, my core values remained the same: applying knowledge and experience to make people feel better and in the process, learn more every day. What more could I want?

However, after working 14-hour days for more than 15 years I developed neck and left shoulder pain. It was not a major issue to worry about, so I tried to ignore it most of the time by keeping myself busy at work. After all, I was in a hurry in life with a need to be productive and efficient. Everybody can do one thing at a time, I wanted to be smart enough to do two or more things at a time. I had to realize my ambitions, my dreams. I had to provide the best life for my family, a life for my girls where they could buy real books, not photocopies. I knew the reasons for my neck pain and stiffness were posture and long hours of work, but I could not afford to cut down. There was a lot to do, a lot to achieve, a lot to prove to myself and a few others. So, I put up with the discomfort, perhaps always too busy to confront an issue that would surely go away.

Although I had no mobility problems, neither physiotherapy nor acupuncture improved the pain. Eventually, after speaking to a pain consultant - a good friend of mine - I tried trigger point injections, then spinal injections, all without success so he referred me to a neurosurgeon.

The only remedy, it transpired, was a surgical procedure designed to free trapped nerves on the left side of my neck, known as Foraminotomy. I couldn't wait! What a relief, I anticipated, to be pain-free, and then I could work even harder. The operation did not concern me. My biggest worry was the recovery period - a fortnight's recuperation followed by part-time hours for a further few weeks. How would I cope with being restricted in this way?

The day of the operation approached. What better way, I thought, to understand the journey and emotions of a patient than swapping roles and being a patient myself, an experience that would surely make me a better doctor. Being pain-free would also enable me to do my job to my full potential. Besides, the dream had to live on, I'd be back.

I organized locum doctor cover and informed both NHS England and the Care Quality Commission of my forthcoming temporary absence. Those duties fulfilled, I eagerly anticipated an absence of pain and returning to the natural habitat in which I thrived: the pressure of a stressful working environment.

But fate had other plans for me.

Adapt to Survive

Two operations down, still unable to walk and an invalid, I returned home in a daze. I was so happy to see my girls and especially my dogs Shadow and Snoopy. However, uncertainties filled the air I breathed. I felt as though I was staring at my future through broken spectacles where everything appeared distorted. I didn't know if I should self-pity or be angry. I was never scared of dying. Who knows what happens after death so why worry about it? I just always wished for a good death, maybe even a valiant one. Didn't someone say, 'Cowards die many times before their death, heroes die only once?

But what I feared was being half-dead, being dependent, being paralyzed, or worse, becoming a vegetable. I saw my dad in that state for 20 years (more on this in the next chapter) and the impact it had on the family, especially my mum. I would never let that happen to my wife and children. How incredible that that is exactly what happened; my worst fear manifested into a harsh reality. Was this the law of attraction coming true?

A family is like a car with one driving seat. For the vehicle to run smoothly, one person needs to be in that driving seat and fully supported by the others. For years, I had been the driver but now, as I came to terms with the changing situation, it was time for Mili to take over and for me to support her fully in this responsibility. As she took charge of the situation and the family, I tried to adjust to a new normal. A temporary bedroom was made for me in our living room. Meanwhile, over the next three weeks or so, our garage was converted into a bedroom. To some degree, this worked. However, without a downstairs bathroom once a week I needed help climbing upstairs to our bathroom for a shower. This was only possible with Mili pulling me from the front and my mother-in-law or my daughter pushing from behind which was both hard work and unsafe. After a couple of tries, we had to give up on this idea. Nevertheless, I am proud of my mother-in-law who has shown great courage in supporting me and her daughter; I realize how difficult it is for her, to worry about what will happen to her daughter's family, especially her grandchildren.

Many things had to be changed regarding the house, and the car, but the most important change that needed to happen was to be within me, my inner being.

During this time, my Labrador, Shadow would sit by me and lick my neck, a strange new habit. He just wouldn't stop. Whatever I did to deter him, he would always come back and continue licking my neck. Neither of my dogs - Snoopy and Shadow - would leave my side even for a minute. It was as if they knew exactly what was going on. They made me feel human again. As desolate as I was, my pets turned into my greatest healers. I'm sure all pet lovers will understand what I mean.

Shadow is a 110lbs chocolate Labrador who used to live with a Brazilian family until he was two years old and then for some unknown reason the family left the country, abandoning him in the garden to fend for himself during two months of winter. Luckily the neighbours looked after him and gave him bits and pieces to eat. I came to know of him through our childminder who is also Brazilian. I could not believe someone can be so cruel to a lovely dog like him or for that matter any pet. Mili and I decided at that instant to give him a new home. By this time the poor chap was skin and bone, wild and insecure. Now, four years later, he is still with us but is insecure as far as going out for walks is concerned in case, we abandon him.

The only place he likes is home and the only command he knows is 'Come' which makes him slobber all over you. He has no awareness of his size and often things are knocked over as he mows his way through the house. I'm glad I named him Shadow as that is exactly what he is, my shadow, following me everywhere and knowing every time I need a cuddle. I just can't imagine life without him and as you will later learn, I think he rescued me more than I rescued him.

Two days after returning home, while trying to get out of bed, I fell, couldn't get up and so was readmitted to the hospital and rescanned. This time I saw a different surgeon. Scans showed that the C5- C7 areas of my cervical scan looked white and different, indicating a spinal cord injury, The new surgeon said he couldn't do anything and advised me to give it time and keep up the hope that things might get better. Easier said than done, right?

Thankfully, my brain seemed to process quite early on that I could not waste time dwelling on this disaster. Instead, it was time to take back control.

Varun, my good friend, and next-door neighbour, who is also a doctor, recommended another Neurologist, Dr Eli Silber. With mixed feelings of hope and despair, Mili drove me to the consultation. As we approached the room, Dr Silber came out to greet me and I immediately had the feeling that this guy was different. We hit on first-name terms straightaway as he told me that he regarded treating a colleague as a responsibility and honour. He took my history, examined me, identified the spinal cord injury on the scan and sorted out the management plan that included urgent admission to Wellington Hospital for inpatient neurorehabilitation for several weeks. I felt I was finally in good hands. I had Varun to thank for this.

Wellington Hospital was quite a story. My room overlooked Lord's, the Mecca of cricket (you'll read later how important this sport has always been to me). The sun shone through the large windows; my room was comfortable but lonely. I knew these weeks would be the perfect time for not only my physical but mental rehabilitation too.

The physios at Wellington were world-class. I don't remember all their names except Maddie from Australia but wish to express my gratitude as it was solely their repeated hard work that enabled me to stand up again and take baby steps with walking aids.

'I can't do it, I'd say, tired after just a few minutes of exertion, embarrassed to make a scene but almost impossible to carry on. 'Oh yes, you can,' Maddie would respond, every day pushing me a little further. I wanted to be their star patient. After all, I couldn't let their hard work be in vain, so I tried my best, with gritted teeth and teary eyes.

There was another assistant physiotherapist, Anna, from Lithuania who used to be a senior in her home country but whose qualifications weren't registered in the UK. I remember her, especially because, during our sessions, she used to tell me about spirituality and her following of Indian spiritual gurus Osho and Sadhguru. We talked a lot and the pain during those sessions was less, probably because of my mind being distracted by our spiritual discussions. 'I've learnt a lot from you,' she told me, but the truth was, I learnt a lot more from her.

Physiotherapy included stretching all the muscles to their limits, lifting my legs, and keeping them in the air for as many seconds as I could, standing on a piece of foam to keep my balance and later trying to walk on a treadmill, holding on to the sides. It was terrifying! I was really scared but they were always there by my side, to stop me from falling over, which happened quite a few times. How grateful I will always be to them and Dr Silber for all they have done for me.

Occupational therapy was even more interesting. I had to learn to write, grip things, lift coins from the table, and eat with a knife and fork. There was lots of foam around cutlery, pens, and pencils (they ended up resembling toys) which enabled me to hold them. What an experience it was to learn to write the alphabet and then cursive writing, like being a primary school student all over again. Thank God I still had my pincher grip intact. Pins and needles, however, were common, and it still feels like razor blade cuts on both my hands due to hypersensitivity. The Occupational Therapist made me repeatedly rub my hands on starched towels to relieve the pain. I marvelled at that idea.

Little by little I was improving every day, yet repeated assessments confirmed the permanence of my disability.

Those days, alone, in Wellington gave me time to think. Life would, in future, be challenging, there was no escaping this fact. To survive, to care for my family, to have a purpose, to retain a sense of fulfilment, I would have to adapt. At that point, I just didn't know how. I began to read lots of books on self-help, motivational volumes, and autobiographies of self-made men, war heroes and Paralympians. Everyone filled me with inspiration. I travelled continents with the characters w h o f o u g h t in wars, laughed with them when they were happy, and cried when they suffered adversities. In short, I lived through every character, every experience, each one giving me company during times of loneliness.

And I thought a lot. Thought about everything. I complained to myself, I self-pitied, I cursed at fate but surprisingly, most of my thoughts soon became thoughts of appreciation and gratitude. What was going on? Had my losses made me more appreciative of the things that I had taken for granted all this time? I was probably getting back on track. Or was I?

There was one quote from a book that remained with me: 'Sometimes you need a freefall to learn to fly high'. Maybe I was in freefall and, one day, would indeed, learn to fly high. But before then I had to deal with the sort of humiliation no one wishes to face.

It was the second night, and I was quite heavily sedated with painkillers when I fell asleep only to be woken by wetness in my bed. Oh no! Reduced bladder control resulted in the most embarrassing accident. I tried to move and sleep on the drier part, but to no avail, the entire bed was soaked. I rang the nurse's buzzer, hoping for a male nurse to help me out. Turned out it was a petite young lady who responded. I told her of my plight, and she calmly said, 'It happens, don't worry. I will change your bed'. She did so in the kindest way but never had I felt so humiliated, being tossed, and turned around, pants changed, bedsheets changed; blankets changed. What a fool I had made of myself!

Often as a doctor, I had witnessed such accidents; nonchalantly reacting while organizing for beds to be changed. How must those patients have felt at such times? Only now did I realize their humiliation. At that moment, in my vulnerability, I made a promise to be more aware of those feelings in the future.

An Unexpected Diagnosis

'Hi Doc, would you like a copy of your reports? I'm going away on annual leave so thought I'd say goodbye before leaving,' said Roxanne, lovingly. She was the Matron of the floor I was on and was a happy-go-lucky, bubbly personality. By then I'd already spent two weeks in Wellington Hospital and had developed a good rapport with the nursing and the physio staff as well as the cleaners. I often joked with them, and many would come to greet me at the start of their shift and bid me goodbye before leaving. I was becoming a part of the family. A doctor, now a patient due to the doings of some other doctor, it was an interesting discussion for the nursing station as I often overheard. 'Of course, Roxanne, that would be great,' I replied, little knowing about the next chapter that was to unfold.

Painting was my biggest passion in childhood, something I hope to rekindle in my life again. Being able to transform a blank canvas into something magical with colours and brushes was, perhaps, the greatest source of happiness I knew as a child and young man. My first earnings were, in fact, by commissions of portraits, initially from relatives and friends and then from others. I would spend days and nights painting and repainting. I would forget to eat and drink until my mum told me off and brought my breakfast plate to my cluttered room where my confinement lasted for many hours as symbolically, I spoke to my paintings as they came alive. Some of my paintings were selected for exhibitions at prominent national venues, and no one was prouder than my father.

I did not know then that there was another painting being created in the heavens above and the subject was me.

I was listening to some heavy metal music when Roxanne returned to my room with a file of papers and said goodbye. I wished her all the best for her annual leave and casually picked up the papers. In the background, Metallica was singing, 'Nothing Else Matters.

The MRI scan report showed the same abnormal area on my spinal cord as was expected as well as the scar tissue from the surgeries. But there was something else, a suspicious tumour on my thyroid that needed an urgent biopsy. Straightaway I knew this was cancer. The doctors were concentrating so much on the spinal cord that they missed this tumour glaring at them on the scan. Mixed emotions danced wildly in my mind. Why did Roxanne offer to get me a copy of my reports? Why did I have these scans in the first place? What would have happened if I had never set eyes on those scans and reports, a few months passing by in ignorance? Was it bad luck that I had a tumour to deal with, on top of my disability? No, it must be good luck. The cancer was at an early stage and could be surgically removed. Maybe it was another miracle I needed to thank life for. Perhaps I was receiving encrypted clues and perhaps, even more importantly, I was becoming more receptive to those clues.

I have gone through several horrifying journeys of cancer as a doctor, losing lovely patients, witnessing their pains and struggles, and nowhere was I in the same situation. Now I would need to go through my journey as a patient, taking my family along with me, too.

The word cancer has a profoundly negative connotation. Most people associate it with pain, suffering and premature death. I didn't know how to inform my family, unsure how they would react. I knew the word cancer would bring on an avalanche of emotions. Instead of speaking to my family, I called my good friend and business partner Anand and told him of this new development. He was astounded, hardly able to believe the sequence of events. That afternoon he came over, leaving his work to push me out in my wheelchair to a neighbouring pub. It was a lovely sunny day, and I was out of my room after several days of confinement.

My God, I needed that drink! We talked for over an hour, and I was so grateful for his company and support that day. I was beginning to know my real friends. One great thing about adversities is that you realize who is with you and who isn't. In the months that followed I have come to recognize this a great deal.

Eventually, of course, I had to break the news to Mili since the health insurance was in her name. As a policyholder, she would need to be the one to organize further treatment and surgery. It was five days after diagnosis that I first told Mili, then my mum. Both cried and sympathized. Out of everyone, it was my brother, Nav, who reacted most violently, as though he anticipated I would die within days. I had to spend a long time consoling him after which he was generally positive, for which I was grateful. I so wanted to spare my family more pain; in fact, my daughters did not know until they needed to know.

Yet for me, cancer was enlightening. I had seen many palliative care patients, 90% of whom were cancer patients. Being on the other side of the fence would, I knew, help me understand the effect of such a diagnosis. For a while I perhaps even wanted cancer to kill me. That would be far better than living a life in pain and being an invalid dependent. But I just couldn't take the easy way out and leave my young family, could I? I must get better. I must stay positive.

I was recommended by my Neurologist to consult M r Simo, a renowned ENT surgeon. He performed the thyroidectomy – the surgical procedure of removing the thyroid gland. That went quite uneventfully, for a change. The surgeon said he managed to take out all the tumours although I would need surveillance for the rest of my life. I was not in any danger. Some good news at last!

The high dose of oral steroids I was prescribed quickly changed my appearance as I put on 14 kg or so in around five weeks. I could hardly recognize myself in the mirror. More than that I was on oral morphine, oxycodone, and several other painkillers to numb the neuropathic pains that sent electric shocks through my body every few minutes. I often experienced tightness in my chest and shortness of breath. Eli told me it was all due to the faults in my circuit board where many fuses had blown. Those painkillers were necessary to control the symptoms, there was no other way. But there were, of course, side effects. The drugs made me severely constipated; I did not open my bowels for two weeks. My belly looked and sounded like a drum. It was so uncomfortable. Every time I ate, it became worse. Laxatives were going in batches, but nothing was coming out. Eventually, I had to have manual evacuation to clear my bowels, another humiliating but humbling experience! Good Lord, what more was left? Life was teaching me lessons fast and I had to keep up. The sooner I learnt to adapt to these changes, the easier it will be, my inner voice told me.

One night I decided I must get out of bed by myself to get to the toilet. That would be my first step towards independence. The lights were off. I tried to move my legs, but they wouldn't budge. Meanwhile, the pressure of nature's call was growing, and I didn't want to wet the bed yet again.

I had seen in movies how people could shatter glass just with their intense concentration. I tried to concentrate hard, but that didn't work. Then, I don't know what made me, but I turned the lights on and, like a madman, started talking to my legs. Crazy, I know. I looked at my toes and ordered them to move and little by little, they responded. Still talking to them and with the help of my hands, I managed to move my legs across and get out of bed, taking four steps to the toilet on my crutches. I managed this on my own! I made it just in time before wetting myself. Oh wow! While in the toilet, the crutches fell, making a loud noise that bought the nurse to my room. She was horrified. 'Oh, my God! What are you doing out of bed without telling us? Why didn't you just ring the bell?' But I was smiling, I had not only discovered a new way of life, but I'd also won my first - small - battle.

While in Wellington Hospital I was assigned to a psychologist who asked me what she could do for my depression. 'I am not depressed,' I responded. 'You should be,' she said. Honestly, I wasn't or at least not yet. I had too much to think about, specifically how to plan the future, to have time to be depressed. 'Maybe I will have PTSD (post-traumatic stress disorder) at some point, I don't know. Meanwhile, I'm trying to practice Acceptance and Commitment Therapy on myself,' I responded. She smiled, clearly impressed with my mention of AC Therapy before continuing, 'It is a pleasure to meet you, Dr Bora, I wish all patients were like you.

Ironically, writing The Second Chance in Life has helped structure my thoughts while sharing personal thoughts and traumas has been a form of therapy for me. Although I have low days, what I am still trying to work through is my purpose from now on, and the reasons behind this trauma. What am I meant to do for the remainder of my years?

I was discharged from Wellington Hospital once I was able to stand and take a few steps with crutches. In those weeks, I relearned how to write, how to hold a knife and fork, and how to sign, all because the complications of my condition had taken away the dexterity of my right hand. Every single day was a struggle, but every small step was an achievement. When I got home, I was so overjoyed to see my children, my dogs and Mili again after the long stint at the hospital. Their smiles and their welcome were priceless. I thanked the Almighty.

It seems incredible that within a short period, I had self-diagnosed two life-changing conditions. How many people have such an opportunity? It's a question to which I will return in Chapter Five.

For the next phase of my rehabilitation, I decided to go to Kerala in Southern India, a beautiful part of the country. My decision was partly influenced by the fact that private treatment is cheaper in India and partly also because the weather was warmer. I had heard from many people that Ayurvedic treatment and regular massages and physiotherapy have helped people with disabilities such as mine, so I wanted to give them a try. I didn't intend to leave any stones unturned in my pursuit to get better. Most recovery from neurological problems happens within the first year; I was in a race against the clock.

Ayurvedic treatment has been around for centuries, b e c o m i n g more popular amongst Westerners who are increasingly looking to the East for holistic treatments.

The 5-star hotel in which I stayed was divided into two wings with a river between them, so guests had to take a boat to the other side for breakfast and dinner. What a lovely experience this was first thing each morning. My days began with rigorous physio then a one-hour massage by two men who used herbs and hot oil. This routine was repeated in the afternoons.

I spent six weeks by myself in a hotel suite, an opportunity for more reflection even though I was worried about leaving Mili and the girls by themselves in London, having never previously left my wife or daughters for such a long time.

Thankfully my family, and my brother's family and parents, whom Jugal bought over, joined me for the final two weeks. How good it was to have everyone together.

This trip taught me many things. First of all, I learned that medicine is not only limited to Western medicine. Alternative medicine including yoga may also play a huge part, as does your psychological state.

Your mindset can so easily be boosted by the right people. A cup of tea cost around £1 but I discovered a small tea stall run by an old couple just 20 meters from the hotel gates where I could take my wheelchair and pay only 10p. And what a cuppa it was, made not only with tea, sugar and water but filled with the heart-warming love of the couple who put everything into that little tin shed of a shop. Nearly every day I was there, both for a refreshing cuppa and to see those hardworking people while mingling with the local crowd. They taught me so much about life. I remember one day the old guy came to find me in the room to make sure I was all right because I hadn't visited them that morning. I learnt from them what caring meant. The day I was leaving, both of them, along with many locals, gave me hugs and wished me all the best. I wanted to pay them some extra money, but they would have none of it. In those six weeks, I almost became a part of them just as they became a part of me forever. The feeling of gratitude that overcame me added to my spiritual evolution to be a better person.

Career End?

Until a few months ago, there I was, prescribing cocktails of medicines for unwell patients, trying my best to make them feel better. For over two decades, I'd had a successful medical career. This included years, initially as a surgical resident, before, in 2006, taking on a new challenge: General Practice. At the time immigration laws and the format of medical training changed in the UK, favouring local medical graduates. This made it increasingly difficult for international medical graduates like me to secure the best jobs. In addition, Mili, who was then seven months pregnant, had secured a good position in a reputable American company. So, while my next surgical job on offer was in Birmingham, I had to make a practical decision. And so, I gave up my dream career in surgery to join a GP training scheme in South London.

In all honesty, it was devastating to give up surgery, but I don't regret the decision to be with my family, welcoming the little angel to our lives, our first daughter Angelina. Years later, my life-changing moment brought my career to an unexpected end, the curtains had prematurely come down on my medical show. In my forties, here I was, a disabled pensioner.

But a sudden life change doesn't have to mean the end. Gradually, what dawned on me was a new perspective, some sort of spiritual LSD that made me thankful for what I still had, rather than unhappy about what I didn't. This sounds crazy, right? Especially given that, at this stage, I had no idea what lay ahead. However, waiting for me was a second chance, an opportunity to build a new, productive life, a chance to find another purpose, to be useful, to feel of value. And this was a chance I was determined to take.

With baby steps and uncertainties in abundance, I started my new life.

When storms come, an eagle flies higher to rise above the turbulence while a mouse hides in a corner. I had to become that eagle and soar higher, not be cornered, and crushed in the storm of life.

Believing in myself was the only way.

Chapter Two

Facing Your Fears

Achievements make us thankful; struggles make us stronger. When we appreciate our struggles, adversities become opportunities.

- isn't that the essence of life?

A Father's Trauma, A Son's Dilemma

After qualifying as a doctor in January 2000, I moved to New Delhi to begin my career as a resident doctor at Deen Dayal Upadhyaya Hospital. Newly qualified doctors earned a lot more in Delhi than back in Assam. During this time, I was also preparing for postgraduate entrance exams to be held later that year. Money was abundant, worries were scarce, and youth was on my side so anything was possible. Life was cool and I was having a good time.

Then, on that fateful morning of 6 August 2000, I woke up with a dreadful hangover. A group of us (young doctors) had partied in my room until the early hours and now the alcohol was taking its toll. When the hostel phone rang, I heard a voice yelling my name, saying it was urgent. Half asleep, I made my way to the phone. It was my mum. 'Son,' she cried, 'your dad is dying.' Now fully awake but stuttering, overwhelmed by her words, I asked for more information. My father had had a massive brain haemorrhage and was unconscious, the doctors predicting he could die within hours.

Only a few months into my first job, ready to take on the world, be the best doctor possible, save lives, and fulfil all my dreams - these things no longer mattered. My only concern was how to reach my dad, my handsome, loving dad, in time to see him alive. The distance between us was more than 3,000 miles. With a few weeks to go before my next salary payment and having spent almost every penny on partying with friends, the realization that I did not have sufficient funds to pay for the most important fight of my life made my mission much harder.

You may not believe in miracles, but I witnessed one that day. It was my good friend Pranab Boro in the hostel who sent out a message and, before I realized what was happening, friends, I knew, and friends I didn't, even people I don't remember being introduced to, came with whatever cash they had. From small change to big notes, soon my bed overflowed with money. All these years later I still do not know who paid what and to whom I managed to return the debt. But such generosity from friends like Pranab, Jayanta, and many other unsung heroes, was more than enough to buy my flight ticket and covered a taxi ride from the airport, too. This truly was a show of humanity one would have to witness to believe.

A two-hour flight and a one-hour taxi ride later, I reached the hospital where the lobby was filled with family and friends who expected me, being a doctor, to have all the answers. My mum hugged me, whispering, 'Keep your dad alive'. Bewildered and overwhelmed with emotion, I closed my eyes and thanked God my dad was still hanging on, and that I could be with him thanks to my unbelievable friends.

I rushed up the stairs to the Intensive Therapy Unit only to be stopped by a security guard informing me this wasn't visiting time. I feel ashamed thinking about this now, but do you know what I did? I shoved the guard and snatched his baton! Hearing the commotion, the doctor in charge of ITU came out. I told him that if my father died before visiting hours, I'd burn the place down! He gave me a long look and then asked me to follow him inside ITU.

For 29 days my dad lay in a coma. Like four of his brothers, he had suffered from high blood pressure for a while. But he hadn't taken his tablets for several days before his stroke.

This was not only a traumatic time but one with severe financial repercussions too. The family didn't even know which bank my dad kept his money in, but we knew he had a second property in town which we had to go for a distress sale, for half price, to fund the hospital bills. At the time my brother was in his final year of engineering training. A middle-class family, we were comfortably off before then but, still, I had to make a choice. That was the day I decided that I would make my future wife fully independent and have joint bank accounts, and joint assets so that if something happens to me, she will know where the money is. Since then, I have made it a habit to piece together an email to my immediate family with every single financial detail and I update it regularly every time there is a change. You must prepare for the future and the best time to prepare for adversity is when things are going well.

Thankfully, Dad was discharged, and we managed to bring him home alive. One battle was won, but that was just the beginning. Now lay the long road to recovery, a time when he needed me.

With my father being the top priority, I decided to leave my job and take a break from my medical career to take care of him. And so began a routine I would never have imagined, each night taking it in turns with mum to look after dad who, at a mere 57 years of age, was dependent on us for changing his clothes, washing him, helping him use the bedpan, cleaning when he accidentally soiled the bed as he was doubly incontinent. To prevent bedsores, he also needed to be turned from one side to another every couple of hours. He often complained of pain, especially in his legs, and I would sit by his side massaging his legs until I fell asleep, only to be woken by my father's groans of pain.

I never wanted my parents to witness my emotions but, as weeks and months passed by, I found it increasingly difficult to cope with the responsibilities of being the elder son and a life without medicine. Thanks to the support of my friends, the depression I experienced never got out of hand although I did, for a period of six months or so, drink quite often in the evenings, a routine that provided a temporary way of blanking out negativity. It was all about escapism, and frustration, rather than the fact that I had to take care of my dad, which I was happy doing. What bothered me more was the year I had lost and been derailed from my career.

The worst repercussion was that I could not appear for my post-graduate exams and was left behind in the race.

Would I ever manage to catch up? In situations such as this, well-meaning people offer plenty of advice, but this often comes across as patronizing. I felt cheated by fate as my colleagues joined their specialities of choice. At the same time, I was full of gratitude that my dad was still alive, still with me. No postgraduate seat and no career could replace that. I lost out on my postgraduate medical exam but there was another exam far beyond the realms of this material world and I felt I did that well. I had to fulfil my responsibilities and feel lucky to have been chosen to do so. Nevertheless, over 21 years later, I still introspect how my future would have panned out if I had passed that ultimate exam.

But back to those months when I was looking after my dad. On a practical level, I had to resort to earning money away from medicine to support the family, including making sure that my brother would be able to pay his fees for the final year of his engineering. That was the time that started my journey as an entrepreneur.

To begin with, I drove a taxi from Guwahati to Shillong, a neighbouring hill station. What a humbling experience this turned out to be. When passengers asked about me and I told them I was a doctor, they responded incredulously, 'Why on earth are you driving a taxi?' This experience educated me about the dignity of labour. No job is ever beneath you and you need to leave your ego behind.

Another earning opportunity came along when, with some friends, I started an agency, selling tickets for long-distance bus journeys from which I earned a little commission. Some bus companies wouldn't agree to give their tickets to us, sometimes we had to force them to. Also, there was a big coal depot locally and many of the coal dealers were from other parts of the country. Some needed odd jobs or 'protection'. I, together with my gang of friends, for a modest fee, provided that protection. I was probably one of the smallest of the guys so while all the others were musclemen, I was the one doing all the thinking, talking and negotiations. All this taught me about the struggle for existence while, more than anything, I made friends for life, friends who not only helped me through some of the darkest times but also looked after my parents. They were there whenever I needed them.

At the same time, I and a few local boys formed a charity organization named Udayan (Sunrise), created to help the poor by collecting and distributing old clothes. It was such a fulfilling endeavour. Then there was a massive earthquake in Western India and Pakistan. Thousands of people died with many more rendered homeless and in poverty. I'm so proud of my friends with whom I worked day and night, gathering relief materials to be sent off to the earthquake-affected areas.

These money-earning ventures provided an income, enabling me to support my family. Yet medicine was my first love. How I missed it! This is why I was down in the dumps when I met my future wife Mili, who came as a saviour to get me back on track. My mum gave birth to me, but it wouldn't be wrong to say that Mili gave me a second life.

Never Alone

As I mentioned, at the time of my father's stroke, my brother was studying engineering near Mumbai. Having completed my studies, my first thought was to ensure that Nav was able to continue his course. He arrived at the hospital the day after me and stayed for a couple of weeks before returning to his university for his final year.

The responsibility we each sensed brought us closer, though both Mum and I sought to shield my little brother from the impact of what had happened. Sometimes, however, I wonder whether we did too much shielding. He needed a lot of money for different projects and assignments in his final year and, as the elder brother, it was my duty to make sure he didn't get derailed as I had been. I was struggling to make enough to make ends meet, let alone send money to him. Then he wanted to change his motorbike for a new one. I couldn't afford one, but I didn't want to let him down. Mum also insisted that

I needed to do my best otherwise he would be upset. Finally, after earning more and borrowing from friends, I managed to send him the money. It was a struggle but on the other hand, I was happy to fulfil his and my mum's wishes. Sometimes the happiness in fulfilling your loved one's wishes is so much greater than your own.

Our relatives kept insisting dad needed specialist treatment and should be taken to a Metro city. I knew, as a medical person, that Dad was not in a state to be transferred, nor could I afford the treatment. It was almost always my fault that I was not able to provide the best treatment for my dad but none of the relatives, who were good at giving advice, would provide any financial help. I was at the end of my tether. I had by now done everything I could, but no one was satisfied. Fortunately, my mum understood. And dad received good treatment; in fact, I'm grateful to the hospital staff for keeping him alive. He could, though, have received better help, such as specialist physiotherapy, in the community. What prevented this? Well, everything had to be paid for, this was our greatest pressure, alongside the emotional impact. Every day in the hospital we had to pay a certain amount (at the time equivalent to £200-300) which was a lot of money for us. As well as the second house I have mentioned, we had to sell land to meet those bills.

By 2017 I had become a millionaire but by then it was of no use. I wasn't rich when I needed to be. Being rich at a time when you don't need it is like having a comb when you have lost all your hair, isn't it?

My dad remained wheelchair-bound for the next 21 years until his death in February 2021. During that time, I was grateful for my good friends who helped my parents. My great friend, Jugal, became like an elder son to them. For the nearly two decades I have been away from India, he looked after my parents unselfishly. I have never met a more selfless man than Jugal. If my parents needed anything they would call him first rather than me. Night or day, if he had anything important to discuss he would go to my parents rather than his own. He is the biggest unsung hero of my life. Yet the trauma he experienced in his own life is unimaginable - losing his wife at the age of 26 when she unexpectedly died in childbirth, along with their second child. He was the last person who deserved such a trauma. Jugal never remarried and has been raising his son, who is now a teenager, as a single parent. He phones me every couple of days, whether I am in a restaurant or at home, and when I visit India, he is always there for me, driving me around.

Early in 2021, my dad's health started worsening. I knew it was time for a final goodbye. Strange as it may sound, I wanted my dad to be relieved of his suffering. It was only when I began my own experiences of pain and futility, that I understood the magnitude of his frustrations and dependence. I wanted him to die, I was guilty of my feelings because the son in me wanted him to live forever, but the human in me wanted him to be free.

Unlike the time of his stroke in 2000 when I did everything to keep him alive, this time I prayed that he would die comfortably. He was admitted and treated by my classmates. The moment came when we had to decide about intubation and ventilator. I didn't want him to go through all that trauma again. Fortunately, my mum understood. We had to let him go. Mili, Mum and my brother were there with him, but I could not face it. All I wanted to remember was his handsome face with the most heart-warming smile. I could not see him dead. I cried because I will never see him again but also from the relief that he now has the ultimate freedom. I hope he is as free as the bird flying in the skies. The greatest influence on my life, my old man, my best friend and confidante, my dad, shall remain in my heart forever as my shining light to guide me through all the darkness life throws at me.

Sometimes the best thing you can do for the ones you love the most is to let them go.

My dad has gone but Mum is never alone, not with Jugal and my friends around. Such friends and my parents are probably the nearest flesh and blood to God.

Fear of Paralysis, Not Death

I have never feared death. Having watched what my father went through, my only fear was becoming paralyzed, becoming dependent.

Perhaps what you fear most is what you get. That is exactly what happened to me. My worst fears came true. Is this the law of attraction?

Never really a fitness freak, I had nevertheless enjoyed good health until that fateful operation. When I experienced my medical trauma, the thought of telling my mother what had happened to me in the hospital was so difficult, I didn't have the heart to do it and I'm grateful to Mili for taking on that task. Not surprisingly, my mum was distressed, not only because she couldn't visit me, but also because it was as though the wheels were turning again. What had she done wrong in life to go through this experience not once, but twice, she wondered? Dad, too, was upset. He understood my pain. Yet he said to me, 'I'm still living, so you have to live'. Previously I had viewed his symptoms from a medical viewpoint as a doctor and son. Now I could understand his ordeal from a patient's perspective.

Given what my mum had to deal with and knowing the sense of responsibility Mili feels for me, as a wife, is difficult for me; I never wanted her to go through that. Yet I failed. I could not be the husband I should have been. Fate had other plans or maybe it was another test of life to navigate. But sometimes, being pragmatic is the only solution. I try to keep our conversations positive and focus on the future of our daughters, Angelina, and Nikita. As a silver lining, all my efforts in making Mili independent from the day we got married have paid off. She is now able to look after herself and the girls without my active input. I am confident that even if I die tomorrow, she will be able to raise the girls well.

The best gift you can give to your partner is your support and help in making them fully independent.

Childhood Ambitions, Meeting Mili, Moving to the UK

Since my childhood days, I wanted to be a doctor more than anything else but, like other children, I was fond of other things too, painting being the main one, followed by reading and writing short poems, some of which were published in the Sunday newspapers, and I was surprised that I even got paid for them.

I also loved playing cricket, an important part of my daily routine. Every day it was my school bag and the cricket bat. We played whenever we had the chance for the day would not be complete without some practice or a match. There was a great rivalry among the different forms, different years. We had to win or, at least, lose with a great fight. Cricket taught me how to be a team player. It also taught me how to win or lose ethically. It was a religion for me. I remember choosing not to attend one A-level exam because India was playing a match in a World Cup. How stupid!

On another occasion, I did not eat anything for two days because India lost badly to Sri Lanka in a big tournament. Now I cannot play but I hardly ever miss a game of cricket especially when India or England is playing Strangely enough, my painting mentor, Nilpawan Baruah, a renowned artist in India, used to visit our home quite often to check on my paintings. While people were willing to pay for his feedback, he would come to give me his feedback for free. 'With your long fingers, you would make a good surgeon,' he'd say. Comments such as this were, I began to realize, signs to be aware of when decrypting life's clues.

I remember the day when his home help, an orphan girl of 19, died of cardiac arrest. She didn't have any relatives and he asked me if I could help. I called upon my friends and more than 40 of us gathered, all willing to give this orphan girl a decent funeral. Hindus perform the funeral rights as soon as possible after death and this was early afternoon. I remember we dressed her body, placed her on a bed of bamboo and headed towards a cemetery one mile away. In Hinduism, someone must take the lead at the funeral, lay the body on the pyre, and embark the body to its destination by lighting the funeral pyre. It feels like yesterday when I performed the funeral rites of this young girl. I had to turn her body to make sure she was fully burnt and later collected her ashes to take back for the other rituals. That probably was when, for the first time, I understood the vulnerability of life and that death is the greatest leveller of all.

Mili, who would become my wife, came into my life as nothing less than a God-sent angel when I was in the depths of despair. A few months after my dad's stroke when I was driving taxis, doing odd jobs, and gradually becoming a depressed alcoholic, it could only be some sort of miracle to get me back on track and that cryptic miracle came in the form of this beautiful angel.

Mili and I had attended the same college for A levels, but we didn't know each other at that time. When I moved on to Medical College, she studied to be a geologist before going into finance. There is a saying that marriages are made in heaven. It was certainly true in my case. I was invited to be the best man at my friend's wedding, an honour I was thrilled to accept. It was sheer coincidence that Mili was his next-door neighbour. She looked exquisitely beautiful that evening. I didn't expect her to remember me after seven years, but it was a pleasant surprise when she did, and we got talking, catching up on the years. I was impressed by her academic achievements. Beauty with brains is hard to come by, I was told, so it was rather nice to be getting to know a woman who had both. At that time our charity Udayan was growing, and we needed someone to look after the books and finances. Upon learning of her background in finance, I offered her the role of Treasurer and she accepted. From then on, we worked together on various projects and came closer to one another. Gradually I realized I was falling in love but what were her feelings? I didn't want to mess up so decided to take it slowly.

Being in her company and the time we spent together prompted me to reduce my drinking. I started taking care of my appearance again and began to feel worthy. As we were getting to know each other better, I realized that she was attracted to me as well. My friends and the other members of the charity, happy that I was reverting to 'normal', made plans to bring us together. They pushed me to propose to her rather than keep her waiting too long. This was quite scary as I wasn't an expert in the matter of dating and girls.

I remember the day when Pankil, another good friend of mine and, in a way, our matchmaker, declared that to be the day I had to propose, or I'd be in trouble that evening. In a bid to summon courage, I downed two straight double vodkas before going to collect Mili from her home. Pankil was driving and as per his plans, I sat in the back with Mili in the front. By this time, I was sweating with nervousness though the vodka was helping. About 15 minutes into the drive, I gathered the courage and, all in one breath, told Mili that I liked her and wanted to marry her if she agreed. Then I added that she must answer me one way or another before I'd let her out of the car. Pencil carried on driving and laughing at my plight. Mili was taken aback, she wasn't expecting this. It wasn't the ideal, romantic proposal that most girls dream of but after a few minutes, she said yes!

A year had passed since my dad's devastating stroke, he was now able to sit up in bed and talk properly. My mum, increasingly worried about me, discussed my situation with Mili. My medical career needed to get back on track, they agreed. I was keen on this, too, and was confident Mum would be able to cope if I employed a carer for Dad. Just at that time, I was offered the role of Medical Officer at Kakajan Tea Estate, a Tata-Tetley

Garden, one of the biggest in the world with 17,000 workers.

Before moving, both sets of parents insisted Mili, and I was formally engaged. Our engagement ceremony, organized by the family, was attended by more than 200 guests and the following day I left to take on a well-paid job with a good pension scheme. Life's wheel had taken a full turn.

My new job was easy, and the pay was good. I had a large bungalow to myself with seven orderlies for various duties. What a contrast! I oversaw a 40-bed hospital with very limited resources. Even for blood tests or X-rays, I had to send patients 30 km away. I learned a lot clinically but understood quite quickly that as much as life was comfortable, this role did not provide any career progression. In that close community, you were expected to laugh at your manager's jokes and laugh even more heartily at the manager's wife's jokes! It was quite lonely. I missed my family and friends. Life seemed quite superficial. Everything was about clubs, parties, and status symbols. I wasn't made for any of those. I decided to have pets to keep me company. I think animals are better than humans in many aspects and soon I had a mini animal kingdom that consisted of four big dogs, one cat, a parrot and five rabbits. They kept me happy.

Nevertheless, I asked for our wedding to be preponed. My parents teased me. The reality was that I couldn't bear the loneliness and the house needed a woman to take charge. The two maids assigned to me were driving me crazy by asking for things to do.

Mili and I were married in April 2002 in a typical Indian wedding attended by more than 1,500 guests over five days. Getting married was quite a task so I was glad when Mili joined me on the plantation. Life becomes different when you are married. At least I didn't have to deal with the maids anymore.

The workers there were good, simple, kind-hearted people who welcomed me with open arms.

Soon I was invited to all kinds of occasions, and I enjoyed attending those functions more than the club parties. Not only was I their doctor, but I also became their counsellor too. It felt like the British Raj continued with many traditions and rituals. (Back in India people still retain this view of the British Raj, believing all British people are rich which is why there are some things we don't tell our friends; they have no idea that there are homeless or poor people in the UK.)

'Sir, you need to come now, right now,' rushed a plantation worker to my Outpatient clinic. I thought a patient must be very ill. I excused my other patients and got on my motorbike with the worker on the back. To my confusion, he guided me beyond the quarters into the gardens. There was a large crowd gathering. I asked the chap what it was all about and to my utter amazement he told me an injured leopard was lying in the field, and he was taking me there to treat him. 'What? I'm not a vet!' 'No,' he replied, 'but all doctors are the same.'

Lying unconscious on the grass was this magnificent animal, a big leopard. At first, I was scared to go too close. Some guys came from the crowd of onlookers and held the leopard's paws and only then did I dare examine him. He had a long deep cut around his belly that had bled profusely; this must have happened as he tried to get through the barbed wire fence. The poor fellow looked like he would die if I didn't do anything. But what could I do?

Animal and human body systems are not much different. In such a situation I would give an intravenous drip and antibiotics to a human patient and dress up the wound, so I decided to do the same. I sent for supplies from the hospital while trying to find the veins. I knew dogs have the most visible on the belly, so I gambled on this being the same with leopards. The supplies arrived and luckily, I found a nice vein to start the drip, administered an injection of antibiotics and cleaned the wound. It was then the animal gave out a faint groan, making us suddenly aware that he was coming to his senses. We all panicked. Quickly but carefully his legs were tied, and he was lifted and put on a hand cart. By this time the Forest Rangers had arrived and taken over the care of the animal. Everyone was overjoyed and clapped. I had saved a leopard!

That day I became a hero. What an experience!

Thankfully I had no further animal medical dilemmas to deal with and, a year later, it was time to move on. I needed career progression. Mili needed a job too, so we decided to give up our life of luxury and go to New Delhi to look for new jobs, degrees, and new challenges. It is always easier to be a big fish in a small pond than be a smaller one in a big pond. But if learning were to continue, we had to leave our egos behind.

Back in Delhi after three years, things were different. Life had toughened me up and taught me hard lessons, but I was richer in courage and experience. My father was doing well, I had my life partner's support and, most importantly, my dream was back on track with the next chapter of my life waiting to be written.

In Delhi, I joined the medical staff at Apollo Hospital and Mili went to work for a finance company. She was happy to be working again and together with my brother Nav and his friend Jiten, we rented a small flat where we had to do everything ourselves at home and outside. What a difference to life in the tea garden. I was happy that Mili, who originally wanted to become a doctor and academically I would say is better than me, was now able to use her academic qualifications in a proper job and I had returned to mainstream medicine.

Life was quite hard in Delhi given the extreme heat as we couldn't afford an air conditioner, and in cold weather, we had to travel by motorbike to work. Mili and I would ride together on cold frosty mornings with gritted teeth; I'd drop her on the way to her office and pick her up each evening. Often, I would sit on my parked bike near her office, managing some revisions while waiting for her. If only all the current 3g/4g data were available on our smartphones at that time but no, that was the era of Nokia button phones or a Blackberry if you were rich. How times change!

Those companies that then seemed immortal faded away as they couldn't keep up with the rapid changes in the field of innovation. Isn't change the only constant in this world? Those who get complacent in their current state and resist change often fade into oblivion. As for the two of us, when you have a dream and you want it badly, every hardship pales in perspective.

I just wanted it badly enough.

Coming to the UK

It was while working in Delhi that we decided to emigrate. As much as we loved India, something was missing, and I needed more in my career or maybe I was running away from all the patronizing. Mili and I discussed whether our destination should be Canada or England. Canada always seemed like a dreamy place with snow, scenery, and maple leaves. We heard that immigrants are generally welcome there. It seemed ideal. Near our apartment was a Canadian Immigration Advice Centre which gave us all the relevant information. We were close to making up our minds, visualizing ourselves in Canada.

But some things are written in fate and the stars align themselves in a way to make fate happen. We must understand and be receptive to these clues. That is what exactly happened to me, yet again. A great friend, Vikas Gupta, talked me into preparing for the PLAB exam, the medical licensing exam for the UK. Initially, I wasn't too interested but when I understood the model of the NHS (National Health Service), a publicly funded healthcare system with no private practice fuss, I was drawn by it. After all, one thing I was running away from was the politics and some of the unacceptable unethical practices in private medical practice in India. For example, where referrals and medical tests meant the doctor who referred a patient received a cut. Some patients were sent for tests they didn't need, and several of my colleagues earned £8-10,000 per month in cash this way. This did not sit right with me. I must say that not everyone took part in these practices so it should not be generalized but a fair few did and continue to do so.

Vikas sourced all the books and the necessary information, we also subscribed to online coaching. When the exam came, somehow, I sailed through but my mentor and guide on this journey, my friend, flunked his exam. As a result of this failure, he decided to leave clinical medicine altogether and instead decided to become a medical insurance underwriter. He is now working in Saudi Arabia in a pretty good position but still misses his passion for medicine for which he trained. There again some things are beyond our understanding or control. It is because of him that we landed in England.

Despite my ambitions and the excitement of moving to the UK, one of my biggest regrets was leaving my parents as well as leaving my dogs in India. Still, a new adventure awaited us.

On a fateful day of autumnal October, nearly two decades ago, with a bag full of dreams and a pocketful of a pittance, saved over time, Mili and I arrived in London. Like all aspiring international doctors, we reached East Ham in East London where all the fantasies of picturesque London crashed into pieces. The place looked like a poor part of Delhi, not what we were expecting. Still, a new beginning is always a new beginning and we needed to be positive.

We rented a bedsit as we couldn't even afford a room. We had to save every penny until I got a job, even booking slots in East Ham library to send job applications as Wi-Fi was out of the question. We were frugal to the highest degree to survive. I remember a day I bought a slice of pizza for £1 from a local bakery, my extravagance warring a severe telling off by Mili. However, this sort of discipline kept us going through those initial days of being immigrant doctors in England.

I was offered my first clinical attachment at Chase Farm Hospital, North London. Clinical observership was an essential part of gaining experience in this country before going for jobs. I had to travel by bus for three hours each way as I couldn't afford the train tickets which would have made the journey only 40 minutes. This meant my day started at 4.30 am to reach the morning rounds, arriving back home at 11 pm after finishing all the work, unpaid. Having left a lucrative career in finance in India, to support my aspirations Mili started working on the Tesco tills. In the meantime, some of my classmates back home who were beginning to thrive in their private practice called me foolish. But yes, I was happy that we were finally starting to follow our dreams. Reflecting on those days, although we were poor, we were perhaps happier and closer as we were both struggling to achieve our dreams and define the purpose of our lives together as one. Today we are richer financially but are we happier? Have the riches reduced our stress or in fact, increased them?

As well as my role at Chase Farm Hospital, I also did a few days at London Bridge Hospital where Mr Glyn Evans, an eminent Orthopedic Surgeon, helped me write my CV which, he advised, needed to be creative and appropriate for English jobs. His kindness was unexpected and no less than a miracle and I am eternally grateful for this man's generous help. Mr. Evans spent an hour and a half with me explaining how to improve my interview skills while cancelling his clinic which must have cost him a few thousand pounds. My updated CV did the trick! Before long I started getting shortlisted and went for several interviews.

After roaming around the country, and staying in B&Bs or inns, a few unsuccessful interviews were followed by my first job as a Senior House Officer in ENT speciality at Derriford Hospital, Plymouth. It was ironic because I hardly had any experience in ENT, and I didn't want to leave London, but it felt safe to have an option. Moreover, it increased my confidence that if I could secure one job, I could secure many more. Having an option in life always increases your security.

One day, to my surprise, my A&E consultant at Chase Farm Hospital, Dr Geoff Hinchley, summoned me. He was known as an intimidating man, and everyone feared him. Some called him racist, and I had been advised to keep out of his sight. Had I done something wrong, I wondered, as I walked to his office? I could never have anticipated the conversation that followed. He said he had been observing me during the previous month and was impressed with my dedication and hard work while doing an unpaid job. He informed me that there was a job coming up and helped me prepare for the interview. As I have mentioned before, if you want something and you want it badly enough, even the stars align to make it happen.

My interview took place on 31st December when I was offered the job on the spot, making that New Year the best I could have wished for. I now didn't need to leave London and I could work in the hospital that I had already come to know. A couple of weeks into the role, the consultant called again and offered me a promotion and extra responsibilities.

Working shifts and topping up with regular locums, I was able to make ends meet and send some money to my mum and dad back to India.

Our new beginning had started and while so many battles were to be fought, the only way was onwards and upwards.

Some of those battles I could never have anticipated. Now I cannot walk without the aid of crutches, often needing a wheelchair. I am **in constant** pain, and I cannot do most of the things that would be expected of a normal person at my age. Some days I feel immensely frustrated but at the same time, I now realize how beautiful are those days of struggle, how those struggles made us both stronger and bought us closer to one another, not just as husband and wife but as friends standing together steadfastly with one another through all challenges, thick and thin.

Fears don't go away. But with the help of positive thinking, affirmation, and visualization, I manage those fears, diffuse them, and in so doing, feed my inner voice, as life continues to challenge and evolve.

Chapter Three Diversity

It is frustrating for people who have not achieved success in their life but perhaps it is even more frustrating for those who have achieved success only to lose it all. I belong to the latter group. The walk downhill is often more painful and heartbreaking but only with sheer determination and perseverance can we find the way back up.

The Cocktail Maker

Vodka, Pessoa, passion fruit and a dash of vanilla, served with a shot of Prosecco - a perfect Prostar martini shaken, stirred, and served, to be acknowledged by a heart-warming smile.

Another cocktail was served, another happy dinner and another moment of reflection.

Until a few months ago, there I was, prescribing cocktails of medicines to unwell people, trying my best for them. From my childhood, the only thing I ever wanted was to be a doctor, to be able to make people feel better, and I was living my dream. What more could I want?

Then time took a turn, life changed and suddenly I became a patient instead. What better way to understand the journey and emotions of a patient than being a patient myself, I thought? I was still convinced that this experience would make me a better doctor. The dream had to live on, I knew I would be back.

But not for the foreseeable future at least. Instead, the curtains came down prematurely on my medical show and, although, in my prime, I became a disabled pensioner. As they say, if wishes were horses, beggars would ride. Beware what you wish for.

But a sudden life change doesn't mean a full stop. What I had originally believed was impossible merely meant that it would take a bit longer to achieve. What dawned on me was a new perspective, some sort of spiritual LSD that made me thankful for what I still had rather than unhappy about what I didn't. Sounds crazy, I know. You see, waiting for me in life was my second chance. A second chance to feel useful, to help people, to feel happier. I found a new way to bring about a smile.

I became a cocktail maker instead!

Cycle of Life

In 2016 I, along with two partners, opened the Samsara
Cocktail Bar and Restaurant. At the time I didn't realize
the significance the name Samsara (cycle of life) would
bring to my life, literally. It must have been some sort of
premonition to have a restaurant of that name. It was
sometime earlier that my inner voice had repeatedly told
me not to put all my eggs in one basket. Hence it was
time to diversify and invest.

Around this period, I somehow got into the idea of
setting up multiple insurance policies, fixed deposit
accounts and various investment plans. It was almost
like someone forecast rain and I was getting the
umbrellas ready.

Cooking is one of my passions so running a restaurant, I
decided, would be a natural progression. We viewed a
few premises but particularly liked Samsara with its
double entrance doors, the arcade at the front and spacious
interiors, so unlike a typical curry house. It is also
located in an affluent area of Surrey with good business
prospects. Having made our choice, we set about a major
entrepreneurial adventure with mighty expectations.

As well as a business investment, being in the restaurant
was also a good way of unwinding from the stress of my
day job; just being amongst customers enjoying
themselves was quite refreshing. People eating drinking

and making merry was a great way to witness the good side of life. More than the financial benefits, the emotional quotient became more important.

Things, however, don't always go to plan, certainly not with me. Entrepreneurship is a roller coaster with high highs and low lows. Whatever the monetary returns are, it is like raising a baby: not a nine to five, nor a five-day-a-week job. For it to be successful it must be a passion, a vocation, a commitment.

One of the most important factors in the success of any business is to have the right partners. The lesson I learned is never to mix friendship with a business partnership. Whenever you look for a business partner it should be a person who has the qualities that you don't have yourself, therefore enabling you to complement each other. We often make the mistake of partnering up with someone that we know or like because they possess the same qualities but that limits the perspective through which you can analyze your business. I made this mistake. A man who was once one of my best friends, I took on as a business partner which not only ruined the business but also culminated in a bitter end to our friendship.

In any partnership, every partner needs to pull their weight and understand personal limitations as well as strengths. Once someone becomes defensive or finds it difficult to accept any fault, this is when a partnership falls apart.

In our restaurant, one of the partners was not pulling his weight. The two others, including me, tried to support him as much as possible but unfortunately, things did not work out and there was no option left other than for him to step away from the business. What hurts me most is the fact that this also affected our friendship because he could not differentiate between a person and a business relationship. This episode made me learn the hard lesson of not mixing friendship or personal relations with business.

I wish he had remained my friend as I cared for him. Losing a friend is like having a part of your body cut off and it doesn't heal well.

Our foolishness didn't stop there. Anand, my friend, and another partner suggested we change Samsara to a sports bar. Anand loves football so we installed TV screens, but the local clientele turned out not to be football fans! Also, we had gone from being a family restaurant with a local, middle-aged customer base to a venue where girls in miniskirts served drinks. Not surprisingly, many customers complained. 'When I come out for the evening,' said one lady, 'I want my husband to look at me, not a young woman in a short skirt.' Another informed me that they can watch football at home, why come out to Samsara to do so? Indeed, they were right because we didn't do any market research or take feedback from the important people, our customers!

Our disastrous stupidity saw weekly sales slump from £14,000 to £2,000 which was evidence of the old saying, 'If it isn't broke, don't fix it. Before making any changes in a business it is important to undertake appropriate market research, take feedback and implement changes accordingly. Most of the time we need an evolution rather than a revolution, more so given the fact that our business was already doing well and just needed some tweaking, not a massive uproot. It is important in running a business that we do what the clients want, not what our fancy brains tell us. Yes, this was another learning curve.

It was at this point the decision had to be taken for me to either walk away from the business or ask to take the driving seat. Fortunately, my other partner understood that we had made some wrong decisions and he fully supported me. It is also important to mention that I take equal responsibility for the debacle because I was an equal partner.

Having recognized our mistakes, we moved forward by changing the menu, rebranding, marketing, employees, literally everything reverting to how it was before, back to being a restaurant with a cocktail bar. Of course, by this time major damage was done, we had lost most of our loyal customer base and gained many bad reviews. Nearly three years have since passed and we are still trying to recover from the damage. The business has been growing we were almost back to normal when we were hit another disaster – the COVID pandemic.

What lesson has this taught me? That the glory is not in never falling but in rising after every fall. If someone has never fallen in their life, they are either extremely lucky or haven't tried enough.

It was at this time when all these things were going on that I was hit with my medical condition which left me incapable of making any useful contribution towards the business or to my medical jobs. I was in the hospital for several months and I am grateful to Anand for looking after the business during that time. It was he who first took me to the restaurant after a long gap and how wonderful that day was, to see the restaurant buzzing again with happy customers and to be welcomed by all my staff members. I felt as though my life was going to regain an element of normality.

However, our debts were growing, and we were falling behind in paying both our suppliers and the rent. Every week we had to put in money from our pockets to top up wages and pay bills and even then, this was not enough. Eventually, Anand decided to exit the business which was quite understandable as he had his other more profitable ventures. Then, when the pandemic lockdown started and the future looked even bleaker, we had two options: carry on with our own money or liquidate the business; in hindsight, the latter might have been a more practical option.

But we make some choices from the heart rather than the mind, however impractical they might be. After losing so much of my normal life due to the spinal cord injury and my medical practices business, all I had left was this restaurant and I did not want to let it go. Retaining at the restaurant still gives me a purpose in life, something which does not make much financial sense but provides a huge degree of emotional equity. Now Mili and I are joint owners of the restaurant and have spent several thousand of our savings. I am glad that the restaurant is still alive after the worst of the pandemic is over when so many big names have closed. I pray that we can continue running this entrepreneurship adventure in the future.

Owning a bar and restaurant is ironic given how alcohol was, at one point back in 2000, in danger of consuming me. But sometimes your weaknesses can become your greatest strengths. I was able to turn a drinking habit into an interest in running a bar.

Now that I can walk indoors for small distances with two crutches, I am much more hands-on in the business. I make sure that I go around every table not only to take orders but also to hear direct feedback from our customers. I also manage most of the bartending and enjoy making cocktails. Whatever our business, it is important for the proprietor to be directly involved and to gather as much knowledge as possible regarding every aspect of that business. It is only by being hands-on and getting the right resources, including investing in the right human capital, that ensures success. Running a hospitality business successfully is to give a complete and satisfactory experience to customers. It is not just the food or service or ambience, it must be everything together in its best form. I have seen the direct impact of this when the owner is present physically and the positive impact of this on the customers when the owner makes the effort to talk to them directly and show how vital they are to the business.

It is also important to develop a contingency plan, perhaps two, to fight against all adversities. I am still a long way from being able to pay all those debts incurred due to the pandemic and because of our rash decisions in the past but I can almost see the light at the end of the tunnel. Support from Mili in this venture has been invaluable, but I also need to mention all my staff members especially my manager, Shahid, who has been incredible in every way in keeping this business going.

I enjoy studying personalities and it is a great experience to see and understand every different personality and how to coach them to become a good team. Every member of the staff in the restaurant is a different personality and after hiring and firing a lot of people, we have finally accrued a brilliant core team that bonds and works well together. Learning from my previous experiences and failures, I realize the importance of diversity among staff members and partners.

I also understand that ego has no place in business. My team members comprise Indians, English, Bangladesh, Romania, Kosovo, and many other nationalities. There is so much to learn from each of them and their cultures. Learning never stops and I discover new things from them every day.

Samsara is a wonderful outlet for me even though, as I write, the restaurant remains an ongoing struggle. Maybe by my next book, I will be able to share some success stories.

Don't put all your eggs in one Basket.

Growing up in India, the norm was to build your own house which is where you expect to live for the rest of your life. Here in the West, the concept is to buy a house already built, new or old, and get on the property ladder with the idea of upscaling as a career and life progress then use the equity in the property as a retirement investment. When one gets old it is then usual to sell the property and downsize to release money.

When Mili and I arrived in England, we rented a bed in East London, followed by a room and then hospital accommodation in North London. Securing my first training rotation was when we started renting a small flat, costing almost £1,200 a month. The outlay was a significant part of our expenses since our monthly income was only around £2,300. It was a bizarre and unlikely probability that we would ever be able to buy a house, but I had a dream of having our first child in our own house rather than a rented one. That dream spurred me to explore options and research property investment.

It was around this time that I met a mortgage advisor which was no less than another miracle in my life. By talking to him I understood that, even given a slight risk, it is better to invest money in buying rather than renting. Rental money is like water going down a drain. If, however, you take out a mortgage and make monthly repayments of the same amount then you benefit from a property whose value will appreciate over time, eventually seeing a return on your investment. This made good sense to me and thanks to Mili too. My friends, however, when I spoke to them, were horrified. They couldn't see any reason why I would be willing to put my savings into buying a house when we weren't even sure if or where we would be living in the country, which depended on the next job. To them, it was almost outrageous that I could even think of taking such a risk. They advised me against making any rash decisions.

However, I reasoned that, wherever I worked, I would still have a house, and I would do everything possible to live in the house we bought. Mili had landed a great job in finance in the city just after she found out she was pregnant. Fortunately, again, that was the time before the worldwide recession. Professionals were being offered 100% mortgages up to five times their gross salary and both my wife and I were recognized as professionals.

And so began a new first - house hunting. I did not have much of a clue. I liked the first house that I viewed and asked to go back there with Mili, the boss, to confirm it. That was it, we put in an offer on that first house we saw. The estate agent was astounded, he had never made an easier sale. Sometimes in life, it is important to take risks. The more calculated the risk, the better the odds. We didn't have anything to lose. The bank was going to pay the whole amount, we just needed to pay instalments that were less than our rent. The house wasn't big or anything fancy, but it was in a nice neighbourhood with a good school nearby and a five-minute drive to work. It ticked all our boxes. The offer was accepted and about five days before Mili was due to deliver, we moved in. What a grand day that was! Our first house, one we would make into a home, plus we would fulfil our ambition to have our baby in our place. Life was just cool.

Fortune favours the brave, they say. It certainly, did in our case. We had made a big decision, but it was just as well because soon after came the deep recession and 100% of mortgages were stopped. As a result, my friends had to wait for more than five or six years before they could buy their own homes. Once again, I felt listening to your gut instincts and wanting something desperately, can make things happen.

Our home was soon filled with the coos of our baby, our beautiful angel, the happiest moment in our lives. We named her Angelina, the word meaning pure. She made our life meaningful. I now had a bigger, better purpose in my life. I had to give her a good life, a life better than mine. My parents gave me the best childhood they could, now it was my turn to give my angel the best start in life. I thanked Mili for everything. She had made my life complete. (I agree with my Assistant Manager, Liam, when he says it is strange that to drive a car you need a license, yet you don't need one for being a parent who is surely far more responsible?)

I had an ideal job, a beautiful wife and daughter, and a home to call our own. Mili got her dream job, and we were getting settled in England just the way I wanted. I had so much gratitude to offer, and so much life to appreciate. But maybe I wasn't sincere enough in my Thanksgiving or my appreciation. Maybe I was so happy that I started taking things for granted. My inner voice was trying to speak again but I was too busy to listen and decrypt the clues.

Life had taught me quite a lot by now with my experiences in recent years, particularly my father's sudden illness which left him disabled and unable to work, thus leading to profound financial difficulties for the whole family. Now that I had my family it was my responsibility to secure their financial safety and to give them a good future. I did a lot of research and studied a lot of books on how to make money grow and how to secure financial independence. As soon as I could afford to, I started investing in all types of insurance including life insurance, critical illness insurance, income protection insurance and health insurance. As much as people tend to run away from insurance brokers, I was becoming their dream customer. Again, my friends were bewildered by my decisions, but my instincts prompted me to prepare for the future and to save money for rainy days.

We had to start saving small. I had read about the compound effect which I wanted to put into practice. I opened several current and savings bank accounts as well as stocks and shares accounts. As I did not have much money to invest, I decided to add small amounts every month and, to maintain this discipline, I set up standing orders for all these savings accounts. As a result, 11 years down the line I believe it was the right decision as over time small savings have grown significantly and helped us during the current difficult times. I became a millionaire in 2016, with a net worth of around £2 million. I know that is not a lot for rich people but for me, it was because we had started from zero and every penny was earned honestly and ethically. I was the sole proprietor of businesses with around £2.4 million in annual turnovers and worked my socks off to keep growing.

I knew my parents and my family had by now become proud of me but strangely I wasn't. Instead, it felt like I was earning money only for family security and for the sake of it. It was almost like I had to prove something to all those people who doubted me and prove something to myself too. Over a period, providing financial security for the family became an obsession. I became so worried about their future that I could not live in the moment or enjoy my present. Worrying about the rain to come, I forgot to enjoy the shining sun. But maybe again, that was just the right thing to worry about because if I hadn't made money when I was able, then my family would have been a lot worse financially today and that would have been even more painful than my trauma.

It is important to keep sight of the future while enjoying the present, but it is equally important to live in the present while keeping yourself prepared for the future.

Those insurances, which amused my colleagues, particularly the critical illness insurance, paid out just at the right time when I had no income, and we were struggling with our finances. Yet again this proved that gut instincts take us in the right direction, we just must be receptive to the signs. (Now those insurance brokers use my name and story to advertise the need for appropriate insurance to the customers.)

I had a responsibility not just to my immediate family but also to my parents and in-laws, who were now quite old and lacked significant means of income. It was my mum's dream to be able to work in a bespoke kitchen of her design. My dad asked me if I could build a house, and her dream kitchen, just as my mum wanted. I was honoured to oblige. Thank God I had, at the time, the means to do this. I built the house where my mum is now living and where my dad spent the last six years of his life. My mum got her dream kitchen, and my dad was so proud that he used to tell everyone how his son had fulfilled his wishes. I was so happy. I must thank my wife for her continued support for these expenses and my best friend Jugal who oversaw the construction of the house as all I could do was send money. I hope I have been able to fulfil some of my duties as a son.

When we got married, as part of our wedding vows, Mili and I made a pact that we would look after each other's family, come what may. Mili is an only child. Unfortunately, society still makes a distinction between having a son and a daughter, in some cultures more than others. My mother-in-law always missed having a son even though Mili went above and beyond her duties as a daughter and still does. I took it upon myself to support her in making sure she can look after her parents. Perhaps I filled their void of a son, becoming more their son than a son-in-law. Of course, this massively increased my responsibilities, but I guess I was blessed, and lucky to have two sets of wonderful parents when some don't even have one.

Like everyone else, we have a love-hate rapport with our in-laws, but the love goes much deeper than any troubled surface waters. I have always supported Mili whenever she had to look after her parents financially or otherwise and I know she has equally done the same.

While my family continue to be a strong influence in my life, others also play their part.

'I take you as my idol in life,' declared Rony, one of my team members in the restaurant. 'I think you have everything in life and the way you have come back fighting is inspiring. There is only one thing missing,' he continued. Quite bemused by this conversation, and keen to know his answer, I asked, 'Really? And what is that?' Rony is a nice guy and quite intelligent, so I often like talking with him. 'The only thing you don't have is a son, otherwise, your life would be complete.'

That caused me to reflect. Do we need to have a son to carry forward our name? Why? I had never thought about it before. I am happy and proud of my daughters and have never treated them differently or less than my sons. Is carrying on our legacy so important? Can this only be done by sons? Surely that is not the right way to think, not in this day and age, not ever. I couldn't agree with Rony. The conversation has carried on and we are still debating those points, now with all the other team members adding their own opinions.

As parents, we often try to live our dreams through our children. We want to see our best in them although that might not always be what they want. Sometimes our love may cause more conflict and hindrance than help in their progress. Isn't that so? I have decided that I will not impose my dreams and ambitions on my children. The only thing I would hope for them is they do their best in whatever they chose. My job is to give them safety, love, solid values, and a good life. Some people say to me that with two daughters, I need to save for their weddings. A typical Indian attitude, I know. But I'd much rather save for their education, and help them to become independent and self-sufficient. That's what my dad did. Am I abnormal in thinking like that for my children because they are girls?

If I do something sufficiently worthwhile to be remembered after I die, then this will be because of my achievements, and not because I have sons to carry forward my name or legacy. Let's think about this life first for it is upon us to make it hell or heaven on this earth itself rather than thinking about the afterlife.

Parents are the nearest thing to God in flesh and blood and I believe it is our utmost responsibility, within our ability, to make our parents happy and keep them safe.

Work Hard, Play Hard

At the peak of my GP career, I would leave the house at 7 am, drop off the girls at school then Mili at the station before driving to my practice. All those years I was the first one to reach my office so that I could catch up on all emails, blood test results and other paperwork before opening the door to patients. There was always management work to do then I'd see more patients in the evenings, finishing at 7 pm. Two or three times a week I'd drive straight to the restaurant, not arriving home until 1 am then restart at 7 am the next morning. Weekends were frequently taken up with bookkeeping and catching up on work from that week. Before I knew it, I was in a spiral. Success was my goal and that involved creating more work for myself. Saying no was my weakness which I'll come back to in Chapter Five.

What I've come to realize is if you can't say no to those who take advantage of you, you end up doing more and more work and being taken for granted.

Angelina was now four years old. Mili was settled in her job. I had settled into my role as a partner in the practice and a senior doctor. We were earning well enough and getting older. It just seemed like the perfect time to complete our family. In 2010 our second daughter Nikita was born, but not before giving us many scares. In her second scan, the gynaecologist told us her kidneys may not be working properly and that we should prepare for some bad news. Both of us nearly went into depression with anxiety. Mili had to go for frequent scans and reviews, each of them preceded by visits to the temple and lots of prayers. Eventually, the time came for her delivery, and we were very tense. On top of that Mili kept bleeding, her haemoglobin levels eventually coming dangerously low (four). The labour wasn't progressing, and she was only semi-conscious. She had to be given an urgent blood transfusion and taken to the operating theatre for delivery. The baby was stuck, and it was too dangerous

to perform a caesarean section or use forceps. Three
senior gynaecologists gathered as they wrestled to deliver
the baby. I thought I was going to lose Mili forever. What
happened with my friend Jugal was going to happen to
me, too. I prayed to God, deep in my heart, 'Let me suffer
the pains rather than her or the baby. Take away
whatever you want from my life but give me a healthy
mum and baby.

Miraculously, my wish was fulfilled. Nikita was born a
healthy baby with normal kidneys. Mili stabilized after
the delivery and a blood transfusion. I was over the moon
at having another daughter. I always wanted girls and my
wish had been fulfilled. She was such a beautiful baby. I
remember being in the baby suite when a Nigerian nurse
unfurled the curtains and announced her name, 'Hello
Mum and Dad, I'm Happiness'. Wow, what a name and
how timely her entrance was!

Although it sounds unbelievable, I sometimes suspect
that my current sufferings are a result of the business
pact I had with God at that time. He kept his promise,
now I must keep mine. My responsibilities had expanded.
I had to cater not for one but two beautiful daughters. I
had to be the best person I could be, a father they will
forever look up to. Now I wonder, with my current
disabilities, will I still be able to fulfil their expectations?
But they are the ones who have inspired me to go on. I
cannot play football with them, nor can I walk the dogs. I

cannot accompany them on a normal shopping trip to a mall or a hiking trip as in the past, and I can see the disappointment on their faces, but I know they have been bravely facing this crisis and have supported me in every possible way.

The bonds you develop as a family take many forms. Like most husbands and wives, Mili and I agree only on a few things and one of them is travelling around the world. It was a dream we had dreamt together during our days of struggle, a way of keeping ourselves motivated. But to do these things, I had to earn even more money so, for me, working hard and playing hard had to go hand in hand.

On a more philosophical note, I believe a person is rich if he can spend his money or give it away for a cause without needing to worry. I have been fortunate enough, within my means, to help several family members and friends financially: one of Mili's cousins had a kidney transplant which I partly paid for. I was also able to help a few friends who were facing enormous financial difficulties during the pandemic, and we did it all at a time when I did not have any sort of income myself. It wasn't because I was a higher spiritual soul or doing something great. I just believe that by doing good things for others you attract good for yourself. There is no greater pleasure than being able to give, a pleasure that currently I am not able to afford due to my current circumstances. One inspiration that motivates me is to be able to afford to 'give' again.

Before my trauma, I had become a workaholic. Mili and I were both so busy with work and children, that our spare time was limited. We prepared the girls for their grammar school exams as our one aim in life was to get them into good schools. There were also activities to take them to (as I write this, I am about to drive Angelina to Worcester for two nights for the National Taekwondo Championships) which left little time for us. In a way, our relationship became quite mechanical.

Now both girls attend grammar schools, so we have more time. Plus, during the pandemic, we worked next to each other at the dining room table, giving us more opportunities to be together.

But previously, in the obsession with securing the future for my family, I almost missed the present. Some of my friends and colleagues thought I was turning into a snob because I rarely had time to socialize, but the reality was that I had spread myself too thin and taken on so much work that there weren't enough hours in the day.

My constant challenge to prove myself did, at one point, get too much. I realized this when I double-booked myself at different places at the same time.

A healthy work-life balance was alien to me at that time. All I knew was to make hay while the sun shines. I don't know now, in retrospect, whether I should feel sad that I missed seeing my daughters grow up or be happy that I have been able to ensure a safe future for them as a parent. And as luck would have it, now I cannot work at all, and I have plenty of time.

Financial Security

Nothing can change what I achieved having become a self-made man and among the top 5% of doctors in terms of earnings. This wasn't something I boasted about, not because I am humble but rather, because I didn't have any feeling of success.

Perhaps I peaked too early after which it was all downhill.

Honestly, when I first realized the lasting extent of my disability, I feared many things. The biggest being negative financial implications. I had to give up my practice and I was not able to earn as a doctor. All those years I had worked harder and harder to build up my practices and my relationship with patients. Medicine was my passion, my vocation but also my bread and butter. In an instant of bad luck, everything was taken away from me. Because of my physical limitations, I did not know what to do to keep earning and provide financial security for my family.

My main concern was my daughters' education - would I be able to afford it? Nikita, my younger one, plans to become a vet. Angelina, the elder daughter, who is intelligent, ambitious, and hardworking, wants to go to the US to study or to an Oxbridge institution. She has her heart set on a career as a barrister. All this will need a lot of money. 'Will I still be able to go?' she asked. Without hesitation, I assured her: 'Yes, even if we have to sell our properties, you will.' I made her a promise and I promised myself to keep that promise. How I will do it, I don't yet know but I will.

But then, I know in my heart that something will work out. First, I must have my gratitude for what I still have and the positivity that keeps me going.

One of the greatest influences during the hardest of times has been my friend Sumit. He is perhaps, the most pragmatic, positive-thinking person I have ever come across in life. He can make even the saddest person feel happy with his contagious smile and his 'glass-half-full attitude. When everything looked bleak and uncertain, his words gave me the strength to just hang on. He assured me that just like good times don't last forever, bad times won't either. He lent me money when our financial problems were at their worst. He is the one who encouraged me to write about my life experiences and struggles. I owe a lot to Sumit, for being my friend in need and someone upon whom I can always rely.

At home, we are much more frugal than we used to be. Mili has a pressurized job and, what with our home life, and extra responsibilities, gets tired and upset. I try to avoid discussions regarding finances, but she is aware of our reduced income and increasing debts. We have both tried our best to limit our outgoings as much as possible.

Family Support

My father had been a geologist, working in senior management for a corporation that sold agricultural goods. He was so happy when he met Mili, who had also trained as a geologist, and immediately took to her.

Mum and Dad were close. Dad loved my mum so much that he wanted to take care of everything for her. When she wanted to work, he took it upon himself to work harder and earn more. When she wanted to learn to drive, he employed a driver for her. This wasn't necessarily right but it was his way of expressing his love. What he did not realize was that he didn't leave a contingency plan. As a result, Mum could never be independent, but she was happy and content with their loving relationship and her two children, not knowing what lay ahead of her.

As a doctor and a business owner, I spent more time at work than with my family. I'm grateful they put up with me. One day Angelina asked, 'Daddy, you are like the moon'. I was surprised and intrigued. 'Why?' I asked her quizzically. She responded, 'Because we only see you at night'. That hit me hard and bought tears to my eyes. I tried to explain to her, 'Baby, I'm doing this all for you and your sister so that you can fulfil all your dreams. As she fell asleep, I think she understood in her mind.

Things are so different now. My changed physical condition has had repercussions for all of us. The burden of care falls to my wife who has handled the situation maturely. Our home, of course, needed to be adapted so we converted the garage into a bedroom for a few months as I could not climb stairs by myself. I remember one morning managing to reach the kitchen on my own and make tea - that was quite an achievement!

However, even now I cannot go upstairs without the support of my crutches and either my wife or daughters because of the risk of losing my balance and falling backwards (which has happened a couple of times). The situation was precarious and so our only solution, we realized, was to find a more disabled-friendly house.

Finding the right property was a struggle and finding a mortgage for a disabled, retired person on a pension was more challenging than I had expected. There was a time, not too long ago when many high street banks would have offered me a mortgage, but now nobody wanted to know. This didn't stop our house hunting, however, and Angelina found a perfect place: beautiful, our dream home with downstairs bedrooms, a massive bathroom with a wet room and whatnot. But as a mortgage out of our reach?

Normally it would take eight weeks to complete the process of a house sale but for us, it took seven months. Fortunately, the previous owner was a nice lady. Seeing our situation, she was prepared to wait. After multiple rejections, we finally secured a mortgage but for only half the amount. We needed the house badly, so I had to put all our savings as a down payment. Finally, in October 2020, we moved to our new house where we made our home. I could finally sleep in a proper bedroom. Once again throughout this experience, I realized that if you desire something and are prepared to persevere, chances are you will eventually achieve your goals.

There was a time when I was able to help many people financially, enabling them to go on holidays, buy nice dresses for the girls, invest, and grow my money but now I have mounted multiple business debts from the time I was in the hospital. This has resulted in several calls asking for money. I've even been threatened by bailiffs. I am astounded at the dramatic, almost overnight, change in my life. At one point I was angry with myself, disappointed at my failures; I felt cheated and frustrated with the situation but now I feel that this is a phase I must pass through and come out stronger. Perhaps this is a period of redemption or maybe a test of my strength of survival. Either way, I must win this and come out on top. I have faith that I will, eventually. As Keats wrote, 'If winter comes, can spring be far behind?'

My mother-in-law has been a vital lifeline during our most difficult times, staying with us for nearly six months when I first came out of the hospital, and helping us cope with the new normal in our lives.

Indeed, I have been blessed with great in-laws, and lovely, simple, honest people, especially my father-in-law. I was always told by my parents that marriages happen between two families, not just two individuals. To me, my in-laws were just at parental as my parents, and I mattered to them as their son. I learned from my father-in-law how someone can be happy with the simple means of life. He loved me so much and he loved to talk, telling me fantastic stories from his childhood and younger days. He was a legend at telling stories. As tragic as it was, I was lucky to be the last person to spend a whole day with him, sitting in the sunshine, talking our hearts away. That night he experienced massive heart failure, fell in the bathroom and died unexpectedly.

'I'm not going to push you in that wheelchair, you must walk. Otherwise, we are not taking you to the mall,' ordered Nikita this time, all puffed up and red in the face. Life had become different in so many ways and I was trying my best to get used to it all, but it has been much more difficult for my daughters to witness their father in such a different physical state. I ended up not going to the mall as it wouldn't be fair on them. Since then, we have hardly been out shopping together, but I did promise myself that I will live up to my little daughter's expectations and make her proud of me.

The girls only visited me once while I was in Wellington Hospital and they didn't want to hug me. At first, I couldn't understand this and was very upset. My elder daughter was in denial; my younger one wondered why I was lying in bed and looked fat and needed help to go to the toilet, and why I wouldn't be able to be able to play football. She had so many questions, none of which I could answer properly. You need to be prepared for everything in life, I told her, you have no idea what's going to come next. Sometimes on the road of life, we just must follow the bend and try and do it with a smile.

Mili has been my pillar of strength, taking on all responsibilities on top of her full-time job. And during the lockdown, when she worked at home, she also had to taxi the girls to their swimming, ballet, taekwondo, and tuition. I felt so useless. I was just a burden on everyone, especially before I learned to drive again. Now I can drive Angelina in an automatic car to taekwondo championships where, towards the end of 2021, she won a second bronze medal. The long journey to Worcester took over four hours because I needed several stops, but it was worth it. Witnessing your children's achievements surpasses any personal success.

What happened to me has changed all of us, of course. Mili has become very spiritual, doing lots of fasts and prayers, and reading spiritual books.

My brother, far more pragmatic and business-minded than me, has been supportive, most of the time insisting I am lucky since I can still look after my family. Perhaps he hasn't quite understood the impact this has had on me. But, you know, we are very different personalities: I am an open book, like my dad; mum is more diplomatic and practical, would never have trouble with relatives but wouldn't be close to them either, preferring to sit on the fence.

Of course, regardless of personality, no one can anticipate how they might cope with trauma. Occasionally when I wake during the night it takes a few moments before I remember my physical limitations. How disappointing when reality kicks in! I try not to let this get me down and am grateful for the ongoing love of my family. One of the other consequences at home is spending more time on my own, something I don't particularly like but is now the norm. On the other hand, I quite enjoy relaxing on the sofa with my dogs on either side of me.

Feeling supported by loved ones is invaluable. They provide a sense of security which enables me to concentrate on survival. I could not have survived without my family's support or achieved what I have achieved, without them.

Healing Power of Pets

I grew up with dogs, mostly large breeds such as German shepherds, the most majestic of all dogs, in my opinion. As I previously mentioned, when I was the medical officer in the tea garden, I had not one or two but four big dogs along with a cat, one parrot and a handful of rabbits. I loved it when they all came bounding over one another to greet me when I came home from work. I was not very hot on discipline and, being a bachelor with a king-size bed, I slept with all four of them, and it was such fun. They were my furry pillows!

Thankfully Mili is equally passionate about dogs. Our pets are everything to me. They are the biggest stress relievers and my most loyal friends. If human beings could understand the meaning of loyalty and love from these animals the world would be a much better place. One of my biggest regrets when leaving India to come to England was the fact that I had to leave my dogs with my parents and in-laws Each of the dogs died within three years, more than likely due to sadness than anything else. I cannot forgive myself for that.

I mentioned in Chapter One that my family includes two large dogs: a 110lb chocolate Labrador, Shadow, aptly named, as he follows me wherever I go, and Snoopy, a two-year-old German shepherd who is intelligent beyond words. Shadow is a rescue dog and has been with us for four years. It still amazes me how he was left behind in the garden to fend for himself after his previous family left England in a hurry.

It was by sheer luck that we found him. Without a doubt, my dogs have been my greatest healers and if they weren't in our lives, it would have been hard to cope with the loneliness when Mili goes to the office and the girls are in school leaving me on my own. These pets continue to play a huge part in my life. Even now as I am writing this, they are lying next to me, Snoopy licking my ears and Shadow with his head on my ankles.

I have mentioned previously that when I was discharged from the hospital after my second operation, Shadow took to sitting next to me and licking my neck, nowhere else, just my neck. He just wouldn't let go. Was it sheer coincidence that I was diagnosed with cancer at the same place where he was licking or was it a miracle? I will never know. After the thyroid gland was removed, Shadow no longer paid any attention to my neck.

Did he save my life? Shadow may have been a rescue dog, but I believe he rescued me more than I rescued him.

Too busy to appreciate my blessings during the good times, too preoccupied to live in the present, it needed a calamity to bring in an emotional evolution. Often, we take the good things for granted and remember only the bad. But our inner voice is always with us if we wish to listen to it.

Chapter Four

Moving Forward

Impossible is just a word, one that means you must fight longer and harder to achieve your goal.

Don't Stand Still

Two years ago, created by life, I was on the verge of deciding that my future warranted little investment. My medical career, which had been a dream since I was a child and to which I had devoted time and energy, would never again be my main profession or earning power. Turning my back on life would, in some ways, have been the easy option. But cowards die many times before their death, the valiant die only once. I did not want to be a coward. Why should I be? What would that achieve? My children were still young, my family was still young, and I could not yet afford to hang up my boots, could I?

During some dark moments, I contemplated ending my life, given the futility of my circumstances. I thought of various ways to die but suddenly m y m i n d flashed with the image of smiley, cute Nikita, my younger daughter, and I realized my stupidity. I had to stop this self-pity; I'm the fighter father they look up to and I couldn't let them down just like that. It was that single image of her that gave me the strength I needed to take back control. I was helped by my father's experience which strengthened me emotionally. You can never prepare yourself for being paralyzed, for your career being taken from you, but I was adamant that I would not make the same mistakes he made.

Although he survived for years following his stroke, in one way I had already lost my father long before he died. I never wanted my girls to feel they had lost their father. Creating memories for them will surely help them cope when that time comes so that's what I'm trying to do. I lost my father and my father and father in law within a short space of time honestly speaking, I have not yet been able to grieve for either. Is it because I still feel them close to me or is it that many years in the medical profession have made my emotions regarding death more stoic? Having seen so many deaths and so much suffering, neither is easy to face, but it is even worse when it is someone in your own family. Witnessing my dad's suffering, and understanding his suffering more after my problems, I need to celebrate his life and remember him in the best way. When someone dies, you can no longer meet them physically but if they are in your heart and mind, you have them anyway. Hindus believe the body is just one part of life; maybe that also contributes to my attitude. I am happy that Dad is now free; when I remember him it is with a smile.

Acceptance is the first step in any emotional fightback, and I was soon able to accept my life-changing events and limitations. I came to understand that certain things cannot be changed, and some things can. It is better to accept the things that cannot be changed and learn to adapt to them. This way you can focus your energies on changing what can be changed to make the most out of the demanding situation.

This is a pragmatic approach, one which will not be natural for everyone. But what is the alternative? You cannot undo what has happened, but you can influence the way you approach the present and the future.

This process of acceptance, which I will revisit in the next chapter, was followed by the realization that keeping my mind occupied and being productive, was my best option. From the moment I woke from my operation, I knew that life was going to change.

I needed to be the agent of change, to be in control. Before changing anything else I had to make sure I was on the way to becoming a better human being.

Lifelong Learning

'Learning place ahead, leave your ego behind. This was written on a plaque at the approach of my brother's Engineering College, and it hit a chord with me. Learning is a lifelong process. Gaining knowledge is always engaging and developmental. Since childhood, I have been an avid reader but somehow in the rat race of medicine and life, reading, painting and other hobbies got left behind.

One of the biggest drawbacks of studying medicine is the lack of transferable skills and therefore one of my long-term goals is to have at least three master's degrees. So far, I'm glad to have a medical degree and an MBA. I did start doing an MSc in Finance but ran out of money to pay the fees so have had to defer it for the time being. I hope I will soon be able to resolve the financial situation so that I can pay the fees and complete my third master's degree. In the meantime, I have received student funding to embark on an MSc in Psychology. I'm looking forward to learning psychology as I feel it would help me understand my mind and the people around me in a better way. It will probably also help me deal with my circumstances more productively. I'd also like to get back to medical teaching, something I used to do at King's College where I was an examiner and taught years 1-5. Some of my students used to come to my practice for tutorials when I would encourage them to interview patients. I love teaching. This is something I had done many years earlier following my A-Levels when I tutored year 10 students, a money earner as well as a satisfying role. I have also been a GP Appraiser and

Education Lead, helping doctors with difficulties, and identifying their learning needs.

After my life-changing injuries, one thing I had in abundance was time and it was up to me how I chose to make the best use of it. The last thing I wanted to do was to waste this privilege of time. Everything can come back but not time once gone. During the last two years, I have invested much time in reading and reflecting on life. While I love reading, it was, initially, hard to find time to sit down and read undisturbed, so the next best thing was to listen to audiobooks. I confess this has almost become a compulsion; as soon as I finish one, I find the next, otherwise, I feel there is something missing something is missing.

Amazon audiobooks have made a huge difference in my life. Now I would much rather listen to a book than music while driving or at home. I quite surprised myself when I counted how many volumes, I have read over the past two years: 190. There is a reason why people say books are your best friends. I have learnt so much from other people's stories and have been inspired by them in every way. My daughter is an avid reader and often reads books too advanced for her age, but I can see her maturity and knowledge developing because of this hobby. Mili reads a lot too and I have read or listened to various books covering such topics as leadership, emotional intelligence, working smart, not hard, managing oneself, motivation, self-help, and war heroes, all of which have been incredible and indeed, I've tried to apply some of these ideas to my own life.

Napoleon Hill, Dan Brodsky, Michael Morpurgo, Andrew Carnegie and Sadhguru are some of the authors and personalities who have made a great impact on my life and given me a lot of strength to deal with adversity . constructively and positively.

Much as I enjoy reading, I also needed to invest time researching an alternative career for years ahead of me. A few months following my disastrous operation, I chose to do an MBA in International Healthcare Management as this would cover elements that I could apply in my life. Fortunately for me, I gained admission to Cumbria University and the course was great.

The first module was about managing oneself, working smart and making the most of limited resources which evolved into organizational behaviour, finance, IT, and sustainability. These skills (I completed the course at the end of 2020) have helped me deal with my restaurant business. I can also see that my daughters have been inspired by the fact that their parents are still studying and trying to earn degrees. At a time when I am looking at all prospective alternative careers, finance, day trading, and motivational coaching are all possibilities. One should always keep an eye open for options and opportunities in life as you never know which might strike gold.

Negativity only attracts more negativity and eventually leads to depression and other mental issues. It would be a lie to say I have never been negative or depressed, but I do try to keep looking for reasons to be positive and thankful and most of the time I find something or another to maintain my positivity. Chronic neuropathic pain and limitations of mobility are the main causes of frustration. Sometimes it can be very depressing. The only way I found to cope is to accept my limitations and symptoms and adapt accordingly.

The process of writing this book has enabled me to reflect. It is as though I am talking to myself in a very honest way, something I haven't had time to do for many years. My reflections are now more structured. At the same time, it has been extremely difficult to relive some things. Events such as wetting the bed, my dad's death, and the moment of feeling suicidal make me tearful. But this cathartic exercise has been of great value in my emotional evolution. As they say, what doesn't kill you, makes you stronger.

In the past I didn't like nostalgia, always preferring to look forward while covering up memories. I once saw a movie in which a character said, 'I never put myself in reverse gear,' and that stuck with me. Now I realize to get your car on track, sometimes you need to reverse and there should not be any shame in that. Looking back, I recognize what I did well and what I did wrong. My biggest mistakes were taking on a friend as a business partner or investing money outside of my area of expertise. I would not do this again.

What I will do is continue both formal and informal learning. I have made my motto, 'Every adversity is a hidden opportunity and am trying to live by it.

The Power of Meeting Customers

Another cocktail served, another happy diner, another moment of reflection.

While I was a GP, being in a restaurant was a great way of destressing. As a doctor, I enjoyed a good rapport with my patients, knowing them, becoming a part of their life, a vehicle in their journey. Dealing with customers in the restaurant is no different. Although circumstances vary, the same principles of interpersonal relationships work in the setting of running a restaurant business. Customers come in many different types, and you must change the way you deal with each person to get the most out of them. There have been a couple of occasions when people have been surprised to find someone in a curry house who can speak good English - aren't people's expectations surprising? Or is it still a fixed prejudice?

Many customers are interested, even fascinated, to know what happened to me. They might offer sympathy, express horror, or ask how I have coped; others hold back, not wishing to appear nosy but are equally caring and curious. My story often seems to inspire some help in building a rapport with them. Most of them have now become regular customers. And, just as with patient, I try to give my customers the same standard of service that I would expect when I visit a restaurant.

One day I was shocked when a customer called out, 'Hey cripple!' but before I could react, he came up to me and insisted he was joking. That was a sick sense of humour. One of my staff wanted to ask the customer to leave but I stopped him. In the past, this comment would have made me angry but now it just makes me realize the ground reality. Yes, he is right. As much as I don't like it, the fact is that I'm a cripple but that doesn't necessarily make me less able than him or anyone else. Pain is objective but how we suffer is subjective and based on our reaction.

I am humbled to say that my physical limitations have not affected the attachment I develop with others. One of Samsara's regular customers is a 76-year-old Yorkshireman who comes in almost daily for two pints of beer. Recently he fell off his bike, breaking his shoulder joint. Over time we have built quite a rapport which is, perhaps, why he summoned me when his wound needed redressing and to help him to get to bed. What a privilege to be trusted in this way. I was, of course, pleased to help him.

A Symbiotic Relationship

Having been both a doctor and patient, during those first few months of recovery I was hopeful the experience would make me a much better doctor. I know as well as anyone that some in the medical profession can be dismissive, or think they are more intelligent than anyone else, regarding arrogance as a virtue. I've known some colleagues to make fun of patients and fob them off. Being on the other side of the fence has made me realize the impact of a doctor's behaviour and words on a patient.

When you are studying medicine, everything is glamorous, like a TV thriller. As a student you have the protection of your seniors then you pass and must cope with the real world. Those doctors who have been through a dramatic time tend to do better. I don't wish to undermine people who went to private schools or who come from rich backgrounds, but they can sometimes come across as entitled.

What we doctors should remember is that usually, a person comes to us because they are not well or at least, they think they are not well so we should treat them with kindness and empathy. What may look trifle to us may be a serious issue in the eyes of the patient. Communication skills are an important element in medical training. Often doctors, with the right approach and reassurance, can themselves be the medicine a patient needs.

As doctors, we deal with uncertainties every day. It is the name of the game. Every diagnosis and management decision involves detection work like putting together a jigsaw puzzle, only the stakes are much higher as we are dealing with human lives.

It is that consciousness that can easily transform into stress if we are not careful. Almost 80% of a diagnosis comes from a patient's history, 10% from examination and the rest from investigations and other work. It is, therefore, vital for all doctors to keep an open mind and take as much detailed history as possible by asking open questions along the lines of ideas, concerns, and expectations. Not surprisingly, many of these principles are also applicable to the hospitality business.

One of the greatest virtues in medicine that can quickly change into a deadly curse is that doctors can become emotionally involved with their patients. I used to be like that. Their pain hurt me, their depression made me pensive, and breaking bad news about a sinister diagnosis affected me the whole day. It took me a long time to get over the death of a patient which would affect me on a personal level.

I was a final year medical student when I started getting house calls from my friends' families at night time. They didn't expect me to treat the patients but as a medical student, thought I would be able to explain to them in a better way their diagnosis and treatment. It was a huge responsibility but a great experience for learning. I was gaining the confidence and respect of my neighbours and my friends' families. They knew they could depend on me at any time.

That was when I experienced my first patient's death. Someone I knew as an uncle and a family friend were suffering from cancer and was terminally ill. The family wanted me to keep him comfortable. He passed away with his hand in mine, a moment I can never forget.

That night, this experience changed my perspective of life and, indeed, of death. The futility of it all dawned on me. Death is the greatest leveller I know. No matter if you are the richest of the rich or poorest of the poor, whether you are highly educated or illiterate, whether you are white, brown, or black, we each die the same and that is the only eternal truth in the universe. This truth didn't scare me, but it did make me reflect that life is a rat race only ending in death. It sounds ridiculous but it is like an onion, as the years go by you keep peeling off the layers until there is nothing. This is why I believe it is vitally important not just to wait for a destination but to enjoy every part of the journey of life too.

There is a fine line between empathy and getting emotionally involved. Every doctor has patients they do or don't like but without boundaries, you couldn't cope when someone dies. This doesn't prevent you from having feelings. I understood this more when fate took me to the other side of the fence when I became a patient myself or even more so as the attendant of a family member as a patient.

Every experience can challenge and shape the individual, to influence, in a positive way, their persona. To benefit, all it takes is an open mind. Nothing should be wasted. I feel privileged to have the opportunity to continually nurture this side of my character. Improving yourself is never-ending. Make the most of it.

Personal Loss

'I'm bleeding,' said my wife Mili. Something was wrong. I didn't want to acknowledge it but straight away I felt this wasn't good news. Sometimes being a doctor can be quite cruel as you tend to know the worst before it happens.

Mili was three months pregnant. Her face was pale, her eyes were grief-stricken and in horror as she too, feared the worst.

Only three weeks earlier we had realized she was carrying our first child. I was over the moon, and couldn't have been any happier. I just prayed for a healthy child but yes, I was a little biased as silently, I also said a prayer asking for a daughter. I always wanted a girl.

As a gift to Mili, I organized a holiday to Paris, meant to be the most romantic city in the world. She was happy, I was happier.

We walked through the city, we lay under the moonlit sky near the Eiffel Tower, and we kissed and held each other in our arms to welcome the new chapter in our lives - a family.

I had my training rotation, I had a lovely wife, and now I was going to be a father. How blissful life was!

We returned to London and there she was with bloodstains on her dress and complaining of feeling unwell. I took her straight from the airport to A&E and was promptly seen by my gyne colleagues. Mili had miscarried. We had lost our baby. A dream decimated in front of our eyes, turning our heights of elation into the depths of depression.

Mili was inconsolable. Which mother-to-be wouldn't be? She said sorry and wept in my arms. But we were together and as husband and wife, vowed to carry on. Life will bring us another life that we'd be waiting to receive at the right time. That day still feels like yesterday.

Since then, I have always been more sympathetic to women patients who suffer miscarriages. As doctors even if we can make a little positive difference, it could change the world for them. Also, fathers are often forgotten in such situations, but they suffer too, and we need to be aware.

Today I'm a proud father of two girls and love every minute but can't help wondering what happened to our first child. It still feels like yesterday.

Many patient stories have inspired me, affected me deeply and even changed my way of practice. Here's one example; a lovely lady who had a profound effect on me.

'I have miscarried again' my patient stuttered, with swollen, wet eyes. She has been crying for a while. This was, not once or twice, but the seventh time that she had undergone the trauma of miscarriage. As I stood up to welcome her to the consultation room, I felt so sorry for her. What has she done to deserve this? She was a lovely lady, one of my best patients.

There was little I could offer her medically. She knew that. She was already under the care of renowned gynaecologists. I expressed my empathy and asked her if I could do anything, being careful not to pity her. That was the last thing she needed.

She said that she hadn't shared the news of the latest pregnancy with her husband, to avoid him experiencing more disappointment but she had to share her sorrows with someone. As her doctor and as a fellow human she found comfort in sharing her grief with me. It was then I realized, yet again, how the analogy of a doctor as a drug holds true and that I may be able to make her feel better, on the one hand not doing anything yet managing to do everything for her. I felt so privileged and inspired by this lady's resilience in the face of suffering. Indeed, pain may be inflicted but how much we suffer depends on how we react to these curveballs in life.

I'm delighted to say that today she is a proud mother of a healthy baby girl after an almost miraculous eighth pregnancy. She thanked me for being a part of her life and for being with her through her most difficult journey when she felt emboldened with every consultation, she had with me. I am pleased that I was there for her. I didn't do much except just listen and reassure. While she was my patient I witnessed her suffering, how much a human being can endure.

She gave her daughter a name that carries the same meaning as my name (Bhaskar means the sun), in her native language.

What more could I have asked for from my vocation as a doctor? Now when I think of her, her resilience helps me in my difficult moments.

A chance meeting on my last flight to London from New Delhi has had a similar, lasting impact on me. Rimy is a most amazing young lady in her early forties with an implanted cardiac defibrillator, following a massive cardiac arrest some 13 years ago. She has been since awaiting a heart transplant but with her associated medical conditions, doesn't stand much of a chance. She gets shocked every few weeks when her heart goes into an abnormal rhythm. She has been told by her cardiologist to not expect a long life.

This lady is not allowed to work, she is not allowed to fall pregnant and, to top it all, her husband left her for another younger girl because he couldn't 'withstand the pressure'.

What, however, was most striking was how remarkably smiley and happy she was. She told me everything as if just narrating a comic story. I told her mine too.

I was awed by her appreciation of life and her positivity. How she is bent on celebrating all the remaining moments of her life and smiling her way to death. And she insisted she was inspired by me! What the universe throws at us, we cannot control but how we react to these curve balls defines our life and who we are.

We tend to think deeply before making big decisions but it's the small, sometimes impulsive, reactions that define our character and strength. As the saying goes, when the going gets tough, only the tough get going. We come alone, we will go alone, leaving all the highs and lows behind. When it's dark even our shadow leaves us alone. We must fight our own battles every time.

When there's much to live for and so little time, I don't have a moment to lose, being sad. Do you?

I have been a doctor to many palliative care patients and have seen them die. After two decades of medicine, I still can't help feeling upset about every patient I've lost. I have been told by many a colleague that this is just part of the job but I'm glad that I never got used to this aspect of my profession. Maybe that's what kept me human. I believe to be a good doctor, for that matter a good anything, you first need to be a good human being.

Do Your Best, Be Your Best

My dad always said, whatever you do in life, do your best and be the best. I had always wanted to be a surgeon, nothing else. But all dreams don't come true. After pursuing surgery for three years, my next jobs were in Birmingham instead of London. Mili had just secured her dream financial job in London and was pregnant again after the traumatic miscarriage. I didn't have the heart to leave her alone. Nothing is more important than family and sometimes you get more happiness by supporting others in fulfilling their dreams than by fulfilling yours. I'd be lying if I said I wasn't upset but with the bigger picture in perspective, I was happy.

Even so, I now wonder whether I gave up on my dream too easily; perhaps I should have fought for a place in London.

My practical decision, to join the General Practice training rotation, was met with incredulity from my orthopaedic colleagues who commented, 'So now you're going to play golf and send all your patients to the hospital?' Is that what he thought about GPs? If this was the case, I promised myself I would be better than their perceptions.

To succeed in my new ambition, I had the good fortune to join the Lewisham GP training rotation where my mentor and trainer, Dr Girish Malde, was not only my professional guide but became a lifelong idol. He trained me in every aspect of General Practice and entrepreneurship. To him, I owe all I have learned and achieved. I am grateful, too, to have trained with some of the most brilliant colleagues.

Three months into my Registrar year, I began to panic about finding a job and supporting my family. Back then I didn't know anything about locums, or that this can be a financially more lucrative option. Having applied for partnership jobs with a 25:1 success ratio, I then met another miraculous man Dr Stephen Langley who invited me for an interview to join a rural dispensing practice partnership. With the help of my trainer, I prepared a business plan and presented it to the interviewing panel, backed by the aim of modernizing the practice and increasing income. Perhaps it was divine luck, but he decided there and then to wait for eight months for me to finish my training and then join him as a partner.

Dr Langley turned out to be my hero, a father figure who took me under his wings, helping me to thicken my skin, build up my network, and support me in every aspect of modernizing the practice. He is retired now, and I never got the chance to thank him properly.

One sure way to success is always to work longer than you are paid. This approach helps in two ways. One is that you enjoy your work more and second you add further value to your worth and make yourself indispensable.

Not that I did everything right all the time. It's true, I got told off a few times for my impulsiveness and impatience. But it always felt like a father disciplining his son. Dr Langley and I worked hard together, enjoying our medicine, our work, and our chats, and in the process increased the registered patient list size from 3,800 to 16,400 and the business turnover from £480,000 to almost £2 million. What an amazing journey!

So, you might be surprised to know that insecurity has always been a part of my life. At the same time, it has been my driver. When I was a GP registrar, I had various exams to complete before the end of the training after which I start looking for jobs. This isn't how I went about my career, however. I was so worried about not having a job at the end of my post-graduate training that I appeared for my exit exams two months into my final year and started applying for jobs. Luckily, I passed and, with eight months of my training remaining, secured a good role as a GP Partner. My colleagues thought I was mad!

Ambition is ingrained in me. But this changed the day I left the surgery. Having felt destined to become a top surgeon, now my mission was to become a partner, then a senior partner, to make money, and to be successful in business. And I was. To be honest, I felt deprived of my ambition to become a surgeon and an academic the day I gave up my surgical rotation, taking, instead, the next practical option, to make money for my family.

My day-to-day role may have changed but being the best is about beating yourself the whole time. Nothing should be beneath us, regardless of role. Only last Tuesday I was taking an order when a customer praised me for being a good waiter. That comment caused my brain to click into action: paradoxically I have gone from being a doctor to a waiter. Even so, given such a compliment, I must be doing the job well. After all, it's not about being the best, but doing your best, whether that is washing glasses in a restaurant or being a doctor. I haven't always been the best, but I always try to do my best.

Unfortunately, the world only looks to winners, and I want to be a winner. More importantly, I want my daughters to be winners, but they also need to learn to appreciate their journey towards winning. They know that irrespective of whether they are winners, if they have done their best, I will always be with them. I also instil in my family another mantra from my dad: sincerity and honesty eventually always payout. I certainly hope so.

For me, physical hindrance is not a barrier to doing my best. And while rebuilding my life I continue to recall past patients and the inspiration they, unknowingly, instilled in me. Who knows, maybe I, too, have unknowingly inspired people. Surely every day we each have the chance to leave a positive mark on others. Making that a mantra could well be the best way to start each morning.

We often think about the past and worry about the future, but we forget to appreciate what lies in the present. Let our past be the bricks and our present be the cement for the building of our future.

Chapter Five Read the Signs

Too busy to appreciate my blessings during the good times, too preoccupied to live in the present, sometimes a calamity is needed to stimulate an emotional evolution. Often, we take the good things for granted and remember only the bad. But our inner voice is always there to guide us - we just need to listen.

Courage to Break the Pattern

When pain travels through generations, it is up to the individual to create the courage, to grasp the opportunity, to break that pattern.

My grandfather was a 'Zamindar', a title conferred by the British Raj to tax collectors. As such he was like the headman of the village as well as the richest. He died before I was born so I miss the love of a grandfather. I know that he used to lend money to poor farmers in their time of need and return or when they couldn't pay back, he would receive their land. Whether or not that was ethical I don't know but he did amass a lot of lands, probably more than 500-600 acres and, along with it, probably a lot of curses too, from poor people who, in losing their property, also lost their livelihood.

All these lands were passed on to the next generation of sons and daughters and I am sad to say that, in my family, hardly any of them did well in their lives except living by selling off those inheritances. My father was the only one who went on to complete a master's degree and earns his livelihood. Four of my uncles, as well as my dad, eventually died from strokes. My paternal family is plagued with numerous chronic illnesses. It makes me wonder whether any of this is connected to the curses of those poor people - karma maybe? In Hinduism, we believe that not only your deed from this life matter but also your deeds from your past lives also influence your present. I am grateful to my dad who educated me to depend not on any inheritance but to stand on my own feet.

The man who taught me independence, sincerity and hard work unfortunately never had much peace in his own working life or with his health. All my childhood I saw him work hard, but he would always be stressed, often bringing his frustrations home where he could be insufferable. Although he never let his attitude affect his fatherhood in any way, it was sad to see him suffering the way he did. It was this continuous stress which led to high blood pressure and then eventually to a massive stroke. During the 21 years my dad survived following his stroke, he was helpless and dependent on us. The person who made all the mature family decisions became a stubborn child. He could never accept his disabilities, and this made him more and more frustrated. My mum bore the brunt of it all, but she never complained. It was so painful to see his suffering that I just wanted it to end.

For years one of my main worries was what would happen if my mum died before my dad. The repercussions would have been immense, not least sourcing 24/7 care for him. The occasion I didn't worry about this was when I was in denial which is a useful short-term strategy to get over your worries. Denial can be healthy in small doses if you are aware of it.

Now I see the empty chair where he sat for most of those 21 years following his stroke and miss him badly. I am a father myself now, but I will forever miss him as a son. How lucky I have been to have a father like him.

When a loved one dies, they take part of you with them forever, but they never leave you completely. It is for us to decide how we celebrate their life and remember them.

Road Trips: Mirroring Life's Detours

Mili and I agree on two important things in our lives – travelling and pets. We had promised ourselves that as soon we could afford to, we would travel the world, and learn about new places and new cultures. Travel broadens your horizons and the more you know about other cultures, the more you respect them.

So, after a few boring, all-inclusive beach holidays, we decided to be a little more adventurous and go on road trips. Once we set the pattern, we haven't stopped. When I couldn't walk or drive, I prayed to God to give me the strength to be able to drive again. The desire of being able to get back on those road trips was one of the biggest motivations to get better. I was unable to drive for almost seven months, a time when I was entirely dependent on Mili or Uber drivers. What a frustrating period. Up until then, I hadn't appreciated the importance of driving and the independence it offers.

With this life-changing injury, I had to learn to walk, drive, write, and even how to hold knives and forks. But the thought of getting back to normal was a strong driving force. Being normal is probably the hardest thing in the world. What an irony that everyone strives to be extraordinary when all I want is to be normal.

If we don't do what we can't do, it is okay but if we don't do what we can do, life cannot be lived to the full. I always wanted a full life and to die without regrets.

Our first big road trip was in Iceland and what a trip that was. One of the most beautiful countries, Iceland is a photographer's paradise. For eight days we drove, stopping in a different part of the country every night, off the beaten track. From log cabins to boats to huts, it was just awesome. The whole family, together in the car, with no Wi-Fi, no screens, just us talking to one another, is the best form of family bonding. Not knowing what our next route would be, our next accommodation, brought a great sense of adventure. Many a time I lost my way which meant it took us longer to reach our next destination, yet those detours gave us insight into more beautiful places and made the journey even more enjoyable.

Doesn't the same apply to life? It isn't unusual to have to take detours but if we keep being receptive, positive, and grateful those detours may bring unexpected rewards that we wouldn't have otherwise ever encountered.

I am probably on such a detour right now yet to find the reason why and what will it bring, I know for sure that I need to remain positive, keep an open mind and be receptive to any clues given by life.

Another beautiful country for a road trip is Norway, a place of astounding natural scenery and lovely people. While on our trip there, I realized that many roads ended up at fjords where you must wait for a ferry to cross. One day, having become rather adventurous, we were delayed and missed the last ferry. On top of that, our satnav didn't work. What were we to do? There was no choice but to retrace our steps and find another way to reach our destination. So, we drove with the girls in the back. It was getting dark and there was light snow. The moon was shining brilliantly and its reflection on the landscape was so dramatic I thought if heaven is a real place, it must look something like this. We kept driving through the tunnels, not knowing if we were on the right track. By now it was getting quite late, and the girls were hungry and tired. We were alone car in a foreign land, late at night with two small children. As much as I enjoyed the drive, I was starting to feel a bit scared. Eventually, after asking at a few shops and knocking on a few doors, we arrived at our log cabin site around 11 pm. What a relief!

That was quite an experience, one which caused some anxiety but also filled me with confidence that, no matter what, with perseverance, we would eventually reach our destination.

My daughters have been to 37 countries so far, most of which as road trips. Not bad I suppose, when you are 15 and 11-year-olds.

My elder daughter, Angelina, keeps travel diaries and has a map on which she adds pins to indicate the places we have visited. She is equally fond of travelling and is my research mate when we meticulously plan each road trip. What a wonderful father-daughter time!

Our last trip was just before the operation after which everything went wrong, and we are all lagging behind schedules. We need to get back on the road again!

I used to take photos while travelling but this evolved into travelling for photography. I developed a passion for outdoor photography and that is one thing that has kept me sane during my most troubled days. Photography can be such a creative art, the next best thing to paint. You must compose the picture in your head and develop editing skills as well. Our road trips became the best opportunities for photography and over the last few years, I have gathered around 20,000 images.

Waiting to restart these road trips is a big motivator for me to get better. I dream of showing people this beautiful world through my lenses, while also having great family bonding time together.

Meanwhile, I sometimes manage to get out with my camera, just around the local neighbourhood or a short drive away to take pictures. I love being creative.

If you have the spirit and are prepared to pursue that spirit, you can fulfil your dreams. In contrast to the usual cliché, I believe, as Buzz Aldrin says, 'The sky is not the limit'.

Strengths - v – Weaknesses

Some people might say I am impulsive, and I wouldn't disagree. I suppose what they mean is that I make decisions quickly, maybe sometimes too quickly. To succeed in life, it is important to keep an open mind and be engaged with change, if not be the initiator. Change is the only constant in this universe so we cannot afford to be averse to it. Often those decisions led by our gut instincts are the right ones and wasting too much time pondering over a decision lead to procrastination and lost opportunities. Nine times out of ten this has been my strength but, at times, it has also been my weakness, particularly when I have, too readily, trusted the wrong people.

One thing I've learnt in life is to never say 'No' to anything, at least not in the first instance. Instead, listen to what the other person has to say, study, analyze and then make your decision. Keeping an open mind and the inclination to say 'Yes', can open many doors. Not all of them will be successful but it will increase the probability. It is said, if we haven't failed, we haven't tried enough. Following this principle in real life, I have been able to invest in various entrepreneurial ventures and acquired some failing businesses which, in time, gave good returns. However, this approach also manifested itself in an unwillingness to turn down work; hence I often ended up with a much greater workload than my partners.

One big problem I used to have was the inability to delegate. I much preferred doing jobs, particularly the important ones, myself, rather than relying on others, particularly after several experiences of tasks with strict deadlines not being met. Inevitably in situations such as these, I resorted to doing the task which was much easier than chasing others. Now, however, since I have recognized my limitations due to my disabilities, I'm much better at delegating and getting results.

Progress in one area, however, doesn't prevent questions from repeating themselves over and over in my mind: Why did all this happen to me?

What will happen now? Will I ever get better? How am I now going to cater for my family, for my parents? How will I survive if I'm not able to work? Ever since my first operation, hundreds of questions such as these have filled my mind leaving me helpless to find any answers. To begin with, these issues drained my mind like the dementors in a Harry Potter movie. The future resembled a blank blackboard. I still had to make the remainder of my life worthwhile. But how?

Let's stop for a moment and look back a little. Remember when I was in Wellington Hospital? One day, while lying in bed waiting for my next physiotherapy session, I stared through the wide window in my room. It was cloudy and drizzling. Everything felt depressing. For several weeks, I had been in this London hospital, mostly by myself, with bundles of thinking time. Then suddenly, something happened, the sun came out and I saw a rainbow. How wonderful it was! At the same time, something clicked in my mind. Maybe this was life's clue echoing the Dire Straits song playing on my smartphone: 'There will be sunshine after rain, there shall be laughter after pain, so why worry now?' Indeed, this was just the inspiration I needed. I had listened to that song hundreds of times but never was a more apt moment than this. The sunshine took away the blank blackboard that, up to moments earlier, had been my future and filled me with some strange happiness that all was not lost. This was not the end; in fact, this was the beginning of something new, a new purpose in my life that went beyond earning money and degrees. The purpose of making my life useful for others and to be an example for my children. To be a good father, a good husband, a good brother, a reliable friend, and a good son. From the depths of despair, my thoughts arose like a phoenix from the burning fire. I felt alive again.

You've probably gathered by now that I'm good at analyzing, a skill that comes with a reflective nature. Yet strangely, I can't love myself and this is one of my biggest drawbacks. Why do I wonder? I've been hard on myself since childhood. Even my brother says he can't remember the last time I enjoyed anything. I always believed I had a good deal of potential but have not achieved that potential. I was quite an accomplished artist but was unable to continue. I wanted to be a top surgeon and, as a surgeon, I wanted to write papers, as some of my peers have done, but things in life took me away from reaching that potential. Then, when I became a GP, I decided to be a good one, compensating for my other dreams by instead earning good money and being a compassionate doctor. Indeed, at one point I was earning ten times more than when I first started work in the UK.

I've always tried to prove things to myself, and others. I realize now that unless you love yourself, you cannot love others. Even on a plane, you are advised to put on your oxygen mask first before attempting to help someone else. Mili is good at this, but I always put myself last. This attitude finds its way into all aspects of my life, even shopping. I can never buy clothes for myself but love choosing outfits for Mili, Mum and the girls.

Remember the incident at school which scarred me for life? Having come second in the class for two years in a row, an achievement of which I was proud, my headteacher castigated me for, in his words, being 'second class all your life. And there I was, thinking I had done well. At the same time, this world only remembers winners, the first ones, which is why I told myself, 'I must be a winner, no matter what.

At the end of year 10, I wanted to move to another educational institution. This would have meant moving away and mom and dad said I was too young to be away from home. The decision derailed me. But, of course, it wasn't the end.

Unexpected decisions often create defining situations. Now I realize that while winning is important it is not everything. The effort, the attitude, and the journey towards becoming a winner are equally or perhaps, even more important. Unfortunately, this is often overlooked. Coming second is not a bad thing, it is vital to keep things in the context of the bigger picture and be appreciative.

Taking things to heart is, I believe, a weakness. At times I have been an emotional fool. Yet emotional intelligence helps me better understand others and therefore build relationships. If I talk to a stranger for 15 minutes or more, they often like me. I am quickly able to establish a rapport, which is how I have made so many friends. I'm also a typical Cancer: emotional, creative (though creativity was, for a while, dormant), artistic, and faithful, and when someone hurts me, my instinct is to return to my shell. It takes a while before I emerge.

I want to stress again something I learned from my dad, as well as my postgraduate mentor, Dr Girish Malde, that you should never say 'No' to anything, at least not in the first instance. What a strength this is. Whenever an opportunity came along, for instance, a failing practice, I would always try to find out more details then, nine times out of ten, I would take it on. This gave me a good return on investment. On the downside, it also culminated in an increased workload. Colleagues would sometimes comment about how I would undertake tasks that I was paying others to do. Why? Yes, we're back to delegating, more specifically how I used to find this challenging. When you tell people once, let alone twice, it is sometimes easier to do things yourself. After all, staff will be staff. I want to foster good relations with those who work for me, but workers and entrepreneurs are different people, with different attitudes. Now I am better at delegating and have taught my managers this skill. To succeed you need confidence, but beware, confidence without clarity is dangerous.

You need to be popular to be effective but as a manager or a boss, it is not always possible to be popular and effective at the same time. As I have already stressed, an inability to say 'No' led me to suffer more than anybody else. It also led to the other person not gaining insight. My business partner, whom I eventually had to ask to leave, was with me for three years; if I had been firmer, I could have sorted out the situation much quicker and in a better way. As an employer, I hired and fired a lot of people as a part of my job. It is always hurtful when you must dismiss someone, but the organization needs to come first, and sometimes harsh decisions need to be taken in the interests of the business.

To be successful or even useful, it's important to optimize the use of individual skills and, most importantly, our brain. Generally, at any time we use less than half our brain capacity. If we wish, we can use more. Research has shown that we are capable of doing eight things at a time, some can do even more. I have tried to educate my daughters that everyone can do one thing at a time, if you want to achieve, you need to be able to do at least two things - successfully - at a time.

I have always believed I can do two things simultaneously. During my medical career, I would work on a dual monitor screen with another laptop nearby. Between patients, I would check blood results, read a medical article, check the news etc. This distraction helped me focus and kept boredom at bay as well as increased productivity. Our brains have potential but how best to use that potential? It has always fascinated me that Leonardo da Vinci could write with both hands at the same time. If he could, surely lots of others can, too. When cooking I usually have four dishes on the go simultaneously, having first done all my preparation. Multitasking was always and continues to be, a keyword for me.

Looking back, one mistake I made was taking on a new GP and, over a short period, quickly becoming friends. I opened up to him too quickly and then he asked for a partnership. I was worried about taking on a friend as a business partner but going against my gut instincts, I did. He also became a partner in the restaurant, taking a third of everything we made. However, after a rocky three years of ego issues and misunderstandings, I had to tell him that the partnership wasn't working and ask him to leave. This decision created animosity; indeed, he still doesn't have any insight into his shortcomings and entirely blames me. I took him as a true friend and still miss that friendship. But one wrong decision, taken against gut instinct, not only impacted my business but also cost me a friend. That has been one of the worst experiences of my life.

I realize the strength in one situation may be a weakness in another. Or weakness in one person can be seen as a strength in someone else. Such opinions are subjective. I would say not being sociable is one of my weaknesses or am I succumbing to society's expectations, I wonder?

One thing, historically, I wasn't so good at was knowing my limitations. For two decades 15-hour days were the norm, my only breaks being holidays and even they were strenuous with so much driving. I wanted to make the most of my capabilities, I was always in a hurry, always wanting to achieve more. Whether that was the right approach to life I don't know. What I do know is that I have always done my best and I have no regrets. Neither should you as long as you have done your best.

I can, however, recognize strengths and weaknesses in others, just as I can tell whether I click with someone. Before I got married, I was short-tempered but marrying

Mili taught me that one must cool down otherwise there could be fireworks every day! Nowadays people ask how I can be so calm.

I was good at recognizing my strengths but perhaps not so good at identifying my limitations. During my phase of expansion and accumulation of wealth, I had spread myself too thinly and took on so much workload that both my emotional health as well as my work-life balance were affected.

I wanted success at all costs, but I didn't know what defined success for me. We often want to be successful, happy, have a purpose etc. but if someone suddenly asks you what it means for you, very few of us can answer honestly straightaway.

Now I can. For me, success is a state of a peaceful, blissful mind. Success now means a good life for my family and parents, to be able to complete my duties.

In any endeavour we undertake, it is important to be involved not just monetarily and physically but emotionally as well. If you don't know your strengths, you will never grasp opportunities; if you don't know your limitations, you are not safeguarding yourself. It is also important to have clarity and an open mind as the eyes don't see what the brain doesn't know.

I easily get bored. Is this a strength or a weakness? Who knows? What I understand about myself, however, despite this paradox, is that distraction is that it fuels focus and productivity for me. I wouldn't have made a good clerk or accountant where you must carry on repetitive

actions and need a lot of patience. Work is my outlet, my escape; the busier I am, the less frustrated I feel.

Decrypting Life's Clues

Wondering why things happen, trying to figure out the point of everything, and thinking about why I was chosen as the unfortunate victim, is a common distraction. I cannot help pondering that perhaps all those decisions are taken voluntarily or impulsively before my first operation prepared me for what was to happen to me from the moment I woke up. Were the cryptic clues already there and I just didn't realize?

The thought of my parents dying and leaving me alone used to scare me a lot. I couldn't bear to face it. But one thing I knew: I wanted my dad to die before my mum. Otherwise, how would he have managed without her? In retrospect, I feel as though, for years, life has been preparing me for their loss. Working as a doctor, particularly with elderly and palliative care patients, witnessing people pass away made me realize the vulnerability of life. We come naked and alone, we go away the same. All the rest is a rat race with no finishing line. Rich or poor, scholar or illiterate, spiritual or atheist, everyone ends up the same. Heaven and hell are all illusions as no one has been there and back to tell us exactly what they are like. All my reading and reflections have taught me that heaven and hell are here. They are upon us; which one we work towards is the most important decision to be made.

My mindset has also been influenced by the reading I have done over the past two years which has affected me in other positive ways, giving me a different perspective on many topics. Along with this development, my personal experience has changed my outlook, making me a much broader thinker than before. And maybe more philosophical.

Life needs to be big, not long. We should live and not just exist on this planet. More importantly, we need to live every day, every moment, because we never know when the next turn will come and what it will bring.

Our psyche is such that we tend to remember the bad, sad things more than the good, happy things which have happened to us. We can easily hate but it takes an active effort to love. In this short life, if we occupy our minds with hate, jealousy and self-pity, there won't be much time left to be happy, grateful, and loved. I know it sounds clichéd but trusts me, my life-changing events have changed my perspective of life. I am weaker physically, and poorer financially but these reflections have, most likely, made me a better person and given me more happiness and peace of mind.

I am a Hindu. Though not a fastidious one, I keep God in my heart. This helps me understand that, even though the Almighty gives you problems, he gives you solutions as well. The solutions may, however, not always be apparent at the time and this can culminate in frustration. On the other hand, there have been occasions when I have been in deep despair and asked for a miracle from the core of my heart and it has happened.

One of the things about medicine is that you are always dealing with uncertainties. Through my own life's uncertainties, I am now better prepared to face the future, however unexpected it might be. In the past, I didn't always appreciate those good times, I do now. Experiences, reflection, and reading have improved my insight and I now have a heightened sense of awareness in decrypting life's clues.

I am sometimes asked, given that my trauma occurred in the UK if I've ever been tempted to leave the country and return to India. This has never been a consideration. Partly because back home, everyone would be pitying me. But also, I have never been angry with the doctor responsible; he has merely taken me from one chapter of my life to another. What happened to me wasn't good, yet it must have happened for a reason, and I need to be receptive with gratitude towards anything that comes my way in the future, always making the most of opportunities and circumstances. Besides, the UK is one of the more disabled-friendly countries and, for the last 20 years, has given me bread and butter so I have nothing against it. Miracles are all around us, but you must be open, receptive to opportunities and decrypt them. Some people aren't sufficiently sensitive to recognizing opportunities, their risk-averse approach to life forcing them to decline every opportunity. I suggest keeping an open mind then you can always decline once you know the details. Unless you take a little bit of risk, you won't achieve anything so go for it, strategize, and then work hard and smart.

Acceptance

The key to acceptance is honesty. Without being honest with yourself, yourself, it is impossible to accept a situation and your place within it.

My symptoms are likely to deteriorate. According to experts, I have at most a dozen years left when I will be able to walk after which I will be confined to a wheelchair. The likelihood of incontinence means I am likely to need full-time care at some point. This is quite a blow yet at the same time gives me greater motivation and a more defined target in which to make something of my life.

As a doctor, I mentored a patient who became a clinical psychologist. She told me about acceptance therapy. For me, acceptance came early so, too, an appreciation of the things around me. But what would I achieve by moaning about what had happened? I had to keep going, to accept what had happened.

Reading about heroes or people experiencing immense difficulties helps me understand there is a reason behind everything that happens - be it scientific or supernatural - which cannot necessarily be explained.

I recently read about a quadruple amputee. Such loss is unimaginable isn't it, yet what an inspirational story. While this and others' stories motivate me, I won't pretend how uncomfortable it is that my lack of independence means, of course, having to rely on other people. It has also been difficult witnessing the pressure on my wife. And we are no longer able to enjoy any intimacy. This doesn't seem fair to her.

And don't think I calmly accept my limitations. On the contrary, certain things continue to frustrate me. For instance, I can't walk from one end of a superstore to another. My legs just won't carry me. Also, the cold affects me a lot so walking through the freezer section in Superstores is extremely painful.

'Get a buggy,' my neurologist suggested. Well, that's quite a change from driving a sports car!

I had already traded my BMW for a wheelchair and a more user-friendly SUV, but a mobility buggy seems a step too far. I'm still too handsome for that! (May I share a confession? I bought that BMW Z4 sports convertible one lunchtime when I went out to buy a sandwich but instead got sidetracked by a car dealership. I didn't tell Mili!)

No, I don't want to give in yet. I walk with crutches whenever I can and try to be part of the whole family thing although I do need a wheelchair most of the time. But we need to be prepared for everything so when it is time for a buggy, that's what will have to be.

Meanwhile recognizing progress, even baby steps, is important and applies to every aspect of life and career. Physically I have improved. From being unable to get out of bed on my own, now I am mobile for short distances using crutches and, thanks to an automatic car, seven months after my first operation I began driving again. I realize further progress is unlikely unless, of course, there's a miracle - you never know!

Meanwhile, as I said earlier, I have been told by experts that, as age advances, my symptoms will worsen with the likelihood that I will be confined to a wheelchair and need an indwelling urine catheter long-term, in no more than a decade or so. I need hardly say that this is not something I look forward to gleefully but on the other hand, I have been given a time-bound purpose to fulfil my responsibilities and my bucket list, something for which I am grateful.

Acceptance is the beginning of a process, one which may be lengthy but vital. My father never accepted what happened to him. Although at times happy and satisfied, he never allowed himself to become independent and never fought to return to normality. This attitude manifested itself in pressure on my mum. Looking back, perhaps we weren't stern enough with Dad, we should have encouraged him to do things on his own. Instead, he became desolate and extremely dependent on my mum, which in turn, affected her health. I used to tell him that Mum cannot do everything all the time. He'd agree but the next day he would be the same. I was always pushing him, and we talked all the time about trying harder. It was amazing that he could speak normally but he had experienced a massive bleed in his brain that must have affected him in ways we don't understand. His temperature control veered from one extreme to the other, he would either have a blanket or a fan.

Or perhaps my father was afraid of trying. After all many people would not be able to accurately define what it is that makes them afraid, limits their goals, and influences their relationships. Here, we're back to acceptance. Recognizing any of these things begins with acceptance. You must be prepared for that process to evolve.

One evening I was sitting behind my bar, down and depressed and unsure of the future yet again when Liam, my Assistant Manager, asked, 'Why are you looking so down?' Without meeting his gaze, I replied, 'It is circumstances that have brought me down. His answer was, 'No, you are letting circumstances bring you down, you are better than this. I looked at him and realized he was right. I was indeed letting myself be dictated by my circumstances. His words were so true and so apt to the situation that I will always remember them. Liam is a realist and pragmatic. We enjoy our worldly conversations. I think if there were more people like Liam in this world, there wouldn't be any racism at all and I'm thankful for his company.

There are certain things you can't change so what is the point in dissipating your energy on them? Instead, focus your energy on what you can do to change those elements of your life which are changeable. This has been my mantra. I have become no wiser over the last couple of years, but I have seen more of life and had more experiences than many of my peers. Coupled with memories of my father's reaction to his stroke, and numerous inspirational books, I have made it my mission to concentrate my energy on the elements of my life that I am still able to influence.

That isn't to say I don't have days when I feel down though Mili is the only person to see my negative side. If I need to moan, I do so to her. She has seen me as a motivational person, these days she accepts I am not the man I once was.

As well as letting off steam to Mili, I have another coping mechanism. As I hinted at earlier, sometimes the only way to deal with things is denial. I reckon this is a survival instinct, something to balance with reality. Being a medical person, I know my pains will worsen with age. What I don't know is how long I will be able to carry on. What bothers me most is the financial aspect of our lives. Even now with a property portfolio, I'm currently cash poor. On the other hand, I accept my permanent disability and want to use this as a cause to help others. Despite the UK being one of the most disabled-friendly countries, there is still a lack of understanding so I would like to make people aware of the emotional aspects of being disabled. I thank God I have not had to ask anyone for money.

Yet I have never been able to accept why bad things seem to happen more often to good people. Why do the good, honest people in life tend to suffer more? Why are some things so unjustified? Why of all people did my dad have to go through what he did? As my acceptance came in stages, I realized how much my dad had suffered over 21 years. At least I can now drive for short distances. Perhaps he gave up rather than fighting. What a lesson I have learned from him.

Maybe without my life-changing trauma, I would not have been so open, nor sufficiently honest, to share my innermost thoughts to help others.

Fighting for yourself is a necessity in the struggle for existence. Fighting for others is a passion that gives you a purpose

Chapter Six

The Present, The Future

We often worry about the future and reflect on the past, omitting to notice what's right in front of us.

Responding to Struggles

Everyone faces struggles in life, it is how we react to those struggles that counts.

Most of the time, inevitably, we all take things for granted. Only when you have lost the use of part of your body do you realize how much you are losing? So many things in life we take for granted, simple things such as walking and driving. Two years down the line I still can't walk properly and have little dexterity in my right dominant hand. I can't afford private physiotherapy regularly so have been doing my own. The pain is worse when I must exert myself or in cold weather or if my emotional state is vulnerable.

I have been told by experts that I have probably reached the peak of my recovery and things are not going to get any better than my current status. What's more, they say that as I get older my symptoms will probably deteriorate. Like my father and uncles, I also have high blood pressure, and this does not respond to medication. I am, I realize, a ticking time bomb. Even so, I must still be joyful for the days I have left.

During the first few months following my trauma Mili and I often talked until a point when I was so depressed and irritable, our conversations veered off course as she had difficulty understanding my mindset, unable to recognize any hope. Sometimes conversations started with how we would cope only to end up self-pitying. This is difficult to explain in words. Perhaps many a time we didn't delve deeply enough. Thankfully, these days our conversations are more mature.

But I have accepted and have tried to rise above all of that. The only thing, however, that continues to worry me is my financials, which are certainly not what they used to be, and I still have not been able to solve that bit of the jigsaw.

I talked about fears in a previous chapter. For me, paralysis was my greatest fear. Paralysis equates to half-death, dependence upon others, and a loss of freedom. That is why I thought it would be for the best if I died rather than be a vegetable. At the same time, I believe I may have unknowingly, subconsciously, prepared myself to face situations such as being dependent on someone. Fear made me more careful, and more prepared although too much preparation can ruin spontaneity.

What I have come to realize, however, is that we all have our fears, fear of uncertainty being the most common. Anything we don't know or understand often translates into fear. We fear death because we don't know what happens when someone dies. It is recognizing your fear and coping with it that defines whether that fear is a limitation or a strength.

Fear, a maker or breaker, is a driver for many people, but it needs to be used positively. The starting point is to recognize and accept your fears.

Sometimes the best way to face your worst fears is to walk through them, if only in your head. To do that you have to let go of your ego and avoid using it as a shield.

It is important to know the impact of our fears on both us and our nearest and dearest. The last thing you want is for fear to become a phobia - that is neither healthy nor helpful. Instead, we should face our fears with a change in attitude, channelling and using them to give us strength. For me, accepting my limitations of mobility and finding ways to adapt accordingly, finding ways to work smart, not just hard, helped me overcome my fears and instead made them my strength.

Perhaps this is the way forward - focusing on our responsibilities rather than those aspects of our lives that are alarming or make us apprehensive.

My children are now my greatest responsibility. Before them, I felt responsible for my parents, particularly following my father's stroke when the sky fell on my head. Of course, from the moment my father-in-law put Mili's hand in mine, I took on responsibility for her, too.

Throughout my life, some small, sometimes seemingly stupid, promises I made to myself helped in maintaining focus during the hardest of times. For instance, after my father's stroke, I promised myself that I wouldn't shave until he could sit upright. I ended up with a long beard, as it took a year before he was able to sit up again. I looked so much like a hippie, a rebel without a cause, I was amazed that Mili accepted me in that condition! Looking at pictures of myself as I was then, I can hardly believe what I looked like but, you know, that small promise kept me focused and motivated to reach my goal.

History does repeat itself it seems. After my spinal cord injury, when I was able to accept my fears, I once again promised myself not to shave or cut my hair until I could take a few steps. Every time I felt my face or saw my reflection in a mirror, I was reminded of my promise which, in turn, empowered my determination. And I could see the results. My beard wasn't quite as wild as the first time, but it was considerably greyer!

The physical change following my operation happened overnight. Mentally and emotionally, I went through all the typical stages of grief. At first, I was angry and upset, asking what I had done to deserve this. Then came fear and questioning my future. For several months I thought I could continue my profession if only part-time; it was the following January that I realized retirement was my only option. Those intervening months caused me harm as staff were putting locum doctors, some I knew, some I didn't, in my place. Then there was a delay in sorting out my pension so financial worries took up a lot of my time back then.

Today I have promised myself to give up something I love very much - all kinds of meat. I have decided to become a vegetarian until I can sort out my financial worries and become abundant again. Crazy as it may seem, there is strength and significance in these self-set goals.

Compartmentalization is a useful skill. To protect myself, I block out some parts of my brain. This was important when working as a doctor; once I left my consulting room, I would never impose my advice on anyone unless they asked. Now, to an extent, I can detach myself from my suffering. People sometimes comment on how I continue to be useful rather than sit at home getting depressed.

The restaurant can survive without me but being there, part of the team is valuable. My staff have even insisted I receive my share of the tips!

I hope the way I have responded to my challenges over the past two years is a positive lesson for my children. Of course, they want to see me in the normal way, the way I used to be, but perhaps even if they don't recognize the lesson that continues to unfold before them now, they will do so when they are older.

Right now, I am less fit and poorer financially compared to how I was. At a spiritual level, however, I am a richer person having learned more about thankfulness and gratitude. Yes, in other ways, I feel I have been cheated. I could have given my family a better life. Physically, I cannot do the things I used to.

If I could turn back the clock, would I decline the operation? Yes. It was the most stupid decision I have ever taken. I put my trust in the doctor, as any patient should, and things happened that shouldn't have. I lost my career, my bread and butter, my physical abilities, nearly everything. But I suppose this was meant to happen. Maybe there is something else being painted on the canvas of my life. I'm still trying to understand what that might be. What I do know is that it must be something good. It had better be!

Meanwhile, cooking remains one of my most therapeutic pastimes, along with books and heavy metal or hard rock music. These days I enjoy classical music as well, two extremes being normal for me!

Desire, Believe, Persevere

Pain is physical and objective, but suffering depends on our reaction and can, therefore, be subjective. Suffering is like a fire that can either burn you to ashes or make you strong like steel. Having read many autobiographies of self-made people, I realize they all talk about their fears and failures, and how these have been overcome. I have fears too, but my plan is for my vulnerability to help others, and for my story to be the motivation to change any adversity into an opportunity.

This transformation came in a strange, unbelievable way too, as if enlightenment, one day during my stay at Wellington Hospital.

Why did all this happen to me? What will happen now? Will I ever get better? How am I now going to cater for my family, for my parents? How will I survive if I'm not able to work? Hundreds of questions like these filled my thoughts and I could not find any answers. I still had to make something worthwhile for the remainder of my life, but how?

In the previous chapter, I mentioned an epiphany while listening to a Dire Straits song playing on my smartphone: 'There will be sunshine after rain, there shall be laughter after pain, so why worry now?' These inspiring words were just what I needed and filled me with the hope of a new purpose in my life; a purpose that replaced earning money with making my life useful for others and being an example to my children.

As goes another cliché, laugh and the world laughs with you, cry and you cry alone. In dark times, how can you expect someone else to be in your shoes? You can't and it's nobody's fault. As another saying goes, only the wearer knows where the shoe pinches. If you must go through something, it's easier to do so with a smile. My staff used to ask how I could still be smiling at the end of a long day. Of course, working at Samsara is hard and tiring but this simple approach makes the job easier and if you enjoy yourself, time goes faster.

I believe the same analogy is relevant for doctors. For me, a patient may be the 45th patient of the day but for that person, he or she is the only one that matters. Often it is hard to understand this because of the circumstances and the pressures we work under but if doctors put ourselves in that person's shoes, only then will we realize what it means. Similarly, in the restaurant each customer thinks he is the only one, that is his expectation. So, in a way, a doctor/patient and a customer service encounter involve the same psychological principles.

Now that I understand what I am going through is going to be a long game, I might as well continue my journey in the best possible way. On the other hand, when I go to bed at night, in pain and unable to sleep for hours, staring at the ceiling, as well as praying for the safety and security of my family I am thankful: 'Another day is done, one day less to live.

All uncertainties and tragedies have a silver lining, however. Looking at the positives, I now have a better life/work balance. My trauma has brought me closer to my wife and children. Before the incident, I didn't know what happiness meant. I'd forgotten how to laugh properly and had become mired in money-making and seeing patients. I was a workaholic and am the only one to blame.

Now I appreciate that small things can make you happy. What does happiness mean? Being different for everyone, it is important to know what it means to you. Personally, right now, happiness is the well-being of my family, supporting Mili and the girls to fulfil their dreams and taking good care of my mother and mother-in-law.

Day by day I'm rebuilding my life. If, while I do so, others are inspired by reading about my experiences and reflections, my motivation for writing The Second Chance in Life will be fulfilled. Sharing my emotions has been therapeutic but, be assured, I don't want to portray myself as someone invincible, nor do I want to sugarcoat anything. In contrast, I'm driven by honesty about my vulnerability, visually sharing them, despite the challenge of reliving some of those moments.

Measuring Wealth

'Why couldn't you be rich? Then I wouldn't have needed to slog so hard and start from scratch?' I annoyingly asked my dad, frustrated at seeing some of my friends living up to the silver spoon cliché, which certainly didn't apply to me. Calmly, my dad responded, 'I am rich. I have two children whom I have been able to educate enough to stand on their own two feet. What more wealth could I have wanted?'

He was right. Of course, he was. Dad was proud, too. At the time I may not have realized it but how blessed I was to be born to parents who toiled hard for us to provide the best, as well as teach us to fight our own battles. We were neither wealthy nor entitled but we were rich in love and closeness. Unlike some, I never had a lift so had to take the stairs. Look at the benefits though: I got to enjoy looking through the window of the world and appreciate every step of life.

My parents gave me the freedom to dream and the strength to pursue those dreams. They instilled in us the ambition to reach for the sky while disciplining us to keep our feet on the ground. If, one day, my daughters ask me, why aren't we rich, I know exactly what to tell them: who can be richer than the one who has freedom and peace of mind?

I didn't anticipate what would happen to me, but I continue to deal with the consequences in a positive way. I am full of gratitude; for me, life, like a glass, needs to be seen always as half full, not half empty.

However, I would be entirely dishonest if I said I never felt resentful. I didn't do anything to deserve what happened to me. I have never shied away from responsibility, have always gone out of my way to help patients and have made sacrifices for my dad, parents, and family. I came to this country as an immigrant with a pittance and became a millionaire having worked my socks off. But everything was taken away from me. I feel I deserved better.

Maybe in the past, I was too money-minded, too career-minded. At the time of writing, I haven't been able to work for two and a half years which disappoints me. If I hadn't created assets at the time when the sun was shining, things would have become even more difficult. Now with those assets, I hope my daughters' education and future are secure.

Just like my father, I have come to measure wealth in terms of my family. I am the father of two beautiful daughters while still recalling the trauma of our loss of our first miscarried baby.

As of now, my restaurant is my biggest financial liability, a liability compounded by the pandemic lockdown. This financial liability, however, is balanced by emotional profitability. I find pleasure in being at Samsara in the evenings, meeting and conversing with customers, helping the staff, making cocktails, and seeing people enjoy themselves. It also gives me a routine and purpose, one that will be even better once it starts paying me some money.

I used to believe wealth equated to happiness but not anymore. My life now revolves around my family; if they are happy, I am happy. When I was in the driving seat, Mili was the one who supported me. Her job gives her independence, and she can financially support her parents. Her employer, Gallup, is a family-friendly organization with a flexible attitude which has been a real blessing for us. When I was dependent on her, her flexible work made a huge difference. I thank all her friends, especially Peggy, who has been so supportive of her and kept her going.

I believe it is important to be thankful and appreciate what you have. Perhaps this is where I was lacking previously. I had success and was always productive with my time, but I wanted more, failing to pause and appreciate what I already had.

Sometimes I think it is more difficult for those who have been successful to lose everything. I worked incredibly hard. What I have since realized is it is not just working hard that matters but working smart and being in the right place at the right time.

When it's sunny, enjoy the sunshine but also use the sunshine to prepare for rainy days.

While I am clutching at straws to discover the next way to earn a living, I believe your earning power doesn't mean you should keep all your monies for yourself.

Giving is important. I always try and help others, and give what I can. The more you give, the more you receive, not always in monetary terms but in blessings and friendships too. This attitude, along with reflection, faith and the role of fate, the value of relationships, keep me grounded.

A Voice for Others

I had a long-held dream of writing a book and whilst in school and college I wrote articles for the local press. I loved the idea of taking a reader on a visual journey. Michael Morpurgo, my favourite writer, is so good at this. Since my trauma, as more and more people suggested sharing my story, I gradually realized this was an opportunity to be a voice for others, particularly given the overwhelmingly positive feedback on my blog http://www.thesecondchanceinlife.com/ and a few posts on social media sites.

My time in the hospital allowed me to think, to plan my future. So, too, the six weeks I spent in India. Until then, I was too busy working. How valuable, I now realize, was this time of reflection.

We make our destiny, and every person has a story. Sometimes we just need to dig a little to find it. I decided this was the time to tell my story. But what about the practicalities? With non-functioning fingers on my right dominant hand, touch typing is a no-go so by typing with one finger, writing this book has been a long marathon rather than a sprint.

Being positive about the future might be tough for many people which is why being a voice for those who have, or are, battling their challenges has become a purpose in my life. I'm doing this both through my book and via motivational speaking, both ventures being immensely satisfying. But Mili? She wasn't so sure, her worries centred around my becoming high profile once more and how this might stimulate more bad luck. But once again I decided to follow my instinct.

As you know by now, I have not been able to overcome either my physical disabilities or financial difficulties. On the other hand, I have managed to conquer depression and emotional negativity. That doesn't mean I don't continue to face days when I feel depressed. Seeing other people walking their dogs, and seeing Mili go for a run every morning, of course, makes me down if not a little envious. But somehow, I have developed a completely different perspective on life. I used to put too much pressure on myself, always trying to be a high achiever, a perfectionist. Winning mattered the most. Now I have a more balanced perspective. Winning remains important but I can appreciate it beyond winning. The journey has become as important as the destination. I have learned to live in the now and become more dignified in failure. Hope is the breath that carries us every day, struggles are how we survive. When you reach rock bottom and the only option is to go forward, but the road is not straight, gratitude and faith are the navigation and headlights to take us through the midst of dark times.

When the journey itself is the destination, when the pain is physical suffering, depending on our reaction, the world can still be a better place with the thought that, despite all adversities, there is always someone worse off. We are still in a better place.

So, let's just carry on doing what we can do best – live life, in the true sense of the word. Easy? No, not at all. But possible.

I share my thoughts and experiences in a bid to help others, never failing to be humbled when people tell me that I have inspired them. Nowadays, I receive plenty of messages from people I have never met or known personally, my writing and my experiences have made a positive difference in their own lives. Everyone's challenges and circumstances are unique. What I want readers to take comfort in is that despite the inevitable sense of isolation when going through difficult times, no one should feel they are alone. Vocalizing thoughts and emotions make them more real. In this book, I have talked, for the first time, about several things that I've experienced. Although painful, this has helped me face my problems. I know I come across as a positive

person but from time to time I am still quite vulnerable in terms of depression, and a lack of clarity for the future. But one of the first things is to know your problem, only then can you solve that problem.

Before my operation, I probably wouldn't have thought myself capable of writing like this, but I hope this book proves how much I must give. If I can be a voice for others who are experiencing crises, then that is my mission.

Recently a female medical colleague wrote to me to say how my writings inspired her to carry on running the last few miles of the London marathon when she was fatigued and suffering from cramps. One other colleague, who was suffering from depression due to forced medical retirement following an amputation, had now decided to overcome his depression and revived woodwork talents as his path of expression. What wonderful art he is now beginning to create!

The best yet is when another person, who had been going through a tough time in her career due to medical complications and had been depressed, travelled from Yorkshire to London with her husband, to meet me in my restaurant. She told me how my words have opened a new perspective on life for her. Since then, we have formed a good friendship and I promise to help her in every way possible.

When I originally shared the experience of our miscarriage, I was surprised when more than 30 women felt inspired to open up about their own experiences of going through similar or worse traumas, experiences they had kept bottled up for years. They insist I have become their grieving voice. Many also wrote to me saying that they hadn't considered the impact of a tragic occurrence such as a miscarriage on the father-to-be. Some of those experiences were profound. Whether I had inspired them or not, they have made a deep impact on my life.

I have been helped by so many genuinely miraculous people during my hours of need. Many of those appeared in a flash and disappeared before I could express my gratitude, so my work in being able to help inspire others is redemption and thanksgiving to those heroes. I may not be a practising doctor anymore, at least not now, but it feels awesome that I can still make people better in other ways. Blessed am I for having been given this second chance in life.

I am also open and receptive to advice, from which I have often benefited. Whether or not I follow that advice all the way is another matter as sometimes it might be

trumped by my gut instinct, my inner voice.
Nevertheless, there is nothing to lose by listening. If we
can train our subconscious mind via visualization,
affirmation, and positive reinforcement, most of the time
our gut instinct and inner voice will lead us in the right
direction.

Linked with this is the ability, or willingness, to ask for
help. This is something, years ago, that was alien to me.
Did my ego get in the way? Did I see it as a sign of
weakness? Let's be honest, we cannot do everything
ourselves. Now if, after several tries, I cannot do what
needs to be done, I ask for help.

Motivational Speaking

As a doctor, I influenced many lives. My audience may
now differ, but I remain determined to be a positive
influence on others.

With the sort of social media and blog
(www.thesecondchanceinlife.com and
www.drbhaskarbora.com) following I mentioned in the
previous section, I have been greatly encouraged by
numerous medical and non-medical colleagues, friends,
and family to explore a new career as a writer and
motivational speaker. Will I be able to, do you think?

Maybe your feedback and reviews will answer my question.

During my time as a doctor, as well as a mentor, appraiser, and education lead, I was charged with the responsibility of hosting monthly education events for GPs and nurses in the area. That role gave me a huge opportunity to rid myself of my fear of public speaking. In fact, with experience, I became a good public speaker, soon realizing how naturally I connected with an audience and going on to host several public events with high attendance and feedback that my talks were engaging and enjoyable.

As I mentioned in Chapter Three, evolution is always better and longer lasting than revolution. My physical change happened overnight, followed by an emotional change a few days later. As soon as I knew I could not walk, something clicked in my mind; I was determined not to make myself as dependent on others as my dad. That motivation happened almost immediately. Now I want to use my experiences to motivate others.

I do not know the reason behind what happened to me. While I try and figure this out (will I ever?), I continue moving forward and, in so doing, want others to benefit from my experience and the insights it has given me.

Life-Changing is Not Life Ending

On 17 July 2019, when I woke up from my first operation and could not feel my legs, I had an instinct that things were going to change. While taking time to decide my future and coming to terms with what that future might be, one thing I knew I needed was to keep myself busy, to have a purpose because an empty mind is a devil's workshop. I've always been like that, focused on multitasking as my brain needs to be compulsively active.

As a child, I needed to watch TV or listen to music to be able to concentrate on my studies. As an adult I continue to be the same, needing, as I mentioned before, several computer screens to concentrate. Oddly, distraction helps me focus.

Whenever I require complete silence and to be away from this material world, I play heavy metal at a loud volume because, for me, only noise can silence noise just like only a diamond can cut a diamond. Abnormal maybe, but this is the way it is. I thrive on productivity and efficiency. I have taught my daughters and medical students the same.

With changed circumstances, my methods of productivity and efficiency may have altered vastly but their importance remains the same. These days I am trying to be just as productive as ever by running the restaurant and reading numerous books, as well as writing one. And once My Second Chance in Life is finished, I plan to start painting again. The canvases and oils are ready. I just hope my fingers will cooperate. But that will be another motivating challenge, won't it?

I have always taken pride in hard work because this is something my dad instilled in me. I have also been reflective and ambitious and remain so. It is just the balance, the perspective that has altered. I used to make good money but became a machine, something I never intended. Was I in a war with life or with myself? Was I deceiving myself with a façade of so-called success and riches when deep inside, I knew I was depleting myself? Was I obsessed with controlling my and my family's future even when I realized that everyone must fight their own battles in life? Was I becoming so big-headed that I thought I could fight their battles and save them all from pain?

Having asked these questions so many times, maybe as a part of my emotional evolution, I now realize what life is meant to be. As the saying goes, you can take a horse to water, but you cannot force it to drink. Similarly, you can only do your best for your loved ones, you cannot control their fate. Nor can you control yours.

Not that fate is something I have always believed in. I used to think you need to be in the right place at the right time to progress fast and make a name for yourself. I have seen people work harder than others, yet the latter has had an easier progression. Perhaps it's what fate wants to make of you. I believe half your destiny depends on fate; the other half depends on you.

Without my trauma, I hope I would still have wanted to write. However, I have had some unique experiences that few people my age has gone through. Are these experiences a blessing or a curse? Who knows?

Physically, the struggle of walking, and using crutches, means I cannot do anything else with my hands. Pain in my neck, shoulders and legs is constant and affects my sleep. Although medicine can take away the pain the side effect of drowsiness makes me feel like a drug addict. My bladder is also a big problem.

At an emotional level, I am at home when everyone else is going to work. Yes, I have the restaurant, but I'm still faced with a lack of purpose and usefulness. Only recently I asked my daughters what they expected of me as a dad. Angelina replied, 'Duty comes first Daddy, that's what you have taught us. I was overjoyed.

There is no point in being held back by the past, is there? Everything that has happened prepared me for the next step. Yes, I do miss my patients and miss making a difference in people's lives. Perhaps at some point in the future, I might be able to work part-time for a charity, meanwhile, I can still make a difference with my cocktails and words, can't I? And that is exactly what I intend to do.

'You are a good waiter,' one elderly gentleman complimented me at Samsara as I was explaining our dishes and which wines go best with which dish. Instantly, his comment stimulated a range of emotions. Which was the right one? I couldn't decide. On the one hand, I felt disgusted with myself. I'd gone from the heady heights of being a doctor to waiting on customers; on the other hand, I realized I must have done well to be complimented so should be proud.

In the end, I decided to be proud of myself, not just for myself but on behalf of all my colleagues and staff members in the restaurant. In my new life, I have at least succeeded in something.

But for how long, I wonder? Ever since childhood, I have had a premonition that my life would end at 55. I know it sounds strange, but I used to have dreams about it. At school, I wrote several poems which were published, including a couple about death. Maybe that's why I have always been in a hurry to live my life and plan everything accordingly. I still have life energy even though I don't desire a long life, don't want to grow old, and don't want to be lying in a nursing home. Do something valuable, have a useful life, and then, once you have finished your purpose, you should go. Death is a great leveller. However rich or poor you are, regardless of your race, we all end up in the same place as everyone else.

I may not be able to run or walk towards my dreams, and I may feel cheated by life, but I can still be the best in everything I do. As my dad told me, 'Always be the best, do your best.

Life throws many dilemmas to test us. How we respond defines our life.

If you are honest, sincere and behave with dedication, it is more than likely you will succeed. Life is about exploring different facets of one's self. There is more to you than what you see, but often we fail to explore our full potential by limiting ourselves to one profession.

We must also explore and appreciate life itself. Writing has resurrected a structure in my life, as well as given me food for thought and put things into perspective. Patients may not think they inspire doctors, but they inspired me. Now I am on my journey as a patient. Someone once asked me if I saw myself as a hero. No way! A lack of self-worthiness has always been an issue for me but if this book can, in some small way, help others, I would consider myself useful and being honest is part of that deal.

I receive many messages from colleagues (or rather ex-colleagues - will I ever get used to distinguishing?) about how they are drowning under paperwork, how they are being asked to work harder, see more patients, and feel undervalued. Of course, many of these concerns are genuine as the whole health system in the UK is on its knees and all doctors are struggling. But I just want to say to them that they don't know how lucky, how privileged, they are that they are still able to do what they are doing. What I wouldn't give to be a doctor again! I would consult patients all day, every day if need be. I would do anything to resurrect the privilege of living my dream again.

So many patients have made my dream worthwhile and inspired me. Unfortunately, sometimes for us doctors, some patients are reduced to mere cases or numbers. When doctors say they have a nice case, it is unknowingly, usually an ominous sign for that patient. In my forthcoming book, I will share those patient experiences which have not only enriched my life but also inspired many others.

Maybe, with my life-changing injuries, time has unravelled new and different subjects to study, live and learn, to add many more volumes to my life experiences.

Surely there are bigger things in store for me and, I hope, for all of us.

When time leaves us memories, we gather strength from the past to prepare for battles ahead, savouring the sunny times as an umbrella for the cold, dark days.

The sun will be out again, and soon.

If we want something badly enough, there is always a second chance.

Letter to Life

Dear Life

This letter is something I should have written a long time ago so please forgive my procrastination, but I want to thank you for all that you have given me over the years. Being busy with my career, daily living, and everything else, I nearly forgot about you. It is only right that, by the turns of the wheel of destiny, you have now given me ample time to reflect and appreciate you. It was long overdue.

I had a lot of questions for you, wanting to know why it was me chosen to go through all these difficult times, why did I have to be the one to give up my career, why is it me that had to suffer, why am I poor? I was angry and upset with you. I didn't want to talk with you anymore.

But all that has changed somehow. I don't feel angry or bitter anymore, nor do I harbour any of those questions. Maybe time, and emotional evolution, have made me a different person. Or maybe you did!

I thank you for the strength you have provided which has enabled me to live through the toughest times and come back stronger. You have taught me the definition of success and spirituality within our daily busy routine.

I understand that a beautiful life is a collection of beautiful memories. A beautiful life is when you can fulfil your responsibilities and make your loved ones happy. A beautiful life is to be able to 'live' the moment, not just exist. It is about counting your blessings, listening to the sounds of birds singing, soaking in the warmth of the sun and dancing in the rain.

Life, you have, by your methods, taught me that although wealth is very important, as is ambition, it is not just material wealth that matters.

The wealth of character, health and love are sometimes bigger than money. Ambition doesn't have to be only in self-advancement but also to be able to support your loved ones in realizing their dreams.

With this second chance in life that you have given me, I promise to be a better person and use my adversities to become a voice of inspiration for others, especially the disabled and depressed. I hope this book will be the start of my new journey that will take me to places where I can share my stories to motivate others and in my small way, help make this world a better place.

Life, you have taught me the role of fate and the importance of faith. You have given me the good luck of meeting some miraculous people to whom I shall remain indebted forever. You have given me pain but also the strength to suffer, you have turned me into a brick from clay by making me go through the burning fire. You have shown me who my real friends are, and the strength of friendship. You have taken me through the depths of despair to the heights of elation. I have always wanted you to be big, not long and you have obliged me. Lead me to the rock that is higher than I and give me the strength and perseverance to scale it.

My dear life, I thank you for everything you have done for me and one day, I will make you proud.

Yours truly

Bhaskar

ACKNOWLEDGEMENTS

Some so many people have made such a huge difference in my life over the last few years, each playing a role, without whom I would not be where I am today. I want to acknowledge all their help in not only helping me complete this book but also in inspiring me to still be alive and look forward to my second chance in life.

I thank my mum and dad, without whom I would not have come into existence or appreciated the valued ideals of life.

I thank Mili, my beautiful wife, for being my pillar of strength through thick and thin. For being the one who has given me my second life. I thank my beloved daughters Angelina and Nikita who have been my constant source of happiness and inspiration. Also, my brother Nav without whom my life, from childhood, would not be complete.

My thanks also to Dr Eli Silber for being so kind and caring and helping me in the most difficult of times. I wish all doctors were like him.

I thank all the staff of Samsara, my bar and restaurant, who have helped in more ways than they can imagine: Shahid, Liam, Mamun, Muhibur Bhai, Lablu, Roney and everyone else.

My heartfelt thanks, too, to the best friends one can ever wish for, especially Jugal, Sumit, Varun, Rupant, Vineet, Anand, and countless others for being there for me whenever I needed them.

Samsara Cocktail Bar and Restaurant is located at 23-25 High Street, Cheam, Sutton, London,

SM3 8RE

www.samsararestaurant.co.uk

Please give me the honour of being your host one day.

I hope I have touched your heart and have given you a new perspective in Life. I look forward to meeting you soon.

www.drbhaskarbora.com

www.thesecondchanceinlife.com

Printed in Great Britain
by Amazon

22703917R00116